MYTHS IN ADVENTISM

Myths in Adventism

An Interpretive Study of Ellen White, Education, and Related Issues

George R. Knight

REVIEW AND HERALD PUBLISHING ASSOCIATION

Washington, DC 20039-0555
Hagerstown, MD 21740

Copyright © 1985 by
Review and Herald Publishing Association

This book was
Edited by Gerald Wheeler
Designed by Richard Steadham
Type set: 10/11 Melior

PRINTED IN U.S.A.

Library of Congress Cataloging in Publication Data
Knight, George R.
   Myths in Adventism.

   Includes index.
   1. Seventh-day Adventists—Education. 2. Adventists—
Education. 3. Seventh-day Adventists—Doctrines.
4. Adventists—Doctrines. I. Title.
LC586.S48K55   1985   377'.8673   85-11889

ISBN 0-8280-0277-0

To Betty,

who encouraged me

to think about the questions

after I was already happy with

the answers.

Abbreviations

General

AUHR	Andrews University Heritage Room
EGWRC-AU	Ellen G. White Research Center, Andrews University
EGWRC-DC	Ellen G. White Research Center, Washington, D.C.
GCAr	General Conference Archives
GCDEd	General Conference Department of Education Microfiche Collection
LLUHR	Loma Linda University Heritage Room
MS	Manuscript
RH	*Review and Herald* and *Adventist Review*
TMC-AU	Teaching Materials Center, Andrews University

Ellen G. White Books

AA	*The Acts of the Apostles*
AH	*The Adventist Home*
CG	*Child Guidance*
COL	*Christ's Object Lessons*
CT	*Counsels to Parents, Teachers, and Students*
CW	*Counsels to Writers and Editors*
Ed	*Education*
FE	*Fundamentals of Christian Education*
GC	*The Great Controversy*
LS	*Life Sketches of Ellen G. White*
MH	*The Ministry of Healing*
MYP	*Messages to Young People*
SC	*Steps to Christ*
1SM	*Selected Messages*, book 1 (2SM, etc., for books 2 and 3)
1T	*Testimonies for the Church*, vol. 1 (2T, etc., for vols. 2-9)

"The greatest hindrance to knowledge is our adjustment to conventional notions, to mental clichés. Wonder or radical amazement, the state of maladjustment to words and notions, is, therefore, a prerequisite for an authentic awareness of that which is."

—Abraham Joshua Heschel

"The insidious thing about myths is people believe they are true. People never doubt their assumptions and so they cannot account for errors or failure to achieve hoped-for results."

—Arthur W. Combs

"To explode a myth is accordingly not to deny the facts but to re-allocate them."

—Gilbert Ryle

"Every human being, created in the image of God, is endowed with a power akin to that of the Creator—individuality, power to think and to do. . . . It is the work of true education to develop this power, to train the youth to be thinkers, and not mere reflectors of other men's thought."

—Ellen G. White

"In Adventist circles thinking has often been treated as a virtue in rhetoric and a sin in practice."

—Arnold Reye

"Wisdom is the principal thing; therefore get wisdom: and with all thy getting get understanding."

—Solomon

Contents

Preface

"Myths," wrote Arthur Combs, "are false or inaccurate beliefs that are generally held to be true." Because people behave in terms of their beliefs, inaccurate conceptions can cause us to make mistaken plans or attempt erroneous or impossible tasks. One way to avoid such problems, therefore, is to examine our myths so that we can move beyond them. Truth, after all, makes a better foundation for Christian living and education than does error.

The purpose of *Myths in Adventism* is positive rather than negative, constructive rather than destructive. While using popular misconceptions as starting points, every chapter advances beyond the misconceptions to a positive perspective. The focus is on truth rather than error, even though we must often deal with errors before we can clearly grasp truth. In each chapter I have sought to emphasize the positive aspects of the issue being discussed and to give practical suggestions where appropriate.

In one sense *Myths* presents an "unsystematic" philosophy of Adventist education, and related issues, using the myth motif as a literary device to generate more reader interest than a "systematic" presentation would have elicited. The myth motif, however, is much more than a literary device, since it begins with actual misconceptions in Adventist thinking that are causing us difficulty in achieving our denominational goals. Some readers may consider some of the myths to be "straw men." They may be "straw men" for them, but for other readers these same myths, in one form or another, are "living men" that need to be adequately treated.

Not all readers will agree with every position taken in this book, but all, I trust, will find themselves forced to *think* about the issues raised and the solutions proposed. My purpose has not been to present the final solution but to raise our collective and individual levels of consciousness regarding the issues involved in the task of more closely approximating Christian ideals in both thought and practice. In some ways people can learn just as much by disagreeing with the positions presented in this book as they can by agreeing with them *if* they know why they disagree and on what basis they have reached their conclusions.

It is my hope that *Myths* will stimulate thought and dialogue on significant issues. I realize that it is safer not to write books that create serious thought. But then, safety is not my goal. The safest and most nonthreatening form of existence is death—a state in which there are no thoughts, challenges, or disturbing practices. Christian living is the antithesis of death. A dynamic way of life in an alien environment, it demands constant thought and action for its vitality and even its existence.

I have written for thinking Christians, both lay and clerical. My original title was "Myths in Adventist Education," but wise editorial counsel indicated that the topics covered ranged far beyond the realm of education, even though many of my illustrations came from that field. I responded by changing the title to *Myths in Adventism* and adding *An Interpretive Study of Ellen White, Education, and Related Issues* as a subtitle. This subtitle brings the title into sharper focus by noting the themes emphasized. "Related Issues" is a catch-all phrase that includes a Christian approach to such disparate topics as literature, recreation, and hierarchy. *Myths* especially seeks to develop principles for interpreting Ellen White and to apply those principles to current practice. In seeking to accomplish these goals I have set forth an approach to Ellen White (and the Bible) that has applicability in all areas of Christian-Adventist living.

Having aimed the book at an Adventist audience, I have quite naturally relied heavily on Adventist sources and Adventist understandings and misunderstandings. The writings of the Bible and of Ellen White, since they form the basic foundation of Adventist thinking, appear extensively. Beyond these sources, I have used sociological, psychological, philosophical, theological, historical, and pedagogical literature as needed to support and develop the various points.

For the sake of brevity I have cited Bible and Ellen White statements in the text. Other sources appear at the end of the book in traditional footnote format. All Bible quotations come from the Revised Standard Version unless otherwise noted. References to the writings of Ellen White use the standard abbreviations. Wherever possible I have used published Spirit of Prophecy books for the convenience of those who do not have ready access to the original manuscripts in the White Estate research centers.

Some readers will probably label me a hopeless conservative, while others will undoubtedly believe that I am a wild-eyed liberal of the most dangerous proportions. I trust that I am neither. It has been my desire to follow the evidence to its natural conclusions and lay the issues out for further discussion. Such is the nature of progress. I freely admit that I do not have all the answers—I don't even have all the questions. The best learning process, however, is one in which we all learn from one another. I will learn from my readers, just as I have learned (and am learning) from my students. My hope is that my readers will let this book speak for itself and will react to its message, rather than to their perceptions of the author as a liberal, conservative, or anything else except a Christian Adventist who is seeking a fuller understanding of mankind's needs as they relate to God's eternal truth.

Myths is the second step in a three-part exposition of Adventist educational philosophy. The first step was published in 1980 as *Philosophy and Education: An Introduction in Christian Perspective. Philosophy and Education* explored basic philosophic issues, examined philosophic theories as they relate to those issues in the field of education, and developed a Biblical-evangelical approach to both philosophic issues and education. With its focus on issues related to Adventist education, *Myths* has moved beyond the general approach of *Philosophy and Education*. The final step will be *Redemptive Education*, which will be a systematic presentation of Adventist educational philosophy from the Bible and Ellen White. *Redemptive Education*, however, awaits the completion of more extensive exploration into the historical context of Ellen White's writings, since the full implications of her counsel on education and related issues are impossible to grasp without understanding the historical situation in which she wrote. Preparatory work in this historical area is represented by the volume I edited entitled *Early Adventist Educators* (1983) and the doctoral research of Gilbert Valentine, Allan Lindsay, Milton Hook, Craig Willis, Arnold Reye, Warren Ashworth, and others.

As an author, I am indebted to many people for their inspiration, encouragement, and insight. A foremost acknowledgment is due Arthur W. Combs, whose *Myths in Education* arrived in my office in December, 1979. His treatment of myths in general American education from the perspective of humanistic psychology inspired me to critique Adventist education using the myth format. Within twenty-four hours after receiving his book, I had my "myths book" outlined in essentially its present form. While differing radically from Combs in philosophy and topic selection, I have found his format to be both helpful and provocative.

I also extend my gratitude to Donald Yost and Bert Haloviak, of the General Conference Archives; Louise Dederen, of the Andrews University Heritage Room; Jim Nix, of the Loma Linda University Heritage Room; Robert Olson, Hedwig Jemison, and their staffs at the White Estate research centers; Charles Taylor, "keeper" of the General Conference Department of Education microfiche files; and the librarians of the James White Library on the campus of Andrews University. They, along with others, provided me with the documents that undergird this book. Additional thanks goes to Patricia Saliba, who did the bulk of the manuscript typing; to Gail Valentine, who did some of the typing; to Gilbert Valentine, who functioned as my research assistant; to Jeff Brown, who helped with the proofreading; to Paul Denton and his staff for preparing the illustrations; to Richard Coffen and Gerald Wheeler, of the Review and Herald Publishing Association, who shared their editorial counsel with me; and to the administration of Andrews University for providing me with financial support and time to develop the manuscript.

My special thanks goes to Sue Schwab and Arnold Reye, who read the entire manuscript and provided me with a large number of helpful suggestions—many of which I resented at the time. The book, however, is stronger because of their input. They have a share in its virtues, but not in its faults.

I trust that *Myths in Adventism* will be of benefit to its readers as they seek to approximate more closely Christian ideals in both their personal lives and their corporate existence.

—George R. Knight

PART I

HISTORICAL
AND
PHILOSOPHICAL MYTHS

1 The Myth of the Inflexible Prophet

*O*ne of the most destructive myths in Adventist thinking is that of the inflexible prophet. It views Ellen White as an unbending interpreter of her own writings and implies that her true followers will be just as inflexible and rigid as she in their application of the "straight testimony." Both assumptions have their roots in misunderstanding. The problem with the myth of the inflexible prophet is that it has lost the balance between prophetic authority and the divine gift of human reason. As a result, it confuses honest reasoning with unsanctified rationalization. Furthermore, the myth overlooks the distinction between the letter and the spirit of the law—a distinction that formed the very foundation of Christ's life and teaching.

Belief in the myth of the inflexible prophet tends to lead religious believers to isolate authoritative statements from the Bible and the writings of Ellen White and apply them in an unthinking manner in their daily lives. Following this procedure often leads to the taking of extreme positions that prove to be detrimental to both the cause of God and the individuals involved. The myth can affect every part of a person's religious experience.

A corollary of the myth of the inflexible prophet in Adventist circles is that of the blueprint. The blueprint myth has usually been thought of in terms of education. It is an extension of the deeply rooted American belief in "the one best method" of education that will meet the needs of the entire population. Throughout its history American education has jumped from one educational bandwagon to another in its attempt to find the pedagogical panacea. The truth of the matter is that the concepts of the blueprint and the one best way are blind alleys.

Christian living is more than collecting and relating to proof texts from inflexible authorities. Likewise, developing a system of Christian education is more complex than measuring educational specifications against a blueprint. On the contrary, the Christian life rests upon intelligent understanding, adaptability to changing circumstances, and a firm faith in the unchanging principles of the Bible.

The Myth of the Blueprint

The blueprint myth undoubtedly arose out of the statements of Ellen White concerning Avondale College. Adventist education in the 1870s and 1880s had not perceived its purpose clearly and had not followed her counsels in its operation. In 1891 Ellen White went to Australia, where she helped found Avondale College as an institution that would implement a well-rounded spiritual, mental, and physical education.

At last Ellen White had a hand in establishing a school that reflected the educational concepts that her writings had suggested, beginning with "Proper Education" in 1872. In varying contexts she later referred to Avondale as an "object lesson," a "sample school," a "model school," and a "pattern" (LS, p. 374; CT, p. 349). In 1900 she categorically stated that "the school in Avondale is to be a pattern for other schools which shall be established among our people."—MS 92, 1900.

Even though Mrs. White never used the word *blueprint*, it became the belief among many Adventist educators that she meant *blueprint* by such words as *pattern* and *model*. *Blueprint*, however, is not a synonym for *pattern* or *model*. It has a much more rigid meaning. Webster defines a *blueprint* as "a photographic reproduction . . . of architectural or engineering plans." On the other hand, a *pattern* is defined as "a person or thing so ideal as to be worthy of imitation or copying," and a *model* as "a preliminary representation of something, serving as a plan from which the final . . . object is to be constructed."

It is evident that the notion of blueprint as a photographic reproduction is much more rigid than the concepts of pattern or model, which imply copying and imitating. The unfortunate substitution of *blueprint* for the looser concepts used by Ellen White has obscured her true meaning and has not always produced the best results.

The fact is that Mrs. White's concepts little resembled the notion of an educational blueprint that some claim for her. In 1901 she penned that *"the Lord has not designed any one, special, exact plan in education."*—3SM, p. 227. (Italics supplied.) Again in 1907 she wrote regarding the Madison School, which was doing its best to follow the "pattern" under Adventism's most zealous educational reformers, that *"no exact pattern can be given for the establishment of schools in new fields.* The climate, the surroundings, the condition of the country, and the means at hand with which to work must all bear a part in shaping the work."—CT, p. 531. (Italics supplied.) Significantly, in this same article she noted that "God will bless those schools that are conducted according to His design. When we were laboring to establish the educational work in Australia, the Lord revealed to us that this school must not pattern after any [Adventist] schools that had been established in the past. This was to be a sample school. It was organized on the plan that God had given us, and He has prospered its work."—*Ibid.*, p. 533. In short, she recognized that Avondale was an example, but not an exact pattern.

These statements make it clear that her mind did not confuse blueprints with models. Her statements imply the opposite of unbending, mechanical rigidity. Unfortunately, some of her followers have never caught the breadth and balance of her perspective.

An Inflexible Prophet?

Ellen White often found herself plagued by "those who," she claimed, "*select from the testimonies the strongest expressions and, without bringing in or making any account of the circumstances* under which the cautions and warnings are given, make them of force in every case. Thus they produce unhealthy impressions upon the minds of people. There are always those who are ready to grasp anything of a character which they can use to rein up people to a close, severe test, and who will work elements of their own characters into the reforms. . . . *Picking out some things in the testimonies they drive them upon every one, and disgust rather than win souls.*"—3SM, pp. 285, 286. (Italics supplied.)

Such a choosing of the "strongest expressions," while divorcing them from their historical and spiritual contexts, has occurred in nearly every area of Christian living. It was so concerning the dress question. To this Mrs. White replied that times and circumstances had changed, that "no one precise style has been given me as the exact rule to guide all in their dress," and that the style of dress should be appropriate for the time (*ibid.*, p. 254). Others sought to make a fetish out of some particular diet. She replied to them that "one rule cannot be made for everyone" because people differ (*ibid.*, p. 294). She also remarked that "in the use of foods we should exercise good, sound common sense," and should take occupational and geographical factors into consideration. Her plea was for us to behave like "intelligent human beings" on the diet question (7T, pp. 133, 134). In regard to the training of gospel workers, she wrote that colporteuring is the best preparation. She also recognized, however, that not everyone has the ability for such activity. Those not so adapted must not be regarded as faithless and unwilling. "The Lord is not unreasonable in His requirements. The church is as a garden in which is a variety of flowers, each with its own peculiarities" and value (6T, pp. 330, 333, 334).

The list of unbending solutions and interpretations that some of us would like to enforce upon others could go on and on, but the point by now should be obvious. The concept of an inflexible prophet is a myth that distorts both the integrity of the prophet and the character of God. God is seeking to clothe us with the robe of Christ's righteous character rather than the straightjacket of unbending fanaticism.

In the area of education we find several helpful examples of the commonsense approach that Ellen White took to her own statements. One of the most enlightening is her interpretation of her statement that "parents should be the *only* teachers of their children until they reach eight or ten years of age."—3T, p. 137. (Italics supplied.)

Notice that her statement is quite categorical. It contains no "ifs," "ands," "ors," or "buts" to temper or qualify its impact. This makes it an excellent candidate for inflexible interpretation if we separate it from the larger message of Christianity. Ellen White first published the statement in 1872. The fact that it reappeared in her writings in 1882 and 1903 has undoubtedly had the effect of strengthening what appears to be its unconditional nature. But Mrs. White's interpretation of her own statement took place in a school board meeting near the St. Helena Sanitarium on January 14, 1904. The dialogue between the board members and the remarks of Ellen White preserved in the minutes of this meeting constitute one of the clearest records we possess of Mrs. White explaining the meaning of her own writings.

The Adventists living near the St. Helena Sanitarium had built a church school in 1902. The older children attended it while some careless Adventist parents let their younger children run freely in the neighborhood without proper training and discipline. Some of the school board members believed that they should build a classroom for the younger children, but others held that they should not do it because Ellen White had said that "parents should be the *only* teachers of their children until they have reached eight or ten years of age."

One faction of the board apparently felt that it was more

important to give some help to the neglected children than to hold to the letter of the law. The other faction, however, believed that it had an inflexible command. Beyond this, it is evident that the pastor felt that the statement might be justifiably used to save some money for the church. At any rate, the school board requested an interview with Mrs. White to discuss the question of school-age attendance and the responsibility of the church for the education of its young children.

During the meeting Ellen White reaffirmed her position that the family should be the school for young children. But she also interpreted the statement within the broader context of Christian responsibility. The whole discussion is most enlightening, and every member of the Adventist Church should read it.[1]

The first thing she did was to qualify her original statement. "Mothers *should* be able to instruct their little ones wisely during the earlier years of childhood. *If* every mother were capable of doing this, *and* would take time to teach her children the lessons they should learn in early life, *then* all children could be kept in the home school until they are eight, or nine, or ten years old."—3SM, pp. 214, 215. (Italics supplied.) Unfortunately, she noted, many did not take their responsibilities seriously. It would have been best if they had chosen not to become parents. But since they unwisely did bring children into the world, the church should not stand by idly without giving any guidance to the children's characters. She held that the Christian community had a responsibility to train such neglected ones, and she even went so far as to claim that the church needed to reform its ideas in regard to establishing kindergartens.

During the interview she remarked that "God desires us to deal with these problems sensibly" (*ibid.*, p. 215), and that part of the reason she gave the instruction in the first place was because there had been no Adventist schools in 1872 in which the Adventist Church could educate its children (*ibid.*, pp. 216, 217). Also she became quite stirred up with her readers who took an inflexible attitude and sought to follow the letter of her message while missing the underlying principle. She evidenced disapproval of both the words and attitudes of her rigid interpreters when she declared: "My mind has been greatly stirred in regard to the idea, 'Why, Sister White has said so and so, and Sister White has said so and so; and therefore we are going right up to it.' " She then added that "*God wants us all to have common sense, and He wants us to reason from common sense. Circumstances alter conditions. Circumstances change the relation of things.*"—Ibid., p. 217.

(Italics supplied.) Ellen White was anything but inflexible, and it is a point of the first magnitude that we realize that fact.

Later in the interview her son W. C. White stated the problem of the day quite nicely when he pointed out "that our people throughout the States and throughout the world . . . sometimes make very far-reaching rulings based on an isolated statement." He then illustrated that every specific ruling rests upon a principle, and that it is the consideration of principles in relation to circumstances that is the proper mode of interpretation for inspired statements (ibid., p. 221). W. C. White's statement was, in effect, a summary and reinforcement of his mother's attitude, method, and message during the interview.

Rationality in both the interpretation and application of inspired messages stood at the root of Ellen White's educational activity. Yet others constantly misinterpreted her. For example, on March 21, 1895, she wrote an extensive and hard-hitting article entitled "Speedy Preparation for the Work" (FE, pp. 334-367) aimed at some of the improper emphases and attitudes in evidence at Battle Creek College. The article had some strong statements in it because she was combating some deeply entrenched misconceptions. One month later, however, she penned two balancing articles (ibid., pp. 368-380) because some of her readers, apparently using the "I have a Sister White quotation" method, faced the danger of going to the opposite extreme. As a result, they wanted to lower the standards of education and do a superficial job. What she was really trying to tell them was that they needed to come to grips with the essential foundational principles of what made Christian education Christian within the context of a quality education (ibid., pp. 368, 373). The essentials in Christian education—the place of the Bible in the curriculum and the missionary motif—became the recurring theme of her educational writings in the 1890s. She pounded it home with surprising rapidity and frequency during this period because Adventist educators had been so dull in arriving at an understanding of the foundational principles of Christian education during the previous twenty years.

Building Sensibly Upon Principles

Henry Thoreau once described a reformer who had written "a book called 'A Kiss for a Blow'" and who "behaved as if there were no alternative between these."[2] It is unfortunate that many reformers have a tendency to go to the opposite extreme from what they seek to change. Perhaps it is because of their determined nature, the inertia of the status quo, or a form of pride that has pushed them into an intellectual corner. No matter what the reason, however, we must consider it as a possible distorting factor as we seek to develop a better educational system. Rigidity in our thinking and actions may be a symptom of the onset of intellectual and spiritual rigor mortis.

A central problem all of us face in our lives is that of balance. In the case of Christian education, one polar extreme is to rely unthinkingly on prophetic authority, while the other is to lean on rationality in an unhealthy manner that allows it to become an excuse for what we really wanted to do anyway. Scripture must always guide our rational understanding. On the other hand, we must always understand and apply the truth of Scripture through the aid of our rationality.[3] To rely either on Scripture or rational understanding without the other is a fatal misconception. Authoritative revelation and sanctified reason go hand in hand as we seek to understand God and develop a Christian educational system. God gave us the power of creative thought, and He expects us to use it for His glory (Isa. 1:18; Ed, p. 17).

In *Education* we read that "with us, as with Israel of old, success in education depends on fidelity in carrying out the Creator's plan. Adherence to the principles of God's word will bring as great blessings to us as it would have brought to the Hebrew people."—Page 50. Our first task as Christians, therefore, is to seek out the principles of Christian living and Christian education through Spirit-guided study of the Bible and the writings of Ellen White.

Our second task is to seek to relate the principles we have found to our personal lives and our unique educational setting. To do so, we must have some understanding of the historic situation that originally called forth the counsel. This will enable us to differentiate better between the universal principles underlying the inspired statement and the particulars that it suggested to deal with a problem in a historic time and place. Furthermore, we must have a good grasp of the situation to which we are going to apply the universal principles. Only with such understanding can we intelligently put the prophetic principles into practice in our daily lives, our church, or our school. Application must not take place without understanding.

Ellen White recommended the approach that applies revealed principles with understanding. In writing concerning some problems in the Fernando School, she claimed that "it would be a sad mistake for us to fail to consider thoroughly the purpose for which each of our schools is established."—CT, pp. 203, 204.

(Italics supplied.) Thus, even though the "pattern school" at Avondale had several hundred acres, she was still able in 1904 to approve the site of the new Washington Training College (Columbia Union College), which consisted of only twenty acres. It is important to recognize that she made this statement during a period in which she was encouraging the founders of Madison College, Emmanuel Missionary College, Pacific Union College, and other educational institutions to buy hundreds of acres so that they could function according to the Avondale pattern. Yet even in this context she could write of the Washington Training College and its twenty acres (the Washington Sanitarium had an adjoining thirty acres) that "the location that has been secured for our school and sanitarium is all that could be desired. The land resembles representations that have been shown me by the Lord. . . . There is on it ample room for a school and a sanitarium, without crowding either institution." We might ask, "How can this be?" It seems almost like a contradiction of principle. Before we become too hasty, however, we should also note that she claimed that "it is well adapted for the *purpose* for which it is to be used."—LS, p. 397. (Italics supplied.)

Purpose had an impact on Ellen White's educational thinking just as did other considerations such as climate, surroundings, the condition of the country, and the means at hand. She saw no rigid pattern (CT, p. 531). One more illustration might be helpful. Writing in February, 1894, during the search for the land upon which to build Avondale, she remarked that proper education can "never . . . be given to the youth in this country, *or any other country*, unless they are separated a wide distance from the cities."—FE, p. 312. (Italics supplied.) She apparently interpreted her straightforward statement, however, in terms of an ideal to be approximated rather than an absolute that could never be violated. In actual practice she adapted her counsel to come as close as possible to the ideals she had set forth. On the other hand, she recognized the fact that circumstances often prohibited the accomplishment of the ideal. In such situations she did the next best thing in terms of her basic principles. Early in the twentieth century, for example, she wrote that schools should be established outside the cities, *if possible*. "But in the cities there are many children who could not attend schools away from the cities; and for the benefit of these, schools should be opened in the cities as well as in the country."—9T, p. 201. Her underlying rationale was that circumstances alter conditions and the Lord expects us to use common sense. She practiced what she preached.

Principles must guide our thoughts and endeavors. The principles don't change, even though the ways of applying them vary with the circumstances. D. Elton Trueblood has illustrated this by picturing two men trying to reach the same island in the middle of a stream by swimming from opposite shores. In order to reach a common goal they have to swim in different directions.[4]

Christian living is a dynamic experience inseparably linked to thinking and acting upon one's thoughts. Christianity is therefore a moral enterprise in which men have responsibility in the eyes of God. Rigidity and inflexibility of thought and action are the antithesis of living Christianity. The Christian's task is to search out God's revelations and then to seek to put them into practice in current living without doing violence to the intent of their underlying principles. This takes personal dedication as well as sensitivity to the guidance of the Holy Spirit.

It was in connection with the Spirit that Ellen White lived and sought to guide the Adventist Church. Christ, who, in His flexible manner, was able to meet all classes of people, exemplified this same stance. His adaptable yet principle-based life and teachings burst the old wineskins of pharisaism.

The myth of the inflexible prophet has had some deplorable results. Fortunately, however, it is a myth. The truth of the matter is that the rigidity is the property of misguided interpreters rather than that of the prophet.

2 Historical Myths

*A*dventists have developed two historical myths that have confused their understanding of their heritage and have failed to provide them with a strong historical base upon which to build a progressively stronger and more adequate educational system. The two myths are (1) the myth of the good old days, and (2) the myth that the educational ideas of Ellen White were one hundred years ahead of her time.

The Myth of the Good Old Days

The Myth in General Society

All societies seem to suffer from a nostalgia that we might describe as historical myopia. People have romanticized and continue to romanticize those people, events, and places that are "long ago" or "far away." As a result, they dream about the good old days when life was simple and nature unspoiled. Many of the youth of the 1970s fled the luxuries of suburbia for the dream of log-cabin living in mountain meadows, adults talked of the grand old pre-Watergate times of American politics when politicians were open and honest, and many fantasized concerning the nineteenth-century world in which honest and hardworking citizens came out on top in the daily struggle of life. Such nostalgia carries over into the field of education, as men glorify the accomplishments of the little red schoolhouse, note how the public school helped the immigrants succeed in society, and make calls for education to return to the basics. The popularity of such television programs as "Little House on the Prairie" illustrates the strength of such nostalgia.

The fact of the matter is, however, that the mythology of the good old days distorts the truth. The minds of both individuals and entire societies play tricks on them through the psychological process of repression. Repression allows our minds to forget the unhappy events of the past while remembering much of the good. This process, we should note, is helpful in that it gives us courage to move into the future. On the other hand, it can be destructive and depressing if we fail to remember that it produces an incorrect view of a past that we must take into account as we face the hard facts of today and tomorrow. Failure to realize consciously the effects of such distortion will only discourage us as we contemplate present conditions and wonder why society, the church, and the educational system have "gone to pot" in spite of our best efforts.

The truth underlying the nostalgic myth appears in the title of a fascinating book on nineteenth-century America by Otto Bettmann: *The Good Old Days—They Were Terrible!* Bettmann utilized vivid and revealing photographs, terse commentary, and nineteenth-century sketches and cartoons from every aspect of cultural life to illustrate his thesis. His book leaves its readers thankful that they live at a time when sewage and garbage are adequately cared for in their communities, when medical practice has risen above drugging, when surgery no longer has a high percentage of deaths as a result of a lack of belief in antiseptics by even leading physicians, and when child labor laws prohibit the employment of 8- to 9-year-old children at twenty-five cents for a fourteen-hour day. Bettmann noted that "the good old days were good for but the privileged few. For the farmer, the laborer, the average breadwinner, life was an unremitting hardship."[1]

C. P. Snow reinforced this concept of the good old days by quoting J. H. Plumb: "No one in his senses would choose to have been born in a previous age unless he could be certain that he would have been born into a prosperous family, that he would have enjoyed extremely good health, and that he could have accepted stoically the death of the majority of his children."[2] The point is that even the wealthy were helpless in the face of man's ignorance of medicine and sanitation.

The myth of the good old days has also colored our recollections of education. Beyond the myth is the fact that the little red schoolhouse was often a dilapidated structure with inadequate ventilation and lighting. It was red because red ocher was the cheapest paint available. Teachers at the elementary level frequently had not graduated from high school, and brawn was more important than brain as a qualification for teaching, because the teacher's foremost task was to keep order. A common conception argued that "lickin' and larnin' goes together. No lickin', no larnin'."[3] Teaching methodology, furthermore, was primitive, and the pupils had to memorize their lessons whether they understood them or not. Finally, a great deal of truth exists to the claim of Colin Greer, executive editor of *Social Policy Magazine*, that many of the nineteenth-century immigrants to America succeeded "in spite of, and not because of, compulsory public education."[4] Immigrant children dropped out of school in great numbers and succeeded because of the customs and skills that their families brought with them to the New World.

Whatever we may say about American education, it will not do to desire to go back to the good old days of the little red schoolhouse. It was in the context of nineteenth-century education that Ellen White wrote of educational conditions and methods so poor that they led to widespread nervousness and disease among schoolchildren (3T, pp. 135-138). She aimed her reforming ideas at the problems of the little red schoolhouse and the good old days of education.

The Myth in the Church

The myth of the good old days in the realm of religion also besets us. I would be a wealthy man if I received a dollar every time I heard inferences about the good old days in the Adventist Church, and how the younger generation has let the church "go to the dogs."

If this is true, we might ask, What prompted the nine volumes of the *Testimonies?* The truth is that they, along with thousands of unpublished testimonies, reprove every conceivable sin. These reproofs went to conference presidents, pastors, physicians, teachers, and the people in the pews. The fact is, believe it or not, that nineteenth-century Adventists were sinners in need of the saving grace of Jesus Christ, just like you and me. One hardly gets a picture of the past as being a golden age of Adventism by studying our history. The pioneers had many of the same strengths, weaknesses, and feelings that we do. Our task is to seek to build upon their strengths while learning from their mistakes. Mrs. White has written that "we have nothing to fear for the future, except as we shall forget the way the Lord has led us, and His teaching in our past history."—LS, p. 196.

But, you might say, the real golden age of Christianity occurred before early Adventism—it was back in Biblical times. We cannot deny that those may have been golden times, but they were hardly the good old days that the critics of today's church would have us believe. Take David, for example, as the foremost leader of Israel and a man after God's "own heart" (1 Sam. 13:14; Acts 13:22). How would you react if we caught the president of the General Conference (or the Lord's prophet) in adultery and delegated murder, as David was with Bathsheba and Uriah the Hittite? Or what about Peter and his post-Pentecostal public denial of the basic principles of Christian brotherhood (Gal. 2:11-14)?

The truth is that human nature has continued to respond to sin in much the same way down through history. The Bible is a meaningful book because we, in our fallen natures, can identify with its spiritual heroes. This statement does not imply that we are to excuse our sin or to justify twentieth-century vice. Rather it means that God thought so much of us that He gave us a record of His church in the past so that we might learn about forgiveness, conversion, justification, and sanctification from the struggles, failures, and successes of its members. Paul wrote that the experiences of the former days were "written for our instruction, that by steadfastness and by the encouragement of the scriptures we might have hope" (Rom. 15:4; cf. 1 Cor. 10:5, 6, 11).

The Bible is a book of hope—hope as hopeless men relate to their hopeful Creator. Its revelation of the condition of both church leaders and members was not intended to discourage us, but rather to give us hope in the fact that others faced problems and God helped them develop their characters for that better day when "this corruptible shall have put on incorruption" (1 Cor. 15:54, K.J.V.).

In the same way it is true that the problems in our contemporary society, church, and personal lives should not cause us to lose our faith. Rather, such problems, in the light of the Biblical revelation, should cause us to put faith in God's infinite power to save us from our desperate condition. The message of the Bible is not that this is a perfect world, but that our only hope is in Jesus Christ.

The Myth in Adventist Education

Adventist education has not escaped the myth of the good old days. Some would like us to return to what they perceive as better times. Once again, however, the good old days, upon historical scrutiny, appear to have been terrible.

The good (bad?) old days of Adventist education began officially in 1872 when the denomination sponsored the Battle Creek church school, which it transformed into Battle Creek College in 1874. The General Conference leaders spared no pains to define what they hoped to accomplish in their first school. The school committee suggested that there were plenty of places where students "could go to obtain an education in other languages, grammar, rhetoric, logic, history, philosophy, and the sciences in general." What they proposed was a school that would uplift the principles of Bible truth as Adventists held them. "This," they claimed, "is the point which this school is especially designed to meet," and they believed that it was the only justification for even establishing an Adventist school.[5] The founding fathers wanted a school that would train Christian workers in a relatively short time.

In addition to these goal statements by church leaders, Ellen White penned her first major exposition on education for the young school. "Proper Education" (3T, pp. 131-160) devoted four fifths of its space to the necessity of a physical-mental balance in education and stressed the need for vocational training in education. Mrs. White took the time to read her statement to the school board and President Brownsberger, but they didn't understand how to develop such a school. So, claimed W. C. White, "it was agreed that the work of the school should be organized on the ordinary lines" and that the industries be introduced later.[6]

What actually developed at Battle Creek College was the antithesis of the stated hopes and purposes of its founders. The college's curricular focal point was a classical studies program for the Bachelor of Arts degree that varied in length from five to seven years throughout its history. The study of Latin and classical (not Biblical) Greek and the "heathen authors" (e.g., Cicero, Virgil, Homer, and Quintilian) formed the skeleton and most of the flesh of its most prestigious course of studies. The administration did not require study of the Bible and the Christian religion or even recommend it in the major courses, although students could elect to sit in on the Bible lectures offered by Uriah Smith, whose main responsibility was the full-time editorship of the *Review and Herald*. Early records indicate that relatively few students bothered to avail themselves of the opportunity. It was a strange curriculum for a college established to teach Bible from a distinctively Adventist point of view and to prepare ministers and other church workers.

The practical-physical-industrial side of education fared equally poorly during the first two decades of Battle Creek College. During both the 1870s and the 1880s the school made attempts to establish industries and practical subjects, but during those same decades the board finally put the struggling programs out of their misery.

The good old days of Adventist education got off to a rough start. Not until the 1890s did the Bible and manual labor find a significant role in the curriculum of Battle Creek College.[7]

Meanwhile, Battle Creek College had false starts in other areas. Even though James and Ellen White had desired a larger piece of property, the school board voted in 1874, when the Whites were in California, to buy a twelve-acre site in Battle Creek across the street from the sanitarium. The board felt that even this was too much land. They therefore sold five acres so that the faculty and Adventist families could live close to the school. In addition, they saved money by not building dormitories. Boarding students had to live with Adventist families in the community. The upshot of it all was that school discipline was unequal, since it depended on individual families, and school activities, through gossip, became the business of the entire Adventist community.

Sidney Brownsberger, the college's first president, resigned in 1881, vowing that he would "never again enter . . . [denominational employment] except on the basis of the lines and reforms set forth in the testimonies."[8] In his place the denomination hired Alexander McLearn, who only recently had come into contact with Adventism. Under McLearn, the situation at the college deteriorated rapidly.

In December, 1881, Ellen White had a blazing speech read before the General Conference delegates and the leading employees of the Review and Herald, the sanitarium, and the college that must have made the faculty and board of trustees quiver in their chairs. She noted that Battle Creek College had missed its mark, and that the Bible should receive its proper place in the curriculum. If that made the school unpopular, she claimed, the students could "go to other colleges" that fit their taste. She then remarked: "If a worldly influence is to bear sway in our school, then sell it out to worldlings and let them take the entire control; and those who have invested their means in that institution will establish another school, to be conducted, not upon the plan of popular schools, nor according to the desires of principal and teachers, but upon the plan which God has specified."—5T, pp. 25, 26.

By the spring of 1882 the state of the school had degenerated to chaotic conditions. The board finally voted to close the institution for the 1882-1883 school year. Battle Creek College reopened in the fall of 1883.

The years between 1883 and the late 1890s saw the gradual integration of Bible into the curriculum, the progressive rooting out of the pagan classics, and even the eventual establishment of viable manual labor programs. Meanwhile, other Adventist educational institutions opened. The unfortunate example of Battle Creek College generally influenced them to a certain extent. The most significant exception was the Avondale School in Australia, which, as we saw in chapter 1, Ellen White hoped would become a "pattern" school, since it had implemented the principles of a uniquely Adventist approach to Christian education.

Avondale and the writings of Ellen White given in connection with its founding and development had an impact upon Adventist schools in America. On the positive side, for example, Edward Sutherland moved Battle Creek College to a large rural acreage in Berrien Springs, Michigan, where it became Emmanuel Missionary College. In addition, he and his colleagues succeeded in destroying the stranglehold of the Greek and Roman classics on the curriculum, gave the Bible the dominant role in the course of studies, and uplifted the value of practical manual labor in education.

Unfortunately, however, Sutherland tended to go to the opposite extremes in his attempt to correct entrenched evils. Thus, to escape from the overemphasis that Battle Creek College had placed on the mental side of education, early Emmanuel Missionary College went overboard on the physical-practical aspects of education. Students performed long hours of vigorous physical labor, lived on a two-meal-a-day program that was insufficient for the exertion they were putting forth, and tried to keep their eyes open and their minds focused as they attended their three-hour recitation period after supper. In like manner, in seeking to avoid the evils of the overuse of the classics, the reformers created extensive controversies as to how one could use the Bible as the only textbook for every subject. Again, in a desire to eliminate the objectionable aspects of degrees, the educators at Berrien Springs chartered their school as a "charitable institution" rather than a college. They apparently failed to realize that extremes at one end of the educational spectrum are just as wrong as those at the other. All extremes missed the sensible balance that Ellen White called for.

We could hardly refer to the early experience of Emmanuel Missionary College as the good old days of Adventist education. From one point of view, we could regard the development of Adventist higher and secondary education in the twentieth century as a process of working out the balance between the extremes of Battle Creek College and early Emmanuel Missionary College. This has been an ongoing process in Adventist institutions around the world.

Another aspect of the good old days in Adventist education is the fact that until just before the turn of the century Seventh-day Adventists had only a handful of elementary schools. The church had almost totally neglected the formal education of its younger members. This was particularly unfortunate in that students are most impressionable and are refining their attitudes, values, and world views during the elementary years. The elementary experience is, in many ways, the most crucial step (outside the home) on the educational ladder. Ellen White wrote in the 1890s that the church should have established elementary schools years before it actually began them (6T, p. 203; cf. CT, p. 46).

Few of us would choose to return to the good old days of Adventist education if we had all the facts. It is undoubtedly true that Adventist education is not all it could and should be today, but it is also true that it is, in many ways, considerably better than it was in the nineteenth and early twentieth centuries. From the perspective of historical study, it appears that Adventist education has continued to advance toward its goals through the years. It may, in fact, be closer to the ideal today than during most of its previous history. This does not mean that Adventist education does not have some glaring problems today or that it may not have retrogressed in some areas. But it does imply that we should have a great deal of hope in the future. One of our greatest perils is that we will become complacent over the fact that we have advanced beyond some of the problems and misunderstandings of our pioneers and thereby feel justified in maintaining the status quo.

Our success, however, is probably nothing to shout about—after all, we are still holding classes on Planet Earth. The real challenge still lies before us. That involves learning the lessons of the past and moving beyond our present position in implementing the development of the fine balance of the mental, the physical, and the spiritual in education. The task before us is to build upon our understanding of both the successes and the failures in our past history so that we do not continue to make the same mistakes. It is true that the good old days may not have been all that good, but it is also true that the Lord expects greater advances in the principles of Christian education in the future. To remain where we are is to stagnate and eventually die.

The Myth that the Educational Ideas of Ellen White Were Ahead of Her Time

As a young teacher I can remember going to conventions and hearing the myth that the educational theory of Ellen White was a hundred years ahead of her time. It sounded good as long as one did not read educational history. Those who did, however, discovered that this destructive belief does not rest on fact.

It is extremely important to realize that Ellen White never made such claims about her educational (or other) writings. The responsibility for the myth lies with some of her misinformed followers who have mistakenly thought they were doing her a service. Good intentions, unfortunately, are not always related to truth.

Other nineteenth-century educators also espoused Ellen White's educational reform concepts. Mrs. White was not unique in the individual ideas she set forth, a fact that should not surprise us, since both she and her contemporaries were fighting the same enemy. We should expect that they, in their sincerity and their common Christian and social heritage, would come up with similar basic concepts of reform. Furthermore, Ellen White never stated that her ideas were unique. On the contrary, she wrote that "as far as their teaching is true, . . . the world's great thinkers reflect the rays of the Sun of Righteousness. Every gleam of thought, every flash of the intellect, is from the Light of the world."—Ed, p. 14. Her statement implies that God is the source of true reform ideas, whether they come through revelation or through the rational application of human study. God has many channels for His blessings.

Ellen White knew she was in harmony with the educational reform ideas of her age. For example, her writings on the role of physiology in education and on proper ventilation and lighting in the classroom resemble some of the ideas in Horace Mann's annual reports. But then, why shouldn't they, since both Mann and Mrs. White were fighting the health-destroying educational abuses that Bettmann graphically portrayed in The Good Old Days—They Were Terrible!? Mrs. White never pretended to be unfamiliar with Mann's work. On the contrary, some of his material was published along with hers in Health: or How to Live in 1865. In addition, in 1899 she requested James Edson White to bring some of Mann's writings with him should he come to Australia.[9]

D. E. Robinson set forth the role of Ellen White as she related to the reformers in health care and medicine in The Story of Our Health Message. The same sort of positive contextual history could be done for her educational ideas, since they were not peculiar to her. Even a casual reading of the first volume of Robert Samuel Fletcher's History of Oberlin College From Its Founding Through the Civil War[10] indicates that Oberlin College had attempted nearly all the Seventh-day Adventist reform ideas during the 1830s and 1840s. It also becomes quite evident that most of them had failed, and by 1865 Oberlin, along with many of its sister institutions, was well on its way back to more traditional approaches to education.

What is special about Ellen White's contribution to educational reform is the total salvational package in which she couched it. Even this, however, is not unique. Other Christian educators have stressed the redemptive aspect of education and the restoration of the image of God motif for education. Both formats are implicit in the Bible. It is important to note this point—that Mrs. White based her educational ideas upon Biblical principles and they are therefore in harmony with others who have built upon the same foundation. On the other hand, she did not follow the false leads of those educational theorists who built partly upon Biblical concepts of education and partly upon those inherited from Greek and Roman classical thought. In other words, her harmony with the educational reformers of her day was not a blind one. She was quite willing to agree with those aspects of their reforms that harmonized with Biblical principles, while rejecting that which she deemed to be error in the light of those principles. As a result, we can say that the total educational reform package of the Spirit of Prophecy, rather than its individual ideas, is Ellen White's real contribution to Christian education. Her contribution is outstanding because of its unity rather than its originality.

It is important that Adventists do not fall into the pit of claiming more for the writings of Ellen White than she did for them. To do so merely leads us away from the message of the writings and sets us up for probable disillusionment. Adventists have at times wasted considerable energy seeking to explain what is unique and original in Ellen White's writings, while she herself claimed that her total teachings are implicit in the Bible (5T, pp. 663-665). We would do much better to put our energies into actualizing the principles in the writings rather than seeking to defend that which no one has asked us to defend. And we can best put these principles in practice when we grasp the historical context of her writings in terms of what was taking place in Adventist education and in the larger contemporary culture. Historical understanding will keep us from succumbing to historical myths and will help us apply the principles to our own personal and social educational context. Ellen White's educational writings did not come into existence in a vacuum. It is therefore important, just as it is in Biblical study, that we seek to learn that context so that we will be better able to separate the universal principles from the historical particulars of a given situation. Only then will we be able to continue to develop a valid and well-balanced program of Christian education.

3 The Accreditation Myth

A myth that has received wide publicity by that sector of Adventism that would like to see denominational schools get "back to the blueprint" involves accreditation. The myth has various forms. Perhaps its two most popular formats are that Mrs. White said that we should not accredit our schools, and that she made the statement that before the end of time Adventist schools would be operated as they should be—that is, without accreditation.

The accreditation myth throughout its history has had a close link to a mythology regarding the inappropriateness of granting degrees. In fact, the problem of accreditation in collegiate education was not an issue in American higher education until the twentieth century, when regional accrediting associations came onto the educational scene with the purpose of developing quality controls in literary and professional education. Before the arrival of accrediting associations, any school (in most States) could call itself a college, set up its own standards, and grant degrees. From this perspective the question of granting degrees was a forerunner to the issue of becoming accredited. Some saw both as a bowing to the standards of the world.

Nineteenth-Century Roots of the Myth

One of early Adventism's most energetic educational reformers was Edward Alexander Sutherland, who went from the presidency of Walla Walla College in 1897 to transform Battle Creek College into a reform institution. During the latter's early years the classical curriculum and degrees based upon that curriculum had formed the core of the most prestigious programs at Battle Creek College. Ellen White and a few of the other church leaders, however, had been calling for an education of a different nature—one that concentrated on the Bible rather than the pagan classics, and one that would focus on the speedy preparation of Christian workers rather than classical scholars.

In the nineteenth century, degrees served as the "bait" to keep people struggling through the years of college. In this role they played upon a person's inborn vanity and pride. It was a pleasant feeling to be able to sport a Bachelor of Arts degree in a society in which most people were doing well if they completed an elementary education. The B.A. signified that the holder had mastered Homer, Cicero, Virgil, and other authors in the original Greek and Latin. A degree was the mark of a cultured gentleman. On the other hand, a college degree was not essential to qualify a person to enter into teaching, nursing, medical school, or the world of business or government. In other words, outside of "snob value" the degree had little usefulness in a culture that did not require it for positions of social leadership and responsibility. Acquiring a degree, however, did absorb a lot of time and energy that one might put to better use.

Battle Creek College, with its classical, degree-oriented curriculum, had been playing the same game as other colleges. Sutherland set out to change this. Soon after his arrival the college stopped offering the classics, the classical languages, and academic degrees.

In 1899 he pointed out that "the first degree was granted by a pope," and that degrees were the "germs" of the disease that permeated the Protestantism from which the third angel's message was calling people.[1] Nearly twenty years later he wrote that "a degree is a sign or seal of authority. In the Christian church 'the conferring of degrees was originated by a pope' as a sign of his authority over the educational system. Today degrees are conferred by the State, and the State has no right to set its seal to the work of an institution unless it can approve the system of education offered by that school. The degree is a sign of its approval. Any Seventh-day Adventist school that grants degrees, thereby invites State inspection, and must accept the world's standard and come into conformity to the worldly system of education. Claiming to conduct Christian schools, we yet seek to so teach that we can satisfy the worldly system. In time the State will either demand absolute conformity to her system or refuse to grant the degrees." Sutherland added that soon the degree granting would be done by the Papacy. Then a degree would come directly from that organization and would be "a seal or a mark of the beast."[2]

Thus Sutherland became, in effect, the antiaccreditation reformer among Seventh-day Adventists in the nineteenth century. Where, we might ask, did he get his "light"? Certainly not from either the Bible or the Spirit of Prophecy. One will search Mrs. White's published works in vain for remarks regarding a prohibition against the granting of degrees. She did, however, make an unfavorable comment concerning students who piled up degree after degree while they were all the time becoming less qualified to do the work of God (FE, p. 356).

In 1896 W. W. Prescott, educational secretary of the General Conference, wrote to Sutherland regarding an interview that he had had with Mrs. White on the subject of degrees. "Sister White," remarked Prescott, "says that she is not aware that she has ever written anything about the question of degrees, and in fact she seemed to know very little about their significance, and so she said she was quite sure that she had never written about them. She said, however, as she has said many times before, that our schools should give a better class of education than the schools of the world, but that it should be of an entirely different character." Prescott also noted that he had explained the significance of degrees in the eyes of educators and that "her idea seemed to be that there was no need that we should pay attention to those things, that what we wanted to do was to educate for usefulness here and the eternal kingdom hereafter, and that the question with our people was not whether a young man had a degree, but whether he had a suitable preparation so that he could be a blessing to others in this work." [3]

Sutherland did not find any direct authority for his stand in the writings of Ellen White. Actually he developed his position from inferences based on selected inspired statements, the historical implications of Jeffersonian democracy, and the reform attempts of Oberlin College. [4] He was also probably influenced by the contemporary Bible Institute movement among millenarians that disparaged academic degrees and focused on the speedy preparation of missionary "gapmen" to fill the place between the common people and the highly educated clergy. [5]

The Changing Nature of Professional Education and the Move for Accreditation

The early twentieth century brought major changes to American education. A pivotal point proved to be the "Flexner Report" of 1910, which eventually led to the closure of more than one half of the medical schools in the United States. The American Medical Association, on the basis of the report, evaluated the fledgling College of Medical Evangelists in 1911 and gave it the lowest possible rating. Eventually the school would either have to achieve a higher rating or close as a medical college, since without American Medical Association approval its graduates could not practice. To receive a higher rating, however, meant that the schools and colleges sending students to the College of Medical Evangelists also had to have accreditation from the developing regional accrediting associations. During the early 1920s a school needed accreditation up through the junior college level. Some Adventist colleges were able to obtain it without too much trouble. By 1928, however, it was evident that they would have to be accredited as senior colleges. This problem proved to be troublesome for many reasons, but the central threat was that college teachers would need graduate degrees and they could earn them only at "pagan" institutions. Some feared that many of those who attended the universities would be intellectually corrupted. More specifically, such individuals believed that some of the teachers would apostatize, while those who returned to Adventist institutions would mix truth with error and thereby provide the basis for an educational Babylon in which the faculty members would serve the true and the false together.

It is impossible for Adventists in the 1980s to realize the emotional impact of this issue on the ministerial and educational leadership of the church in the twenties and thirties. The fact that several Adventist educators who early received graduate degrees did leave the organized program of the church, and even the denomination itself, reinforced the fears associated with advanced degrees and accreditation. Everett Dick has indicated that many of them left, however, because the church did not really want what they had to offer and looked with suspicion upon them. This in turn, he noted, "played into the hands of the nonaccreditation people in high places for they could point to this as an example of the ill effects of attending the university."[6] From our comfortable historical perspective it is quite easy to recognize that some of the Adventist leadership were contributing to their own self-fulfilling prophecy, but this was not at all evident to most of the participants.

The 1920s and 1930s saw the church leadership polarized between those who believed accreditation would be a denominational disaster and those who felt that the church could not operate educational institutions in the twentieth century without it. Both sides drew their ammunition from the writings of Ellen White. Such men as William H. Branson, general vice president of the General Conference; James L. McElhany, vice president for the North American Division; and Warren E. Howell, secretary of the General Conference Department of Education, led the nonaccreditation forces. They believed that Ellen White opposed accreditation. She had urged: "Let us determine that we will not be tied by so much as a thread to the educational policies of those who do not discern the voice of God, and who will not hearken to His commandments."—CT, p. 255. Again, she had written that "there is constant danger among our people that those who engage in labor in our schools and sanitariums will entertain the idea that they must get in line with the world, study the things which the world studies, and become familiar with the things that the world becomes familiar with. This is one of the greatest mistakes that could be made."—FE, p. 534. These and similar declarations, they interpreted to support the antiaccreditation stand.

On the other side stood Percy T. Magan, dean and later president of the College of Medical Evangelists, and several of the college presidents. They had documentation from Ellen White that logically led to nothing but accreditation, even though it had dangers involved. The basis of their position went back to 1910 when the denomination had faced the problem of the type of medical education to offer at Loma Linda. In their concern they placed the matter before Ellen White.[7] Her reply was unequivocal. "We must," she claimed, "provide that which is essential to qualify our youth who desire to be physicians, so that they may intelligently fit themselves to be able to stand the examinations required to prove their efficiency as physicians. . . . *We are to supply whatever may be required,* so that these youth need not be compelled to go to medical schools conducted by men not of our faith."[8] She also indicated that this would affect our colleges. "Our larger union conference training schools in various parts of the field should be placed in the most favorable position for qualifying our youth to meet the entrance requirements specified by state laws regarding medical students. . . . *The youth . . . should be able to secure at our union conference training schools all that is essential for entrance into a medical college.* . . . Inasmuch as there are legal requirements making it necessary that medical students shall take a certain preparatory course of study, our colleges should arrange to carry their students to the point of literary and scientific training that is necessary."—CT, pp. 479, 480. (Italics supplied.) These statements, along with historical developments in professional education, left Adventists with no alternative but to seek accreditation. But this, however, was not immediately apparent to all the participants of the accreditation controversy.

By 1928 the requirement for entering medical school had risen to three years of college, and it was obvious that Adventist institutions would need more than junior college accreditation. The Autumn Council in that year established the Board of Regents as a denominational accrediting association. The church hoped that the regional accrediting bodies would accept the association and that the Adventist colleges could thereby avoid "contamination." Such a hope proved to be wishful thinking.

By 1931 it grew evident that the Board of Regents scheme had failed and that the situation was more desperate than ever. From September 25 to October 23, 1930, the *Review and Herald* had devoted a great deal of its space to the accreditation debate. The fact that even General Conference Educational secretary Howell, one of the staunchest of the nonaccreditation brethren, capitulated indicates the serious difficulties involved in remaining unaccredited. In the *Review and Herald* of October 16, he pointed out that changes in professional standards affected not only the training of physicians but also the education of schoolteachers and nurses. This fact, claimed Howell, had brought the denominational educational system face to face with an emergency. We had, as he saw it, two choices: (1) send our youth to secular schools, or (2) accredit our own schools and colleges. He pointed out that accrediting only meant "*cooperation*," and not "*affiliation*." Howell by now saw no option but to accredit, although it was his hope that eventually the church would have its own graduate school so that our college teachers would not have to study at non-Adventist institutions.[9]

Sutherland, the antidegree champion of the 1890s, had also seen that times had changed in professional education, and that even self-supporting Madison would have to seek recognition as a senior college by the "rating associations" if its graduating teachers, nurses, and premedical students were to be able to continue their professional careers. On January 7, 1931, *The Madison Survey* featured an article by Sutherland emphasizing these points and announcing that Madison would seek approval as a senior college.[10]

Sutherland's announcement brought shock to some of the Adventist community. Clifford G. Howell, a medical doctor living in Tennessee, noted in a letter of protest to Sutherland that "if the man who was called to lead God's educational work out of Egypt, out of Babylon, out of Battle Creek, out of worldly customs, away from centralization, away from worldly . . . methods, has not fallen into the very pit he pointed out as one of greatest danger, then I do not know how to measure values of 30 and 40 years ago."[11]

Otto J. Graf, one of the presidents who followed Sutherland at Emmanuel Missionary College, sounded a similar note of anguish and surprise. "Now, my brother," he wrote, "years ago we looked upon you and your school as bulwarks against things worldly, and now to find you leading out in this matter of subjecting out [sic] school system unnecessarily to the worldly influence and dictation is a tremendous disappointment. . . . I can hardly visualize that the man who wrote that wonderful book, 'Living Fountains or Broken Cisterns' could be responsible for such a statement." [12]

Sutherland's extensive reply shows the depth of the problem. Once again he pointed out the fact of rising standards in professional education. He then went on to state that he had been quietly sending some of his teachers to recognized colleges and universities for advanced degrees since 1923, so that Madison would be in a position to meet the legal requirements. The Lord had not changed His mind, claimed Sutherland, but the failure of His people had made "it necessary for Him to change His plans." Sutherland did not feel that in seeking accredited recognition he was contradicting or repudiating the great principles he had earlier enunciated. Rather, he said, "it is simply an adjustment to meet conditions that have been brought upon us because of failure on the part of our denomination to step forward in educational reform years ago." As a result, he suggested, Adventists were closer to the tail than the head, and our schools had no real choice but to seek recognition or discontinue a large part of their educational program.[13] Both Howell and Graf wrote to Sutherland that his arguments had changed their minds. They said they had come to see that accreditation was the only way.[14]

The accreditation issue was a major item at the 1931 Autumn Council. It gave Adventist colleges denominational approval to secure regional accreditation. Even after such authorization, however, many of the leaders in the church continued to struggle against the idea. William G. White has written that "the 1931 Council decision did not solve the problem, but was only the opening salvo of a five-year war of words as the pros and cons of regional accreditation were debated by church administrators and educators." [15]

A major setback for the accreditation forces came in October, 1935, when W. H. Branson delivered the report of the Survey Commission on Accreditation to the Autumn Council. Branson closed his report by noting that "we are ready to admit that in our action of four years ago we went too far. We find that we made a mistake." The committee's assessment was that "we have departed far from the blueprint." [16] As a result of his speech and the discussion that followed, the session decided to minimize the danger by accrediting only two senior colleges. The 1936 General

Conference session reversed the decision, however. Times had changed, and the significance of the changes was too obvious to avoid. By 1945 all six of the North American senior colleges that had been the focal point of controversy in the 1930s had received their accreditation.

A Perspective on Accreditation

We live in an era when Adventist institutions publicly display their various accreditation achievements. But that is not just institutional vanity. It is rather an essential aspect of advertising, since in the last quarter of the twentieth century an unaccredited degree is not worth the paper on which it is printed if offered for admission to many professions. Such a situation is not incompatible with the position Mrs. White took. She indicated to Prescott in 1896 that the important thing is not the degree, but whether a person has "a suitable preparation so that he could be a blessing to others in this work." [17] In those days accredited degrees were not the pragmatic necessity that they are today. Then a person could serve in the professions quite well without one. Today, however, accredited degrees constitute the "suitable preparation" needed for many lines of Christian service. Ellen White apparently glimpsed our day when she wrote that "in the future there will be more pressing need of men and women of literary qualifications than there has been in the past."—FE, p. 192.

One of the great fears of Adventist leaders earlier in the century was that regional accreditation would cause Adventist colleges to lose their distinctiveness. Part of their concern came from the misconception that accredited colleges would have to instruct within the context of the belief system of the accrediting body. Actually, however, accrediting teams do not evaluate institutions in terms of whether a school is teaching to satisfy the demands of the accrediting body's philosophy, but whether the institution instructs and operates in a manner that meets the demands of its *own* philosophy. An accredited institution, therefore, can have a curriculum just as Christian as that of an unaccredited one. Both types, of course, may also be equally unchristian. Accreditation is not what makes the distinction. What determines whether a given school is Christian or not is whether it has a Christian philosophy and is implementing it in its daily activities. Accreditation evaluation may even help a school see where it has not lived up to its own Christian philosophy. On the other hand, striving after accreditation can blur the distinctive mission of Seventh-day Adventist educational institutions when their leadership does not focus intensely on Christian goals.

A second function of regional accrediting bodies concerns the technical aspects of education. Does the school have sufficient space, safety features, and sanitary arrangements? Are its teachers qualified? Does it maintain adequate records? Is it meeting minimum standards concerning the length of the school year? Evaluations on such items have helped many Christian schools to move beyond sloppy administrative and classroom practices. It is unfortunate that the church has not always maintained high standards on its own initiative, since many of the standards of accrediting bodies are inherent in the concept of Christian excellence.

We should realize that nowhere has the Lord indicated to the Adventist Church that degrees or accreditation are wrong. On the contrary, the advice given by Ellen White concerning the College of Medical Evangelists' medical program has left the denomination with no choice but to accredit its institutions of learning. She does indicate, however, that we face a very real danger when we delight in degrees, and institutions become vain and glorify their accreditation as a human achievement, while losing sight of their purpose for existing. Vanity, pride, and the glorification of that which is human constitute the essence of the sickness of sin. The challenge to Adventists today is to view degrees and accreditation not as ends in themselves to flaunt as evidence of human achievement but as the means of preparing Christians to serve the church and the world in many of life's callings and vocations.

4 Myths About Educational Purpose

Myths about the purpose of education take many shapes. Probably the most widespread examples argue that the true function of schools is to develop intellectual abilities and/or to prepare young people for the world of work. These myths occur widely, both within and outside the Christian community. Perceptive Christians, however, often see beyond such myths and claim that the primary and most fundamental aim of Christian education is to develop character and/or to prepare young people for service. These views are also mythological. They are, however, even more subtle than myths about intellectual culture and job preparation, since they have the trappings of Christianity. All of the above purposes are good in themselves, but they are Christian aims only when related to something much more basic.

The Central Role of Purpose in Education

Why have Seventh-day Adventist schools? Why do Adventists spend millions of dollars each year to support approximately five thousand schools around the world when free public education is often available? How can we justify such expenditures in the light of the other pressing needs of the church and the world that it serves? The answer to such questions has of necessity a link to the purpose of Adventist education. If Adventist schools serve a sufficiently distinctive and important purpose, the achievement of that purpose is worth their cost. Establishing and clearly understanding the true object of Christian education is therefore crucial to the continued support and operation of Adventist schools. In fact, the most important educational understanding a Christian can arrive at is related to the purposes, aims, and goals of education.

Education without an aim is useless, and, directed at the wrong target, is worse than useless, even when it achieves its goals, since it obscures the true issues of life. A marksman can hit only a target he sees. Educators likewise must have a clear vision of their primary purpose if they ever hope to reach their goal. An understanding of our objective makes it possible for us to focus our energies and resources in the most profitable manner, and it allows us to plan in an intelligent and orderly fashion. Educational aims give direction to the education process, motivate us, and provide criteria for evaluating progress. Purpose affects every aspect of education.

Ellen White highlighted the crucial nature of educational aims and purposes when she wrote that *"by a misconception of the true nature and object of education, many have been led into serious and even fatal errors."*—CT, p. 49. (Italics supplied.) Her powerful statement implies that for many people a mistaken notion of educational aims has been eternally fatal. "Such a mistake is made," she added, "when the regulation of the heart or the establishment of principles is neglected in the effort to secure intellectual culture, or when eternal interests are overlooked in the eager desire for temporal advantage."—*Ibid.* It is easy to see that she disqualifies both intellectual learning and job preparation as the primary goals of education. On the other hand, it does seem to indicate that character development and preparation for service might be its fundamental aims.

This conclusion seems especially appropriate in view of the following statements: "The great work of parents and teachers is character building. . . . A knowledge of the sciences sinks into insignificance beside this great aim; but all true education may be made to help in the development of a righteous character."—*Ibid.*, p. 61. "The true object of education is to fit men and women for service by developing and bringing into active exercise all their faculties."—*Ibid.*, p. 493. True education "prepares the students for the joy of service in this world and the higher joy of wider service in the world to come" (Ed, p. 13).

In spite of such statements, however, neither the development of character nor preparation for service is the primary (i.e., first in time and importance, most fundamental) aim of Christian education. Why is this so? Because many have done, or at least attempted, both of them outside of Christ. Many humanistic educators have also sought to make character development and/or preparation for service to humanity the purpose of education. Altruism and human goodness, however, are not Christianity. Separated from a relationship with Jesus Christ, they may be merely another attempt at salvation by works. *Steps to Christ* treats the myths of character development and education for service as the primary goal of education quite well. "Education, culture, the exercise of the will, human effort, all have their proper sphere, but here they are powerless. They may produce an outward correctness of behavior, but they cannot change the heart. . . . The idea that it is necessary only to develop the good that exists in man by nature, is a fatal deception."—Pages 18, 19. What, then, we might ask, is the real objective of Christian education?

The Primary Aim of Christian Education

Perhaps the best way to get at the fundamental goal of education is to examine the needs and conditions of the object of that education—man. D. Elton Trueblood made a most meaningful statement when he claimed that "until we are clear on what man is we shall not be clear about much else."[1]

In the passage that undergirds her entire philosophy of education, Ellen White pointed out that if we are to comprehend the meaning and goal of education we will have to understand four things about man: (1) his original nature, (2) the purpose of God in creating him, (3) the change that took place in the human condition at the Fall, and (4) God's plan for yet fulfilling His purpose in the education of the human race (Ed, pp. 14, 15).

She then went on to explain the four items. First, man was created in the image of God.[2] Second, mankind was to reveal ever more fully God's image by continual development throughout eternity. Third, disobedience badly damaged, but did not destroy, the image in its mental, physical, and spiritual aspects. Man's disobedience also brought death. Fourth, God did not turn His back on man in his hopeless condition; He still intended to fulfill His purpose for the human race by restoring His image in man through the plan of salvation. Education is one of God's redemptive and restorative agencies. Therefore, indicated Mrs. White, the primary purpose of education is to lead students to God for redemption (ibid., pp. 15, 16).

Scripture presents the same picture. Central to an understanding of the Bible is man's fall in Genesis 3. Here is one of the most crucial chapters in the Bible. Neither Scripture nor daily experience makes sense if we explain away as legend the first three chapters of Genesis. According to Genesis, God created humanity in His image and likeness—an exalted state (Gen. 1:26, 27). Man, however, rejected God and chose his own way. As a result, he became alienated and separated from God (chap. 3:8-10), his fellowman (verses 11, 12), his own self (verse 13), and the natural world (verses 17-19). Separating himself from the source of life, he became subject to death (chaps. 2:17; 3:19). Man had become hopeless and *lost* in the fullest sense of the word.

The lostness of man provides the purpose of Christian education. *Man's greatest need is to become "unlost."* Thus Jesus claimed that He came "to seek and to save that which was lost" (Luke 19:10, K.J.V.). Such seeking and saving is the theme of the Bible from Genesis 3 to Revelation 20. The message of the Bible from the Fall to the restoration of Eden in Revelation 21 is the story of how God, through teachers, prophets, patriarchs, preachers, symbolic services, and a host of other means, has been attempting to rescue man from his lostness. We must see Christian education in this context. "In the highest sense," penned Ellen White, "the work of education and the work of redemption are one" because both build directly upon Jesus Christ. *To lead the student into a saving relationship with Jesus Christ "should be the teacher's first effort and his constant aim"* (ibid., p. 30; italics supplied). Here is education's highest and primary goal.

Edwin Rian correctly noted that most writers in educational philosophy, regardless of their philosophical and religious perspectives, "agree on considering the problem of 'sin and death,' which is the problem of man, according to Pauline and Reformed Protestant theology, as irrelevant to the questions of the aims and process of education." Such a position, he indicated, cannot help producing "miseducation and frustration for the individual and for the community." From the perspective of fallen man's predicament, Rian uplifted *"education as conversion."* Herbert Welch, president of Ohio Wesleyan University early in the twentieth century, made the same point when he claimed that "to win its students from sin to righteousness is . . . the highest achievement of the Christian college." [3]

Christian education is the only education that can meet man's deepest needs, because only Christian educators understand the core of the human problem. The redemptive aim of Christian education is what makes it Christian. The primary aim of Christian education in the school, the home, and the church is to lead young people into a saving relationship with Jesus Christ. This heals the principal alienation of Genesis 3—that between man and God. And the healing of the God/man relationship sets the stage for the removal of man's other basic alienations. Education is a part of God's great plan of redemption, or atonement. The role of education is to help bring man back to at-one-ness with God, his fellowman, his own self, and the natural world. The whole message of the Bible points forward to the day when the work of restoration will be complete and the Edenic condition will be restored in the realm of nature because of the healing of man's manifold lostness (Revelation 21, 22; Isa. 11:6-9; 35).

The essence of the Fall was that man chose to place himself, rather than God, at the center of his life. Redemption, therefore, reverses this procedure and reinstates God as the focal point of personal existence. It is a dynamic experience called by many names, including conversion and new birth. The Bible also refers to it as the obtaining of a new heart and mind. Paul vividly captured the experience when he claimed that the Christian is one who has had his entire way of thinking and living transformed (Rom. 12:2). The English language has adopted the Greek word he used for *transformation* as *metamorphosis*, the term we use to indicate the change that takes place when a caterpillar becomes a butterfly. It is a radical change that expresses a discontinuity with the past and a new beginning. Carlyle B. Haynes caught the central nature of the experience when he wrote that "the Christian life is not any modification of the old life; it is not any qualification of it, any development of it, not any progression of it, any culture or refinement or education of it. It is not built on the old life at all. It does not grow from it. It is entirely another life—a new life altogether. It is the actual life of Jesus Christ Himself in my flesh." [4]

The student's greatest need, then, is for a spiritual rebirth that places God at the center of his existence. Paul noted that such renewal is a daily experience, and Jesus taught that the Holy Spirit accomplishes the transformation (1 Cor. 15:31; John 3:5). Christian education can never take place, we must emphasize, without the dynamic power of the Holy Spirit.

Mrs. White wrote that the "all-important thing" in education "should be the conversion" of the students (FE, p. 436). *It is upon the foundation of the new birth experience that Christian education can proceed with its other aims and purposes. If it fails at this foundational and primary point, it has failed entirely.*

Some Secondary Aims of Christian Education

The healing of man's alienation from God sets the stage for the treatment of his other basic alienations and thereby implies the secondary purposes of education. We have noted that it is a part of God's great plan of redemption or atonement. The role of education is to help bring man back to at-one-ness with God, his fellowmen, his own self, and the natural world. Within this context Christian teaching restores broken relationships. The healing of the broken relationship between an individual and God prepares the way for the successful accomplishment of Christian education's secondary purposes, such as character development, the acquisition of knowledge, and job competency. We shall now briefly examine the secondary aims—particularly as they relate to the primary objective of Christian education.

Character development is certainly a major goal of Christian education. Ellen White noted that the character determines the destiny for both this life and the one to come and that "character building is the most important work ever entrusted to human beings."—Ed, pp. 109, 225. C. B. Eavey related character development to the fundamental purpose of education when he stated that "the foundational aim in Christian education is the bringing of the individual to Christ for salvation. Before a man of God can be perfected, there must be a man of God to perfect; without the new birth there is no man of God." [5] In other words, true character can develop only in the born-again Christian. If we equate the primary objective of Christian education—to bring students into relationship with Christ—with such theological concepts as conversion, the new birth, and justification, then it follows that character development, as a secondary aim, must be synonymous with sanctification and Christian growth.

Such an equation is exactly what we find in the writings of Ellen White. "The great work of parents and teachers is *character building—seeking to restore the image of Christ* in those placed under their care. A knowledge of the sciences sinks into insignificance beside this great aim; but all true education may be made to help in the development of a righteous character. *The formation of character is the work of a lifetime,* and it is for eternity."—CT, p. 61. (Italics supplied.) Character development and sanctification are essentially two names for the same process. The only real point of difference seems to be that the world of education and the world of theology have, unfortunately, developed different vocabularies to treat the same process. A misunderstanding of this point has placed some educators in the incongruent position of espousing salvation by grace in religion, while implying salvation by works in education.

At this point we should not need to remind ourselves that the concept of Christian character development is quite opposed to the humanistic view, which implies merely the refinement of the natural, unrenewed man. [6] Christian character development never takes place outside the conversion experience or apart from Christ and the agency of the Holy Spirit (Phil. 2:12, 13; John 15). Only the dynamic power of the Holy Spirit develops the image of God in the individual. The essence of the spiritual element of that image is the reproduction of the fruits of the Spirit—love, joy, peace, patience, kindness, goodness, faithfulness, gentleness, and self-control—in the life of each student (Gal. 5:22-24). Hans LaRondelle has indicated that at least part of the restoration process occurs as we behold the "attractive loveliness of Christ's character." Through this act we assimilate His image.[7] Thus it is imperative that every phase of Christian education—the character of the teacher, the curriculum, the methods of discipline, and every other aspect—reflect Christ.

Jesus Christ is the beginning, the middle, and the end of Christian education. The Holy Spirit seeks to implant the likeness of His character in each of us and in our children and students. The Spirit uses parents, teachers, and other educators as agents, or mediators, of salvation. The individual's part is to continuously surrender his will to God's infilling power and then to follow the directions of the Holy Spirit in his life. Character development is an act of God's grace just as much as is justification.[8] Because of its vital role, the science of character development should form a central pillar in the preparation of teachers, parents, pastors, and others in educational positions.

It should be obvious that Christian education has other secondary goals, such as the acquisition of knowledge and preparation for the world of work. Such goals, however, sink into "insignificance" when compared to the redemptive work of education that relates to conversion and character development (CT, pp. 49, 61; FE, p. 27). After all, "what is a man profited, if he shall gain the whole world, and lose his own soul?" (Matt. 16:26, K.J.V.).

We must always see the acquisition of knowledge in Christian education within the larger context of Christianity. The Christian educator is not nearly as concerned with passing on masses of information as he is with developing the Christian mind—a Christian way of viewing reality and organizing knowledge within the framework of the Christian world view. Gene Garrick pointed out the secondary nature of knowledge acquisition when he wrote that "there can be no truly Christian mind without the new birth since spiritual truth is apprehended and applied spiritually (1 Cor. 2:1-16)."[9]

We will discuss the development of the Christian mind at greater length in chapters 10 and 11, but before we leave this topic we should realize that the Christian never views gaining knowledge—even Christian knowledge—as an end in itself. In his acquisition of knowledge and in the development of a Christian mind, he never loses sight of the fact that his ultimate goal is better service to both God and his fellowman.

Preparation for the world of work, as we shall see in chapter 19, is also a definite purpose of Christian education. Every student completing a Christian educational program should have at least one marketable skill (Ed, p. 218). Occupational preparation, however, like every other aspect of the Christian life, cannot be separated from the issues of the new birth, character development, and the development of a Christian mind. The Christian life is a unit, and each aspect of it interacts with the others and the total man. The Christian will always see an occupation within the context of an individual's wider vocation as a servant of God. This brings us to what we might consider the ultimate and final outcome of Christian education.

The Ultimate Aim of Christian Education

The life of Jesus was one of service for mankind. He came to our earth to give Himself for the betterment of others. His followers have the same function, and the ultimate end (i.e., final outcome) of education is to prepare them for their task. Ellen White has written that "true education is the preparation of the mental, moral, and physical powers for the performance of every duty, pleasant or otherwise, the training of every habit and practice, of heart, mind, and soul for divine service."—3SM, p. 228; cf. CT, p. 493; Ed, p. 13. Along this same line, Herbert Welch concluded that "education for its own sake is as bad as art for art's sake; but culture held in trust to empower one better to serve one's fellow men, the wise for the ignorant, the strong for the weak," is education's highest aim. "The Christian character," he postulated, "which does not find expression in service is scarcely worthy of the name." [10]

Figure 1 (see next page) indicates that conversion, character development, acquiring a mature Christian mind, and occupational preparation are not ends in themselves. Each is rather an essential element in an individual's preparation for service to his fellowman as God seeks to heal the alienation that developed at the Fall between man and his fellows. The essence of Christian love and the Christlike character is service to others. The second great commandment, therefore, building upon our supreme love to God, bids us to love our neighbors as ourselves (Matt. 22:39).

All too often human beings have gotten their educational priorities backward. How often have we heard the following sentiments? "Society owes me a living because of all the years I

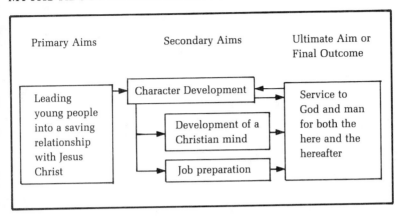

Figure 1. Purposes of Christian Education

spent getting an education." "I deserve more of the good life because of what I have accomplished." Even those who claim to be Christian often make—or at least imply—such statements. Unfortunately, they express the antithesis of the ultimate aim of Christianity. Gaining an education is a privilege, not a punishment, and having a professional role in society is an honor and responsibility. Tuition never establishes or builds educational institutions, and it pays only a small part of the cost of higher education. The bulk of it comes in the form of offerings and/or taxes from the working public. Society does not establish educational institutions to supply graduates with the right to "fleece" the public, but rather to train specialists to serve the public need.

It is morally wrong for individuals to use the gifts of society for self-aggrandizement. George S. Counts has written that "at every turn the social obligation which the advantages of a college education impose must be stressed: too often have we preached the monetary value of a college education; too widely have we bred the conviction that the training is advantageous because it enables the individual to get ahead; too insidiously have we spread the doctrine that the college opens up avenues to the exploitation of less capable men. *Higher education involves higher responsibility* . . . ; this cardinal truth must be impressed upon every recipient of its advantages. In season and out of season, social service, and not individual advancement, must be made the motif of college training."[11] If Counts from his humanistic perspective can so clearly recognize this fact, then the committed Christian should see it even more distinctly.

The message of the parable of the talents is that the greater our natural endowments and the greater our opportunities for their development, the more responsibility we have to image Christ in faithful service to those who have mental, spiritual, social, emotional, or physical needs (Matt. 25:14-26). To gain an education for self-service and self-glorification is the antithesis of Christianity, because it makes the same mistake that Lucifer did in heaven and Adam and Eve perpetuated in Eden. It places the human self on the throne of our lives and leaves us destitute of God's Holy Spirit (Gen. 3:1-7; Isa. 14:12-14; FE, p. 387).

On the other hand, an education that leads us to use our talents for our fellowman builds upon the conversion experience and helps heal the alienation between man and his fellows. Our service to man is indissolubly linked to our service to God. Furthermore, our service enables us to come to grips with our own selfishness, and who we are. As a result, it facilitates the removal of the alienation we suffer within our individual selves. In other words, we help ourselves to wholeness as we aid others. At the same time the kingdom of God grows within us and prepares the way for the second advent of Jesus Christ.

In conclusion, we should emphasize that Christian service is a response to God's love rather than an altruistic humanitarianism that still allows an individual to congratulate himself for his personal goodness. The Christian's gratitude toward God for saving him from his "lostness" inspires him to become a channel of God's love to others. In one sense, as we noted in Figure 1, character development lays the foundation for service. Yet it is also true that such service further develops character. From this perspective, we might visualize the two as working in tandem, each contributing to the other. It is certainly true that character development cannot occur without service. Christian service is not something that begins after graduation from high school or college. Rather, it is an integral part of a Christian's life from the time of conversion. We must introduce it into every Christian family and classroom as we lead our children to love one another and help them discover simple ways of cooperating with one another in their daily activities.

Perhaps one of the greatest challenges facing Christian education is to find ways to actualize the rhetoric of service. This topic is beyond the scope of this chapter. But the same Spirit who empowers us for selfless service will also direct us to ways to bring it into our lives, classrooms, and families as we seek to reach God's purposes for us in Christian education.

A final point that we should make explicit is the fact that the Christian school is an evangelistic agency, since its primary purpose involves leading its students into a saving relationship with Jesus Christ. It differs from other evangelistic agencies, however, in that its main thrust centers upon the conversion, development, and preparation of young people from Christian homes rather than people from the general public. The Christian school functions as a protective environment in which Christian nurture can take place in the context of the Christian world view and away from non-Christian peer pressures. It has both a conservative role, in providing a protective atmosphere for Christian growth, and a revolutionary role, since it seeks to develop evangelistic agents of various types for the church.[12] Many Christian communities have made the sad mistake of viewing the school as a general evangelistic agency rather than a selective evangelistic enterprise. The tragic result has generally been that the values of the non-Christian peer group have unduly influenced many of their children, rather than vice versa. While the Christian school might successfully serve as an entering evangelistic wedge in areas where the church is not yet established, it has proved to be more efficient as a protective environment for the conversion and development of young people from Christian families in places where well-established church communities already exist.

PART II

MYTHS ABOUT INSTITUTIONS AND PEOPLE

5 The Myth of the Omnipotent School

The Myth and Its Roots

Americans have a deeply rooted faith in the power of schooling. The eighteenth-century Enlightenment had bequeathed to the new nation the doctrines of the infinite perfectibility of mankind and the efficacy of formal education to bring about a utopian existence for all men. Thus Horace Mann, foremost founder of the American public system of education, could write: "Education, then, beyond all other devices of human origin, is the great equalizer of the conditions of men—the balance-wheel of the social machinery. . . . It gives each man the independence and the means by which he can resist the selfishness of other men. It does better than to disarm the poor of their hostility towards the rich: it prevents being poor. . . . If this education should be universal and complete, it would do more than all things else to obliterate factitious distinctions in society." [1] The school, from such a perspective, had omnipotent attributes.

This myth continued to gain currency among both professional educators and the general public throughout the nineteenth and early twentieth centuries. Americans equated education with schooling, and largely overlooked the roles of the family and other agents of education. Sociologist Marvin Grandstaff, therefore, could say in the late 1960s that "discussions of the educative role of the family are almost nonexistent." The result, he noted, was that parents generally did not think of themselves as educators. Instead, they tended to view "themselves only as providers and caretakers" who tended the children until they were old enough to go to educational specialists. Meanwhile, the public viewed the home as "an educationally barren place" where the children could spend their time between trips to school. The schools, for their part, often regarded the home and family as obstacles that they must somehow overcome, or, more positively, as adjuncts of the school, willing assistants to the programs of professional educators. [2]

The myth of the omnipotent school, despite some recent unmasking, is still alive and well. The American tendency to add a course or develop a school program to solve nearly every social problem clearly illustrates this. On the other hand, it is also true that the 1970s saw a disenchantment with formal schooling on an unprecedented scale—the myth's mask was beginning to slip.

The Myth Unmasked

The myth of the omnipotent school, which has made such an impact upon the public sector of education, has also influenced, to a lesser extent, the Adventist view of education. Undoubtedly it represents a carryover from the larger culture, but it is remarkable that it has had any impact at all, since the Bible and Ellen White give just the opposite message.

"In His wisdom," wrote Mrs. White, "the Lord has decreed that *the family shall be the greatest of all educational agencies.*"—CT, p. 107. (Italics supplied.) I was personally shocked when I first read this statement, even though I had been a teacher and principal in Adventist schools for several years. Probably my reaction resulted from the fact that I had absorbed the view that the school is society's primary educational agency. My dealings with many parents who apparently held the same opinion had reinforced the concept.

Her statement effected what one might refer to as a "Copernican revolution" in my educational thinking. No longer could I view the homes of the children in my school as supplements to the program. No longer could I see parents as aides to the work it carried on during the day. Rather, I had to take the revolutionary (for me) view that the school was, in effect, an extension of the home and that my teachers and myself were servants of the parents in the educational enterprise.

The primacy of the parents in education has its roots in both the Old and New Testaments. God selected Abraham to be the father of the chosen people partly because He knew he would teach his children and the rest of his household the way of the Lord (Gen. 18:19). Moses wrote to parents in Israel that " 'these words which I command you this day shall be upon your heart; and you shall teach them diligently to your children, and shall talk of them when you sit in your house, and when you walk by the way, and when you lie down, and when you rise' " (Deut. 6:6, 7; cf. chap. 4:9, 10). And Paul admonished fathers to bring up their children "in the discipline and instruction of the Lord" (Eph. 6:4).

The family, wrote Jacques Maritain, "is the first and fundamental educational sphere" because it is "grounded in nature."[3] The family is the primary educational institution of society because the Lord created it to be so. The book of Genesis clearly indicates that the family is the central institution in all social life. All other social institutions exist to aid the family in its task.

Several important and influential research studies in the past twenty years have also highlighted the primacy of the family's educational role. Two of the most significant of the studies were the Coleman Report (1966)[4] sponsored by the United States Office of Education, and the Carnegie Corporation's three-year funded study under the leadership of Christopher Jencks entitled *Inequality: A Reassessment of the Effect of Family and Schooling in America* (1972).[5] Both proved to be major blows to the myth of the omnipotent school.

Coleman and his colleagues surveyed approximately 600,000 students, 70,000 teachers, and 4,000 principals. They concluded, to the surprise of most people, that family upbringing and background was more important in educational achievement than what happened in schools. Furthermore, variations in school facilities, curriculum, and staff had little effect on achievement independent of family background.

Jencks's findings reinforced those of Coleman. His data suggested that schools, no matter how good, cannot do much to eliminate the differences in family background that students bring to school. Both studies cast a shadow over faith in the school's capacity to improve the social, economic, and intellectual status of students. *Implicit in the findings of Coleman and Jencks is that improved families are more crucial than better schools.* Schools cannot solve our social ills—both the root of the problem and its solution lie in the quality of family life and family education.

Frank Gaebelien, former school administrator and associate editor of *Christianity Today*, realized this truth and remarked that the home is the greatest single educational force. "The most influential teachers, whether they recognize it or not, are parents. . . . For better or worse, the home wields more crucial influence upon youth than does school or college. The same is true of parents. No kindergarten teacher, grade school teacher, high school teacher, or college professor, however effective, can surpass the influence of a devoted Christian father or mother. Contrariwise, one shudders at the influence for evil that may be exercised by unworthy parents."[6]

The centrality and power of the family as the primary educational institution comes about because it has the children during their "period of greatest susceptibility and most rapid development" (Ed, p. 275). The parents have the first chance to reach fresh minds, which, as we have all experienced, can be swayed quite easily because they tend to believe what they hear without questioning it. The minds of young children, furthermore, are not full of conflicting ideas and thoughts that blunt the impressions made upon older people. With young children it is especially true that first impressions are lasting. More than that, first impressions also provide the context in which one evaluates future ideas. Thus, first impressions are also powerful.

It is in the home, the child's first school, wrote Ellen White, that "he is to learn the lessons that are to guide him throughout life—lessons of respect, obedience, reverence, self-control. The educational influences of the home are a decided power for good or for evil. They are in many respects silent and gradual, but if exerted on the right side, they become a far-reaching power for truth and righteousness. If the child is not instructed aright here, Satan will educate him through agencies of his choosing. How important, then, is the school in the home!"—CT, p. 107.

The family is a mind- and character-shaping entity without comparison. The attitudes fostered in the family largely determine a child's aspirations, his ability to relate to other people, his attitude toward schooling and learning, his value system, his response to God's love, his sensitivity to the world around him, and every other important human and Christian characteristic. It is the home that provides life's foundation.

Parents can perform their role as shapers of their children's lives well or poorly. But, as we shall see in the next chapter, they can never escape their responsibility.

When I first became a Christian, and later as a young pastor, I had a difficult time understanding what Moses meant when he claimed that children would pay for the sins of their parents until the third and the fourth generation (Ex. 20:5; 34:7; Deut. 5:9). I knew that God did not punish children for the faults and deeds of their parents (Eze. 18:20). The mystery, however, cleared up when I became an elementary school teacher, had the opportunity to work with both parents and their children, and discovered that they shared the same personal difficulties. The plain fact is that our children are like us because of heredity and, even more important, because of the environment we provide for them during their formative years. My children either suffer or benefit because they model after my wife and me. They tend to learn our attitudes and values, both good and bad, and copy our actions for better or worse. It does not mean that the human family is necessarily locked into a deterministic sequence of defeat that passes from one generation to the next. But it does imply that such a thing is a very real probability unless we as parents surrender our lives to Jesus Christ and allow

His Spirit to transform us. Moses, in commenting upon the third and fourth generations, was reflecting upon the power of the home as a socializing and educational agency.

Modern social science has backed up this insight. The findings of Benjamin Bloom, of the University of Chicago, have been especially influential. His studies indicated that 50 percent of the development of intelligence takes place in the first four years of a child's life and that 80 percent has been determined by age 8. Afterward, regardless of schooling and environment, we can alter mental abilities by only 20 percent. He found, in addition, a similar relationship between early development and achievement. As a result, he reasoned that "deprivation in the first four years of life can have far greater consequences than deprivation in the ten years from age 8 through age 17." [7]

Some have concluded from such research that society should not entrust children to their parents during these crucial years. The 1960s and 1970s saw strong drives by educators to create early childhood educational institutions outside the home. Others took a stand more in harmony with the Biblical perspective and suggested that such data pointed more than ever to the crucial nature of quality home environments. Psychiatrist John Bowlby claimed in 1951 that "children thrive better in bad homes than in good institutions." [8] Harvard's Burton L. White uplifted the same theme when he wrote: "In our studies we were not only impressed by what some children could achieve during the first years, but also by the fact that the child's family seemed so obviously central to the outcome. . . . The informal education that families provide for their children makes more of an impact on a child's educational development than the formal educational system. *If the family does its job well, the professional can provide effective training. If not, there may be little the professional can do to save the child from mediocrity.*" [9]

The myth of the omnipotent school has had unfortunate consequences because it has diverted society's attention from the real sphere of educational action—the family. The school is not the miracle worker that many have perceived it to be. The most important and influential part of a child's education takes place before he even arrives there.

Schools Can Make a Difference

Some might conclude, after having read the above argument, that schools don't make any difference. That conclusion, however, is just as false as the myth that schools produce the major impact.

Society has established them because they can and do make a difference. Lawrence A. Cremin, reflecting upon Coleman's and Jencks's studies of equal educational opportunity, remarked that their message is "not that the school is power*less* but that the family is power*ful*." [10]

A realization of the falsity of the myth of the omnipotent school should not prevent our attempting to provide the best possible schooling. Rather, it should lead us to see more clearly the true educational potential of the school in relation to the home.

The school, unfortunately, finds itself forced in cases of family default to take the initiative in the educational endeavor. Ellen White wrote that she strongly urged the necessity of establishing Christian schools "because of the cruel neglect of many parents properly to educate their children in the home" (CT, pp. 204, 205; cf. pp. 153, 154). Sarah Peck, speaking to this issue in 1904, asked Mrs. White whether she could best accomplish her job as a teacher by urging parents to see and take up their responsibility, or to take it away from them by having their young children attend school. Mrs. White replied in an unequivocal manner: "If they have not felt their responsibility from all the books and writings and sermons, you might roll it onto them from now till the Lord comes, and they would not have any burden. It is no use talking about responsibility, when they have never felt it."—3SM, p. 225. Mrs. White had no doubt that schools could and should make a difference. In fact, she indicated that Christian schools are the main hope for those children whose parents have neglected them. On the other hand, the school's function with children from responsible families is to build upon and aid the continuance of the good work begun in the home.

The Cooperative Role of Home and School

It is imperative that teachers, parents, and other social leaders realize the correct relationship between the home and the school. In *Education* we read: "Never will education accomplish all that it might and should accomplish until the importance of the parents' work is fully recognized, and they receive a training for its sacred responsibilities."—Page 276.

Part of what we must recognize is the central role parents play in the educational enterprise. From a Christian perspective the school is not an extension of the State or Federal government. [11] Neither is it a master or adversary of the home. Rather, the Christian school is a cooperative extension of the Christian home. Gene Garrick has written that the function of the school is to "supplement the parents, not to supplant them." [12] In a similar vein Ellen White penned that "the teacher's work should supplement that of the parents, but is not to take its place."—*Ibid.*, p. 283. We need cooperation between the teachers in the home and the teachers in the school.

Christian schools exist because Christian parents have beliefs and value systems that differ from those of the larger culture. They are willing to pay relatively high tuition for their children to attend such schools because they know that it is important to expose them to the same world view and value system at both home and school. A public school teacher wrote the following thoughts concerning why she sent her children to Christian schools to Dr. Paul A. Kienel, executive director of the California Association of Christian Schools. "We believe that God does not cease to exist from 9 A.M. to 3:30 P.M. Monday through Friday, but with the laws and trends affecting public education today, this is the atmosphere in which our children would go to school if they attended public schools. We feel that we want as much continuity as we can get in our children's lives. If one thing is emphasized at home but is contradicted (no matter how subtly) at school, then we lose a great deal of ground." [13]

In this cooperative Christian endeavor the teacher stands *in loco parentis* (in place of the parent). He functions as the student's parent away from home. *In loco parentis* expresses the fact that the Christian teacher, like a good parent, has a concern for the highest good for the whole child. Beyond an interest in each student's academic achievement, the Christian teacher seeks to meet the child's spiritual, social, emotional, and physical welfare. Thus, in the fullest sense, the Christian teacher is one who aids and cooperates with the parents in their weighty responsibility (CT, pp. 145, 146).

Cooperation between parents and teachers for the good of the student implies the need for mutual respect for each other's educational roles. The child benefits most when his parents and teachers work as a team. This means that parents and teachers should take advantage of every opportunity to get to know and understand each other. It would be helpful if all parents, in their concern, would take the initiative to visit the teacher in his classroom before school started for the year or at least during the first few days of school. But, often to the detriment of all, it usually doesn't happen. In fact, I had a hard time getting parents to come to parent-teacher conferences, even when the school scheduled them in the evenings and on Sunday. Most of them apparently felt that education was the business of the school, and they were content as long as their child stayed out of trouble.

Because of this all-too-common lack of concern among parents, Mrs. White penned the following: "Since parents so rarely acquaint themselves with the teacher, it is the more important that the teacher seek the acquaintance of parents. He should visit the homes of his pupils and gain a knowledge of the influences and surroundings among which they live. By coming personally in touch with their homes and lives, he may strengthen the ties that bind him to his pupils and may learn how to deal more successfully with their different dispositions and temperaments."—Ed, p. 284. To be most effective, such visitation should occur during the preschool week or early in the school year. Then it would give the teacher a chance to discover the wishes of the parents and the needs of the child so that he can best serve in loco parentis. If problems develop at school before parents and teachers become acquainted, a strong probability exists that an adversary relationship will develop between the teachers in the home and the teacher in the school. In such a situation everyone loses, but especially the child, who may, to his detriment, use "divide and conquer" tactics with both sides so that he appears in the best light to all.

Cooperation between the two chief educational agencies of society is central to successful education. A good day at school can make the child easier to live with at home and vice versa. Likewise, a poor day in either place makes life more difficult for both parents and teachers. Parents and teachers affect each other's daily lives much more intimately than most of us realize. Friction will arise between them from time to time, just as it often does between parents themselves. The worst thing for the parents or teachers to do in this case is to side with the child. Christians have no ethical alternative but to follow the council of Matthew 18 and go to the other party and openly present their grievance. It may seem like a difficult task, but it is much easier (in the long run) than siding with the child or gossiping about one's "adversary" behind his back. I have often found that the real "problem" was a misunderstanding that was quite easily solved if parents and teacher talked together before things got blown out of proportion.

In closing, we should note that home training is the foundation upon which all other educational experiences build. As a result, those children who have received the best foundation at home will benefit most from the program of the school (CT, p. 118). Teachers often find themselves hindered in their work because their students have not learned to study, to respect authority, or to discipline themselves at home. It is unfortunate that at times parents criticize teachers "because they have not had power to counteract the influence of the wrong example and unwise training received in the home" (*ibid.*, p. 504). It behooves both parents and teachers to be aware of their own shortcomings and to learn how they can best work with each other.

Everybody gains, especially the child, when the parents and teacher cooperate, appreciate each other, and occasionally compromise. The school may not be the greatest educational power in a child's life, but it is a significant power. It is most effective when the home and school work together.

Postscript

Some might choose to fault this chapter because it discussed the home and the school in the educational power structure while neglecting the media and the church, a charge especially pertinent in the light of the report issued by the Carnegie Council on Children in 1977. This study indicated that "by the age of 18, the average American child has spent more time watching television than in school or with his or her parents." [14]

The treatment in this chapter took this into consideration even though it may not have been explicit. It seems to me that the media, especially popular music and television, may be more powerful than the school in the realm of education and/or mind control. The point underlying the development of this chapter, however, is that it is the parents who early determine a child's values and his response to the media, just as they largely mold his reaction to the school. Parents therefore have great control over the child's early relation to the media. By their education in this area, they can utilize a force for great good in their child's life or they can unleash a power that will neutralize much of the positive effect of both home and school. A child's relation to the powerful educational potential of the media has, in most cases, already been shaped by the time he arrives at school. We might say the same about the church as an educational agency.

6 The Myth of the Teacherless Home

Discussing the myth of the teacherless home is something that I would rather not deal with. I would avoid it, in fact, if the issues at stake did not lie at the foundation of a healthy individuality, society, and church. Because the home is society's primary and most powerful educational institution, it is imperative that it has quality teachers who are in a position to devote their energy to their all-important function. All of the other educative forces of society build upon the foundation laid by the parents. We cannot ignore the issues at stake in the myth of the teacherless home in a book on education.

The role of the parents within the home, whether we realize it or not, is the fundamental issue in education. A civilization can face no question more crucial. Carle Zimmerman, in his fruitful study of the relation of family life and civilization, has demonstrated that no civilization has ever survived the disintegration of its home life.[1] Ellen White made a similar point when she noted that "the well-being of society, the success of the church, the prosperity of the nation, depend upon home influences."—CT, p. 396. "No work entrusted to human beings involves greater or more far-reaching results than does the work of fathers and mothers."—AH, p. 182. Psychologist James Dobson expressed his concern regarding the accelerating trend for both parents to work outside the home when he wrote: *"I believe that this abandonment of the home is our gravest and most dangerous mistake as a nation!"*[2] In the same vein, child development expert Urie Bronfenbrenner put his finger on the social (and educational) problem that brings all other problems in its train when he poignantly stated that "the family is falling apart."[3] Human civilization can do without many things, but it cannot continue to exist if it does not perform its parenting function satisfactorily.

This chapter addresses a problem of relatively recent origin. Modern societies have spawned an increasingly larger proportion of families in which both parents work full-time outside the home.

Generally it results in "teacherless homes" during the day, while during the evening the parents are often too busy or too tired to perform their nurturing tasks with much energy and/or enthusiasm. That such a situation provides an adequate educational base for a healthy civilization is an educational myth that is undermining modern society.

Historical Background and a "Less Sexist" Solution to the Problem

Before the industrialization of society both work and family structure were much different for nearly everyone than they are now. Families, for instance, were not the modern nuclear family consisting of a mother, a father, and children. The traditional extended family included them, but also grandparents, aunts, uncles, cousins, and sometimes apprentices and other "attached" individuals. Children had many adults to interact with. Education for most extended families was quite informal, with boys acquiring their trades by observing and working with the men of the family and girls learning their duties from the women. The workplace was the family farm, the family shop, or the family business—often operated in close proximity to the living quarters.

In traditional societies adults did not leave their children when they went to work, nor did they shunt children off to spend the day with peers. Both fathers and mothers had well-defined and well-understood roles to play in the education and nurture of their children.

The system broke down under the impact of industrialism. Specialization and the spread of the factory system progressively took more and more parents away from their families. Males first left the family workplace to create a separate world for themselves. Even though some women followed them, the female half of the adult population usually ended up being responsible for the home, including the care of children. Men and women now had separate spheres of activity. Meanwhile, the shuffle also transformed the social positions of children and adolescents. Even though the workplace had once welcomed and needed young people, they had become unwelcome in the highly organized world of industrial work. This eventually resulted in laws and regulations restricting their work and in compulsory education laws designed to remove them from the labor market through the establishment of juvenile ghettos (schools) to keep them out of mischief.

This whole transition has at least three implications for our understanding of the issues of working parents. First, most twentieth-century adults have a confused concept of the nature of traditional society. Traditional society was not a social order in which men worked outside the home while women remained inside and were responsible for the children. This phenomenon is a relatively recent development. The traditional family was a productive economic unit that involved both sexes in the nurture of children. It was the predominant family pattern from the creation of Adam and Eve up through the recent past.

Second, while the Bible writers represented ideal family life in terms of the integrated extended family, Ellen White, living in the midst of the industrial era, often wrote to meet issues and problems that were specific to family structure in industrial society. Thus, while at times she was emphatic in laying parenting responsibilities on both parents, at other times she emphasized the role of the mother. One would expect this in a society that had largely delegated child rearing to the female sex—if women failed at the task, the failure would be complete. Her writings sought to apply principles to problems in a specific historical time and place. There are, therefore, "less sexist" and "more sexist" implications in her counsel on parenting.[4]

Third, parents must perform at least two major functions— earning a living and adequately caring for their children. The industrial model that has both parents working full-time outside the home may facilitate the accomplishment of the first, but it frustrates the second. While we can call no one approach to family living exclusively "Christian," Christianity implies the necessity of accomplishing both tasks.

Perhaps the ideal is not fathers laboring outside the home and mothers inside. A better way might be for parents to share in both productive and domestic work and in child rearing. That may not seem very practical, but it doesn't mean that it is impossible. Bronfenbrenner pointed out at least one avenue to accomplish such a goal when he claimed that "neither men nor women can combine working and parenting" successfully under a system based on male work rules that stipulate "nine to five, forty hours a week, and if there's overtime you do it or you don't keep your job."[5] He suggested the development of alternative work rules that would allow for the personal fulfillment of each parent in both productive work and family life.

Some Christian couples have successfully made arrangements for a different set of work rules on an individual basis, so that each parent can have a more equal share in both earning a living and raising a family. For example, one couple who teach in an

Adventist college have contracted to "share a job." Both the husband and wife are biologists. Each spends half the day at the school and the other half at home on domestic chores and "taking care of the kids." Such an arrangement is one commendable attempt at approximating (and even going beyond) traditional modes of parenting, but it is probably not an option for most Christian parents.

A revolutionary development holding potential for more parents to share their responsibilities is what Alvin Toffler has called the "electronic cottage." Toffler has pointed out that society has moved beyond industrialism to postindustrialism or superindustrialism. The computer and other advances in technology "could shift . . . millions of jobs out of the factories and offices," into which industrialism swept them, "right back where they came from originally: the home." New modes of production and communication make possible "a return to cottage industry on a new, higher, electronic basis, and with it a new emphasis on the home as the center of society." [6] The "electronic cottage" allows for rural living and flexible working arrangements, coupled with financial security. This lifestyle is already a viable option for many families. It certainly offers possibilities for married couples to share in their dual role of earning a living and responsible parenting. In many ways superindustrial lifestyles offer a more satisfactory solution to Christian family living than do the models of work developed to meet the harsh, inflexible demands of the industrial "rat race."

While Toffler's scenario of massive changes in workplaces is a possibility, it may not be a probability for most people. Social forecaster John Naisbitt, for example, has predicted in Megatrends that most people will still choose to work away from home because of the increased need for social interaction in a highly technological society.[7] Others may shy away from it because it does not lend itself to achieving their particular professional aspirations. Still others—perhaps the majority—have no interest in radical lifestyles. They are comfortable with the familiar industrial model with all of its rigid requirements. In the words of Paul Goodman, "they have ceased to be able to imagine alternatives" to current practices. [8]

The rejection of radical lifestyles by some couples and the nonavailability of alternatives for most parents leaves us with the same old social problem—an inflexible set of work rules that militate against healthy child rearing when both parents have employment full-time outside the home.

The rest of this chapter will face the issue of working parents from the perspective of contemporary social practice, which discriminates against males in the child-rearing responsibility of the family and against females in the area of productive work outside the home. From the viewpoint of industrial society, "the myth of the teacherless home" degenerates into "the myth of the working mother," since the mother is nearly always the last parent to leave the home for outside work. We might as well face it—*the industrial social order is sexist by its very nature.*[9]

If we do not choose to move beyond current practices, then we must seek to act responsibly within present social parameters. The obvious ideal is not to discriminate against either women (in the workplace outside the home) or men (in the workplace inside the home). On the other hand, *in seeking to avoid sexual discrimination, modern society has fallen into the pit of discriminating against children through providing teacherless homes.* A basic premise of the remainder of this chapter is that the last error is worse than the first. The discussion therefore is admittedly sexist. Furthermore, we cannot really avoid the issue, since most people in contemporary society are involved in it.

Within the framework of present practice, the next section does not attempt to give all "the answers" to the issues at stake, but it does highlight certain difficulties with current trends, uplifts some of the principles that point to a viable solution, and provides a foundation for constructive thought. Life is complex, yet we do know some facts through experience and others through divine revelation. In an area of civilized life as crucial as child rearing, it behooves us to use our individual and collective intelligence, as well as our honesty, as we seek possible answers to a vexing problem.

A "More Sexist" Approach to a Contemporary Issue

In shifting from the issue of the teacherless home to that of the working mother, it is important to get two possible misunderstandings out in the open. First, it is not a female problem—it is a family problem with which all modern nations continue to grapple. Russia and some of the countries of Western Europe have sought to solve it differently from the way the United States has, but as yet society has not found a satisfactory solution to the disruption of family living spawned by the industrial revolution.

Second, we do not want to imply that mothers who stay at home do not work. Nothing could be further from the truth. The man who wrote *The Kitchen Sink Papers*[10] found, after a year's experimentation, that housewives labor much harder than he cared to. He was glad to get back to do his job at the end of his trial year. It is more accurate for a husband to say, "My wife is not employed outside the home" than "My wife doesn't work." We might frame the issue of the working mother more clearly if we thought in terms of the mother who has a full-time career outside the home as opposed to the one who sees her parental function, at least while she has children living at home, as her primary career.

Why Mothers Work

Whereas industrial societies expect fathers to work outside the home, mothers choose or find themselves obligated to work away from their homes for a variety of reasons. The blunt fact is that some mothers have to have a full-time job if they are to survive. Situations arise where the husband cannot work or cannot earn enough to meet the genuine needs of his family. In other cases various reasons may have removed the husband from the home. Such situations are obviously not ideal, and mothers caught in such circumstances generally have no alternative but to put their children in the care of others and work full-time. Under the current social mentality these women are doing their best as they seek to fulfill the dual role of mother and wage earner. Of course, it is not too difficult to imagine more enlightened alternatives. If society viewed parenting in the light of its true importance, it might develop adequate and responsible plans so that mothers could be paid to stay at home and raise their children if they so desired. This makes more sense and would generally be more efficient and effective than building and staffing day-care centers.

While some mothers must work, others choose to do so, even though most of them genuinely love their children and many would prefer to be with them rather than being employed away from home eight hours a day. Why, then, we might ask, do so many of them work? And why do so many Christian mothers, who see their task not only as a social responsibility but also as a "sacred trust" and a "religious duty" (CG, p. 18), elect to work? There are at least four main reasons although others are not difficult to imagine.[11]

One reason why so many mothers desire full-time careers outside the home is that modern society generally does not respect the role of housewife and mother. Grace Hechinger came right to the point when she wrote that "Mother's Day is a symbol of our national feeling of guilt for making child care an activity of high rhetoric and low prestige. . . . Mother's job has no status in a society which rewards the single-minded pursuit of money and success. Her role clashes head-on with the real values of an achievement-oriented culture." [12] Burton L. White, a Harvard psychologist, has called mothering "a vastly underrated occupation." [13] This is probably too mild. In terms of its true significance, it is the most underrated occupation in modern society. It is not surprising, therefore, to find that Dobson's survey of American women turned up low self-esteem as the major problem they faced. He noted that "the 'disease' of inferiority has reached epidemic proportions among females" because "their traditional responsibilities have become matters of disrespect and ridicule." [14] In most areas of the country maintaining a home and raising children have very little status. Society has long teased and ridiculed housewives, and their function has often been the butt of jokes. The arrival of certain of the women's "libbers" with their remarks about "supermoms" and "snotty-nosed kids" has not helped the matter. Some of their more radical discussions of bored and restless mothers certainly leave one with the feeling that no one could be a "real person" (or at least an intelligent and worthwhile person) without filling an "important" social position. Dobson has indicated that part of the myth is "that every female who isn't 'working' is being cheated and exploited." He concluded that this "is a lie with enormous consequences." [15]

Psychologists tell us that more than 90 percent of our self-concept comes from what we conclude others think about us. Furthermore, we live in a society in which we are seemingly under the illusion that people get paid according to the value of their services. Housewives, of course, do not get paid. It is therefore not too large a jump in reasoning for them to feel that their task is worthless, since it does not receive a financial reward. With these facts in mind, it is no wonder that so many women seek some significance in the world of work beyond the home. After all, none of us can stand the awful thought that we are not needed or that what we do each day is not worth doing.

The self-image problem may be the most powerful of the forces pushing mothers into careers. A good self-image is necessary for both mental health and the efficient performance of daily duties. Mothers cannot handle their family responsibilities properly without one. Another thing that we should note about the self-image put-down as it relates to being a housewife is its subtleness. The lack of worth attached to the function is all-pervasive—it seems to be in the air we breathe.

A second reason why so many mothers decide to work is

economic. Sociologist Cole Brembeck has pointed out that the economic issue is prominent in modern society because the primary function of the family has moved from economic production to economic consumption.[16] The traditional family was production-oriented. Mothers taught their daughters how to cook, sew, and prepare food for winter storage, while sons worked with their fathers and learned a trade, how to run the farm, or the ins and outs of the family business. The child of the modern family, however, receives an allowance to purchase what he wants, and the supermarket and shopping mall meet the family's needs.

The transference of the fulcrum of family living from production to consumption has increased the modern family's need for money. The fact that consumption has become a social ideal has intensified the financial demand. The pressure to "keep up with the Joneses" is quite powerful and real. Our society leaves us with the feeling that there is nothing worse than to live in a consumption society without the ability to consume. Many people believe that both parents must be gainfully employed if marriage and child rearing are even to be feasible. As a result, many young men put pressure on their wives to work outside the home rather than to lower their lifestyle. Such pressure, coupled with the wife's desire to have nice things and the negative image of the housewife and/or mother, often tips the scale toward outside employment. Among Adventists, the high and constantly rising cost of denominational school tuition further aggravates the problem.

Even though the economic pressures of modern society are very real, we must not, where possible, allow them to rule our lives. Both parents and children need adequate leisure for caring relationships more than they need things.

A third reason why mothers seek careers outside the home is that they don't like the noise, trouble, and "bother" associated with responsible parenting. All normal adults find parenting a "pain" periodically, but some find it to be an impossible ordeal. Fortunately, such situations are in the minority, since they often have disastrous effects on children's self-images and sense of personal worth. Some mothers and fathers could have avoided the problem by seriously considering the wisdom of bringing children into the world in the light of their known attitudes and personalities. Others, even after carefully thinking the matter through, discovered that they couldn't handle constant contact with lively children after the irreversible event had transpired. In such cases, both children and parents might actually be better off if the children spent a portion of the day with a *carefully chosen* parent substitute.

The fourth reason mothers accept full-time work outside the home is the least subtle. Some mothers have professional aspirations that are important to them. While there is nothing wrong with professional ambitions, full-time professional involvement and motherhood bring about their own set of tensions for both parents and children.

We have discussed four reasons why mothers choose to work outside the home. Next we will examine some problems faced by the family of the working mother. Then we will look at some principles that point toward a solution.

Some Issues Facing the Families of Working Mothers

A foremost issue to consider is that each parent has a work to do for his or her children that no one else can accomplish, not even the other spouse (FE, p. 69). According to both the Bible and Ellen White, the responsibility for child rearing rests with the family. The mother, furthermore, has the primary nurturing responsibility, especially of young children. It is built into the very nature of sexual distinctiveness. God designed Eve and her daughters physically and psychologically to perform the mothering task. We should note, however, that, contrary to some traditional beliefs, that was not all that God created Eve to do. Rather, it is one of woman's possible functions—one central to her very makeup.

Psychiatrist John Bowlby, a leading student of maternal deprivation, has demonstrated that a child's attachment for his mother is rooted in nature.[17] Children invariably suffer from maternal deprivation. Bowlby claims that "what is believed to be essential for mental health is that the infant and young child should experience a warm, intimate, and continuous relationship with his mother (or permanent mother-substitute) in which both find satisfaction and enjoyment." The maternal relationship, combined with "countless" other relationships with the father and with siblings, underlies the development of character and mental health. After years of comparing children from warm, loving homes with partially deprived children (i.e., children whose mothers are unable to give them loving care or children removed from their mother's care for any reason), Bowlby has concluded that even partial maternal "deprivation brings in its train acute anxiety, excessive need for love, powerful feelings of revenge," and eventually guilt and depression.[18] We sometimes observe such symptoms in the actions of young children when they realize that their mothers are getting ready for work. Parents assume a serious risk when they seek to find a substitute for their chief responsibility, the children in their home.

The risk gets compounded, points out Peter Blitchington, by the fact that "you can rarely pay another person to make up for the lack of maternal stimulation when the mother herself is not willing to provide it." [19] Or as Dobson so nicely says it: "Now I ask you who disagree with what I have written; to whom am I going to submit the task of guiding that unfolding process of development? Who will care enough to make the necessary investment if my wife and I are too busy for the job? What baby-sitter will take our place? What group-oriented facility can possibly provide the *individual* love and guidance which Ryan needs and deserves? Who will represent my values and beliefs to my son and daughter and be ready to answer their questions during the peak of interest? To whom will I surrender the prime-time experiences of their day? The rest of the world can make its own choice, but as for me and my house, we welcome the opportunity to shape the two little lives which have been loaned to us. And I worry about a nation which calls that task 'unrewarding and unfulfilling and boring.' " [20]

Another issue that we must consider is the fact that each of us has only so much time and energy to expend on our various responsibilities. Dobson has implied that the claim that most mothers of young children can come home after a full workday and still meet their family obligations—possibly even better than if they had stayed at home—is mythological nonsense.[21] Grace Hechinger, a woman who has apparently struggled with the problem, has suggested that "it is time we recognized that there is a harsh conflict between the demands of a career and raising a family, no matter how fulfilling and rewarding both may be. . . . The current chic theory that it is possible and desirable to set aside short periods of 'quality time' for children is baloney. How can anyone do a demanding job by only working at it an hour or so a day? And after a hard day at the office as well! Chalk up another put-down for mother's work." [22] Wives, being finite, have only so much of themselves that they can give. If they channel more to one thing, obviously they have less for other activities. Some things have to be done—especially those related to the paid job if one wants to continue employment. Then, of course, someone must get the dinner, clean the house, and do the wash. Even when the husband helps, lives get spread pretty thin—after all, he has worked all day too. Where do such families *consistently* find time to create the warm, personal relationships that both children and adults need for their healthy development and the smooth running of the family? More often than not, the wheel that squeaks the loudest will get the grease. While it may get us through the day, is it a Christian—or even sane—way to order our priorities? Besides, squeaking wheels get on our nerves—nerves that need personal time for meditation, rest, and devotion. Too often the hectic pace of a home with both parents working full-time helps set the stage for frustration, irritability, and family conflict. It should be evident that our families need our best as parents rather than the leftovers of our time and energy.

One more reality that we must face is that institutional child-care employees, except in extremely rare cases, cannot replace the individual, one-to-one influence of a mother with her child. Young children need the extensive relationship and involvement that is often available from their mother but is seldom given by those running a child-care "business." The consensus of child-development experts is that the mother-child relationship is essential, rather than optional, for the healthy development of children. Russia, Czechoslovakia, and other Communist countries that have extensively experimented with day-care centers have been revamping their ideas and practices because they have been unable to escape the fact that the experiment has not worked. We cannot legislate the crucial roles of parenthood into oblivion or pressure them economically out of existence, because they are central to God's creation—they are rooted in the way God made people and societies.

Toward a Solution

It would be folly to minimize the problems that actually face families in their daily life. To do so would be naive and irresponsible. It is a worse folly, however, to believe that our current solution is the best or only way. We may be "getting by" as a society of absentee parents, but is "getting by" enough? Do society, our children, and the Lord need our minimum or maximum in the crucial area of parenting? No easy answers exist to the problems of modern family living. What might be the correct course of action for one family might be wrong for another. God has not given us inflexible rules, but He has provided us wth intelligence and the ability to make responsible choices and to live responsible lives. Every individual must honestly weigh the principles involved in parenting. The following paragraphs offer some ideas (and some facts) rather than ironclad dictates. God leaves the choice up to you and me.

We noted earlier at least four reasons why mothers decide to work even when they have a choice: (1) the low position accorded the housewife and mother, (2) economic motivations in a consumption society, (3) the desire to escape the noise and hectic problems related to the mothering role, and (4) professional aspirations. The following examination of possible solutions to the issue of the working mother will be developed on the basis of these four reasons.

Part of the solution to the problem of the low social role accorded the housewife and mother might be for people to consciously realize the crucial nature of her task. In *The Ministry of Healing* we read that "no other work can equal hers in importance."—Page 378; cf. FE, pp. 158, 159. She has the first opportunity to shape impressionable minds in the likeness of the divine, a task involving lives that have infinite potential.

It is important for society as a whole to come to grips with the centrality of parenting to the health of the community, but it is just as important for individual husbands and wives to make this breakthrough in values. We need to learn to *demonstrate* in both words and actions our appreciation for each other's parenting role. Too often parenting is a thankless job. The attitude of many husbands is that they have been out doing the "important work" of the world, while their wives have been lying around watching TV, playing with the children, and generally enjoying a life of semileisure. Such men feel they have a right to service when they, as "masters of the house," get home a half hour late—after all, what else are wives for? Such an attitude merely reinforces a housewife's low opinion of herself and her task. On the other hand, wives sometimes feel resentful toward their spouses, who have been out "socializing" with their friends, while they have suffered at home in relative isolation from the adult world.

Perhaps the most momentous thing that husbands and wives can do is to make a practice of demonstrating their mutual appreciation for their multiple roles. A little appreciation and mutual understanding will help us all become better fathers and mothers. The result will be better self-images, more successful parenting, and more-rewarding family living. Successful family living, we need to realize ever more fully, is built upon a dynamic reciprocity.

The economic motivation for working mothers should be viewed realistically. For some mothers, especially those from single-parent homes, and for families situated low on the socioeconomic scale, employment may be an economic necessity. They often have no choice but to have a full-time job. On the other hand, the majority of middle-class husbands and wives do have an option. The following suggestions are for those in this second category.

At the center of the economic issue is the question of values—what is most important in our life. Ellen White placed the issue exactly in this context. "In the children committed to her care, every mother has a *sacred* charge from the heavenly Father. . . . If mothers had always realized their responsibility, and made it their *first purpose*, their *most important mission*, to fit their children for the duties of this life and for the honors of the future immortal life, we would not see the misery that now exists in so many homes in our land. . . . *But Satan lays his plans to secure the souls of both parents and children. Mothers are drawn away from the duties of home and the careful training of their little ones*, to the service of self and the world. Vanity, fashion, and *matters of minor importance are allowed to absorb the attention*, and the physical and moral education of the precious children is neglected."—FE, p. 149. (Italics supplied.)

I have to admit that it is nice to have two cars in the garage, a roomy home with well-appointed furnishings, and four top-quality suits. "But," I am impelled to ask, "is it worth the real cost?" Most of us need to face up to the distinction between our *genuine needs* and our *desires*. Such a thing is not an easy task in a society that has established a massive advertising industry to confuse us on this very point. The media and our social context are continually barraging us with the message that the good life is conspicuous consumption. As a result we ever more rapidly transform the world's resources into rubbish.

It is high time that Christians stand up and ask themselves if this is really the good life or merely one of the devil's diversions to keep them from life's real enjoyments and values. Many people would be shocked to discover that families can still live pleasantly on one salary once they have distinguished between genuine needs and desires.

This brings us to the subject of budgeting. The family that has separated its necessities from its luxuries and has opted to live on less than two full salaries will need to build an adequate budget and stick to it. Family counseling specialists, books on the topic, and friends living successfully on one salary can serve as resources in this delicate but important task.

In the realm of values, only those things that will still be meaningful in a hundred or a thousand years from now have value in the Christian sense of the word. Most of those "important" things for which we currently struggle will be garbage before the end of the decade. Unfortunately, not until the final judgment will parents "realize the almost infinite value of their misspent time" (*ibid.*, p. 29).

The following principles by Ellen White may help put our values in perspective. 1. "Too much importance cannot be placed upon the early training of children."—MH, p. 380. 2. Parents, "especially mothers," should (ideally) be the only teachers of their children for the first six to ten years of their lives (2SM, pp. 436, 437; FE, p. 21). 3. "Parents should live more for their children, and less for society."—MH, p. 386. 4. Parents should not send children away from home too early, and "the mother should be careful how she trusts the molding of the infant mind to other hands."—FE, pp. 156, 157. 5. "Parents should be much at home" to provide their children with love, sympathy, and encouragement (*ibid.*, p. 65). 6. The mother's time, "in a special sense, belongs to her children" (*ibid.*, p. 139). 7. It is important "that the minds of parents be as free as possible from perplexing, wearing care in temporal things, that they may think and act with calm consideration, wisdom, and love, and make the salvation . . . of their children the first and highest consideration!" (*ibid.*, p. 30). 8. "One great reason why there is so much evil in the world today is that parents occupy their minds with other things to the exclusion of the work that is all-important—the task of patiently and kindly teaching their children the way of the Lord."—CT, p. 129. 9. It is better to "deny . . . children anything" rather than the parental instruction and caring that they need so much (*ibid.*).

Before moving beyond the economic motivation of the working mother, we should take a look at the husband's role. All too often the husband exerts strong pressures on the wife to seek work outside the home so that they can get "those little extras that make life worthwhile." Frequently it backfires (particularly if she feels forced into a job). For overworked parents life itself comes to lose its luster, and after a while nothing seems worthwhile. The husband has an important role to play in the decision of his wife's career. No one wins if he pushes her in a direction she would rather not go.

We noted that the third reason why some mothers opt to have full-time careers is to escape the noise and bother of child rearing. Such situations are unfortunate for both parents and children. With adequate forethought and honest self-examination some of those parents might have chosen not to have children. It would have saved a lot of frustration and heartache. But even this may not be sufficient, since human forethought is limited. Some people think they would enjoy parenthood before they experience it, only to realize their mistake after they are "locked into" the task. In other cases, couples make a decision to have children on the basis of false premises. For example, some couples accept what has to be one of the world's most naive ideas—that children will cement a shaky marriage together. On the contrary, most people in unstable marriages have found that children are more like dynamite to blow the relationship apart. Another faulty premise is that every Christian couple should have children if they are to follow the Biblical injunction to "fill the earth" (Gen. 1:28). Mothering, however, is merely one of the possible functions of married women. The Lord has left us with many options. Each couple has the opportunity to select the best one in the light of their unique set of personal and contextual factors.

The issue of choices brings us to a fourth major reason why mothers elect to work full-time outside the home: their desire to have both a family and a profession. As noted above, this option has its own set of tensions built into the very finiteness of human nature. Couples living within the limitations of industrial work rules face several choices in the realm of profession and/or career. One of the most difficult options to carry out successfully is the attempt to combine both a full-time professional career and the full-time role of motherhood. More manageable are several options that see the choice as either a career or mothering; a career the woman interrupts for a number of years; or one put on hold while the children are preschoolers and then followed as a part-time position during their school years. The possible alternatives are numerous enough to allow each couple freedom.

The commitment to responsible choice is basic to Christian parenting. Dobson has cogently remarked that a woman should be free to select the direction her life will take. His "strong criticism . . . is not with those who choose nonfamily lifestyles for themselves. Rather, it is aimed at those who abandon their parental responsibility *after* the choice has been made." [23]

My plea is for each couple to weigh the issues and the principles involved carefully and then to make a responsible decision regarding their combined parenting responsibilities. Next to the one to give their hearts to Christ, it will be the most important decision they will ever make.

Three Myths Related to the "More Sexist" Approach

One of the most destructive myths related to child rearing is that it is the mother's job. This is damaging to both boys and girls. Each child needs to have healthy parental relationships with adults of both sexes for well-rounded development. The development of normal sex identity and the ability to relate successfully to the opposite sex are tasks best accomplished in the home. The ideal is parental teamwork. "The mother," claimed Mrs. White, "must ever stand pre-eminent" in the child-rearing process (AH, p. 184), but "the father's duty to his children cannot be transferred to the mother. If she performs her own duty, she has burden enough to bear. Only by working in unison, can the father and mother accomplish the work which God has committed to their hands."—FE, p. 69. She further indicated that fathers who are not willing to take their share of the task should not take upon themselves the responsibility of parenting (ibid., pp. 65, 66).

A second myth that often leads to disillusionment is that the role of the mother is static. A good mother, so it runs, is one who stays at home for twenty to thirty years and then begins her own life after the children are gone. This myth is destructive. The mother and wife whose life is an unchanging round of daily tasks soon loses touch with her husband and her children and often finds herself disillusioned and purposeless when the children finally leave home.

Ellen White indicated that the mother's role is dynamic rather than static. It demands "continual advancement" so that she can successfully relate to both her husband and children, who must live dynamic lives because of their continual exposure to the larger world at work and school (ibid., p. 149). "Continual advancement" may mean at times taking a class at the local college, reading widely, becoming involved in community activities both inside and outside the church, or even working several hours a week—so long as the family budget doesn't become locked into her extra wages. (It is undoubtedly best if she feels she can quit her part-time employment whenever needs at home make it the best course of action.) Some diversion will not only facilitate personal growth but also will allow her to return to her family with renewed vigor.

A final myth related to the working mother is that our children need us less after they start school than before. Its widespread acceptance we see evidenced by the large percentage of mothers who refrain from work outside the home until their youngest child starts school, then begin full-time employment. We might argue that just the opposite is true, that children need parents with adequate time for them even more after they begin school. The first years of school, when children go through the strains of adjusting to peer pressure and to life in a larger society, are critical to their social development. It is important that someone has the quality time to care for them, answer their questions, and help them through these years. Other parents feel that it is "safe" for the mother to resume or begin full-time work when the child enters junior high or high school. Adolescents, however, may also need an *available* parent in whom they can confide. It is true, if they are maturing properly, that teenagers may need their mothers and fathers less often during this period. But when they do need help and advice, it is important that someone sensitive to their needs be there to give it. Teenagers are learning to relate to both sexes in a mature manner and to work through some crucial aspects of their self-identity. If they can't get the help and care they need at home, they will be forced to look for it elsewhere.

The Western world is raising a generation of "latchkey" children—children who come home to an empty house after school. Urie Bronfenbrenner, a leading child psychologist, has written: "If there's any reliable predictor of trouble, it probably begins with children coming home to an empty house, whether the problem is reading difficulties, truancy, dropping out, drug addiction, or childhood depression." [24] Some women have related to the problem by working only part-time while they have school-age children. In this way they can be home and rested to some extent before the children arrive from school. In terms of a career, it is undoubtedly a compromise, but it brings its own type of reward.

Conclusion

The issues raised in this chapter are some of the most important that men and women ever face. Given the fact that parents are society's most important teachers, the teacherless home is a tragedy. Whether a couple elects a "less sexist" or "more sexist" approach to parenting is not nearly as important as their basic commitment to be responsible in their parenting role. We live in a society that is "playing games" with this most important human endeavor. If ever there was a need for sanctified judgment and the proper use of Christian freedom and responsibility, it is in the area of parenting. It is time that the Christian community began to uplift parenting (in action, not just rhetoric) for what it is: a career of the first magnitude; a career that can be more rewarding and more beneficial than any other; a career that provides the very foundation for all subsequent educational efforts.

7 The Myth of Up and Down

Modern society widely assumes that every social position has a value intrinsic in it. We tend to think of jobs as being hierarchically related—that is, we picture them in terms of "up" or "down" the social scale in the sense of their importance. In the eyes of most people, for example, being a college president is "up" from being a first-grade teacher, being a conference officer is "up" from being a pastor, being a physician is "up" from being a plumber, and being a lawyer is "up" from being a housewife. The world at large has evolved a set of rewards that constantly reinforces this hierarchy upon our minds. The hierarchy has a direct relationship to the amount of money a person is "worth" and the amount of prestige society accords his position.

Christians, by and large, have accepted the hierarchy of up and down. In fact, it seems to be so thoroughly entrenched that we rarely question it. Christians have also developed a system of social rewards that have effectively maintained the myth. Adventist institutions, it is true, have tended to play down large salary distinctions, although they have developed a subtle scale of small distinctions. Less subtle have been prestige rewards and those "extras" or special favors, including such things as fringe benefits and travel allowances. (Some of them are undoubtedly justified, while others seem to function more like smoke screens that rather thinly veil the preferential treatment of those who have "higher" responsibilities.) In the past, ordination of certain types of leading employees (educational, fiscal, and medical) outside the pastoral ministry also served as a reward.

The myth of up and down is alive and well in society as a whole and in the Adventist subculture. Unfortunately, the myth, at least as most people currently view it, has some fatal flaws both sociologically and theologically. From a sociological perspective it often appears to be upside down. It seems to label as "up" that which may be "down" in terms of actual social contribution and vice versa. On the other hand, it might not do society much good to turn the hierarchy on its head. That would create another whole batch of problems. Perhaps the most-needed insight into the hierarchical myth is the Biblical perspective that seemingly rejects the directions of "up" and "down" altogether and replaces it with a model based on aptitudes, gifts, and callings rather than hierarchical rank.

The Myth Partially Exposed

Sociological observation and reflection about social roles leads to a partial exposure of the myth of up and down. It is true that society may pass out social and financial rewards to those having visible positions, but the distribution of rewards does not make those positions more important.[1]

A case in point is the social role of motherhood, which is generally thought of as "down" in terms of the myth. It has been amply demonstrated that in actuality, motherhood is society's most crucial role and should be "up" at the top if we rated roles in terms of their societal importance. If society performed this function correctly, we would not have nearly so much need for "bosses," police chiefs, and authority figures of every type. Ellen White has correctly noted that "no other work can equal" the mother's "in importance" (MH, p. 378). Mothering (parenting) is one of society's most crucial functions, yet mothers receive no pay and little prestige. It makes their role seem rather "worth"less in a cash-oriented society.

Another example that betrays the shallowness of the myth is the position accorded to teachers, particularly elementary teachers, in Western society. Within the formal schooling system educators usually regard "up" in terms of becoming an administrator, curriculum specialist, counselor, or college teacher. But from the perspective of actual impact upon children (and thus on the future of society), the classroom teacher holds the crucial position in the educational system, because he or she stands at the place where the adult world and that of the child meet. It is the teacher who implements administrative decisions and applies curricular suggestions. The nonteaching position, ideal curriculum, latest educational tools, and flawless organizational pyramid have only marginal value unless there is a quality relationship and communicative interchange at the point where the student has the learning experience.

What other group of adults has the powerful opportunity of meeting with the entire youth population for six hours per day, 180 days each year? And yet, strangely enough, the profession generally treats any position outside of the classroom as a promotion, and the further one moves from the scene of classroom education, the larger the social and financial rewards. As a result, education removes a great deal of maturing teaching talent from the classroom. Ideally, we should reverse the whole situation. We should encourage the very best teaching talent that society and the educational system can provide to serve at the junction where impressionable young minds meet the representatives of the adult world. From this perspective perhaps a specialist in charge of curriculum or an assistant superintendent in charge of finance might be "promoted" to the classroom, where he actually receives the awesome responsibility of being entrusted with the care of the Lord's children.

A corollary to such a revised picture of professional values is that the most crucial role in teaching (outside the home) is at the first-grade level. The entry point is where students are most impressionable and where they develop their initial, and generally lasting, attitudes toward school and formal learning. We should find the very best professional talent and the most ideal teaching conditions at the primary level. If we actually valued teaching for what it is (or could be), it is probable that we could avoid many current educational and social problems.[2]

In *Philosophy and Education* I wrote that "perhaps the best way to destroy the potential of the educational system as an agent for restoring the image of God in man is first to undermine the role of the housewife-mother and then to make teaching, especially elementary teaching, a second-class professional activity. With these two strokes the true function of education can be stymied. The challenge in Christian education is to value teaching for its true potential as a powerful and crucial form of ministry."[3]

Further thought and observation continue to reinforce the idea that perhaps we have our educational ups and downs reversed, and that we are reinforcing a false myth by maintaining our current system of social and economic rewards and/or favors. The present social position of the elementary teacher in the mythological hierarchy was impressed upon me when I resigned from the pastoral ministry to teach at a two-teacher church school in west Texas. Many of my former colleagues looked at me as if I had "fallen." To tell the truth, I felt that way myself because of my acceptance of the myth, social pressures, and my own guilt trip. Several years later, the problem of hierarchical values again came to my mind when I was "elevated" from being a "lowly" third-grade teacher to junior academy principal in the middle of the school term. I didn't particularly want the administrative job, but after I assumed it, many people, to my surprise, began to treat me as if I were somehow of more value or more important than I had been before, in spite of the fact that I had moved from ministering intensively to my students to pushing paper, solving problems, and raising money. Now, as an "exalted" university professor and author, I have "evolved" in mythological "upwardness" to a yet "higher" position. Of course, in the process I have lost much. For example, I no longer have the clout of the third-grade teacher who meets with his highly impressionable youngsters every week for as much time as I now see my much less impressionable university students in their entire career.

If I were the devil, I would so mix the "up" and "down" hierarchy that the truly important roles of society came out on the bottom. He was apparently trying to do just that in Christ's day. As Peter Blitchington has pointed out, "Christ's disciples had the same orientation toward children and child-rearing that many people have today." [4] When the Jewish mothers brought their children to Jesus for the customary blessing, His disciples thought the task too trivial for Him to waste His important time on. Jesus, however, took the opposite view. He said: " 'Let the children come to me, and do not hinder them; for to such belongs the kingdom of heaven.' And he laid his hands on them" and blessed them (Matt. 19:14, 15).

Psychologist Arthur Combs shed light on the "lowness" of elementary teaching in his discussion of what he has called the "credentials myth" (viz., experts are better). Combs has pointed out that applying the credentials myth creates a hierarchy of value, prestige, and status. The college professor-research specialist sits at the top of the educational heap. In the pecking order junior college and high school subject matter teachers follow him, with the elementary teacher at the bottom, since he is concerned with " 'Mickey Mouse' matters." Modern society has developed a "specialty-is-better syndrome," which, noted Combs, has had two unhappy effects: "(1) the denigration of the elementary teacher accompanied by the glorification of the subject matter specialist, (2) the flight of the teacher from the classroom to specialist status." [5] What the specialty-is-better syndrome has not consciously recognized is the Christian truth that foundations are all-important (chap. 7:24-27). It is true that most elementary teachers, by the nature of their task, must be generalists in many subject matter areas, but they must be specialists "in understanding children and how they learn." [6] After all, the rest of the educational system must build upon their work (along with that of the parents).

From this perspective the myth of up and down has had disastrous effects upon the total educational system of society and the church. Perhaps it was no accident that a professor of education discovered the "Peter Principle." The Peter Principle states that "in a hierarchy every employee tends to rise to his level of incompetence." [7] The principle arises from the myth of up and down and the belief that whatever society considers "up" is "better." Thus, accordingly, a good teacher in a school should be promoted to principal. Of course, if he is a poor teacher, then he will have to remain as a teacher, since he has already reached his level of incompetence. Likewise with principals, if they are incompetent, they tend to remain as principals, but if they are successful, they can rise to a superintendency, where they may find their level of incompetence. The process removes a lot of good talent from the classroom to other areas, where it is often less effective. The drain will probably continue because of the myth of up and down and the social and financial rewards that sustain it.

What we have said about the educational profession is also true of other professions, including the pastoral ministry. The general feeling, once again, seems too often to be that any move out of the pastorate is a promotion upward. Thus, so the logic seems to run, a good pastor will make a good conference official; likewise, a successful conference official will make a capable union or General Conference official, et cetera. Of course, what actually happens is that many effective pastors leave positions where their talents lie to fill positions where they may be incompetent. Some men realize that it has happened to them, but the social pressure created by the myth of up and down makes it difficult for them to move backward (or "downward") to where they were truly effective, because going back (or "down"), in our mythological framework, is seen as a demotion and a personal failure rather than a possible stroke of honesty and courage.

If I were the devil I would want to get as many successful church employees as far from the scene of action as possible—I would put them behind desks, cover them with paper, and inundate them with committees. If that wasn't enough, I would remove them to "higher" and "higher" levels until they had little direct and sustained contact with the people who make up the church.

One should realize at this point that I have presented only a partial and incomplete perspective. Another side exists to the issue, and there is a true role of administration in the Biblical sense. Stick with me, and we will balance the picture in due time.

Up to now my point in the discussion has been that the popular idea of up and down is a faulty conception. We, for example, would probably say that being a physician is "up" from being a garbage collector. But if we really analyzed the social importance of these two occupations, we might prefer to revise that judgment. After all, what would our urban society be like without efficient garbage collection? Proper waste disposal, sanitation, and knowledge about cleanliness would create much less demand for the services of physicians, but the reverse is not true—that is, proper medical care does not lessen the need for sanitation services. Waste disposal is crucial in modern society. We cannot continue present levels of existence without it. It is not "down" in the level of social importance, even though society may choose to place it in the lower strata of human valuation.

What Christians must recognize is that God sees "up" and "down" differently than man does. From a human perspective, both Moses and Paul made mistakes in their courageous choices in regard to the "up" and "down" scale. They both selected service to God rather than prominent, secure, and respected social roles. But God's evaluation in the light of eternity was quite different (Ed, pp. 68-70). Ellen White has indicated that it is often difficult for us to determine what is great and small. "Many a worker," in what the world considers the lowly places of life on the up and down scale, "by setting on foot agencies for the blessing of the world, has achieved results that kings might envy!"—Ibid., p. 266. Christ never assumed a position that men rated as "up," but His work was of the highest importance. Only in the judgment will we see the results of what God considers the "world's noblest work" (ibid., pp. 305, 306).

Toward a Christian Explanation

The Christian answer to the myth of up and down is not the partial one regarding role and function that humanity derives from sociological insight. If it were, we might seek to solve many of our social problems by rearranging the up-and-down totem pole or by turning it upside down. But this would merely change the social problems rather than solve them. Paulo Freire glimpsed this point when he pointed out that the study of the history of revolutions indicates that a new oppressor class always builds upon the ruins of the structure of the defeated oppressor class.[8] It is the concept of hierarchy that is wrong, rather than any particular ordering of positions or people within a hierarchy.

The Bible and the writings of Mrs. White move beyond the myth of up and down to a social structure built upon a different basis. Ellen White used the idea of "highest calling" in a very provocative way. When she talked about occupational roles she often used superlatives. For example, she made statements that teachers and mothers have the most important work in the world. But if one reads on, she also said the same thing about physicians, ministers, and colporteurs. She even wrote that the cook who prepared the meals at Battle Creek College held the position of "first" importance within the institution, since the minds of the students would not be in a position to operate effectively if she did not do her job properly (FE, p. 226).

Just who is most important? What is society's highest calling? We do not find the answer in the myth of up and down. Rather, the Bible reveals it in terms of talents, gifts, and callings. Paul spoke to the myth directly in I Corinthians 12 (see also Eph. 4:1-16; Rom. 12:3-8). He presented God's social ideal as one of unity in diversity. God has given individual members specific gifts for the good of the whole. Paul compares the gifts to the parts of the body. One of his major points was that *all* the gifts are required for the health of the social body—they are all important. Furthermore, he explicitly rejected the myth of up and down when he wrote that "the parts of the body which seem to be weaker are indispensable, and those parts of the body which we think less honorable we invest with the greater honor" (1 Cor. 12:22, 23). Health of the social body is at its highest when it recognizes and respects the function and contribution of each individual, and when each works in harmony with the whole.

The Bible does not picture the ideal social order in terms of the evolutionary strata of "up" and "down," but as a smoothly functioning organism created by God. This picture, simple as it is, is difficult for us to grasp because of the almost overwhelming weight of the hierarchy of social roles within contemporary society and the material and social reward system constantly used to enforce it. Within the church as a whole we may never fully escape from the false social conception of "up" and "down," but certainly individuals will be able to find a more satisfactory personal adjustment if they begin to see the situation from the Biblical perspective.

The Biblical point of view does not regard the conference president as more significant than ("up from") the pastor. Nor is the teacher more important than the principal or the physician more vital than the garbage collector or vice versa. All are of utmost importance to the social whole. Ellen White has written that "God dispenses His gifts as it pleases Him. He bestows one gift upon one, and another gift upon another, but all for the good of the whole body. It is in God's order that some shall be of service in one line of work, and others in other lines—all working under the selfsame Spirit. The recognition of this plan will be a safeguard against emulation, pride, envy, or contempt of one another. It will strengthen unity and mutual love."—CT, pp. 314, 315.

It would be a sad world indeed if all of us became physicians, garbage collectors, or teachers. God has given to every person certain gifts, or talents, and has ordained that in our work we should supplement one another (ibid., p. 521).

Mrs. White used such superlatives as "highest calling" and "most important work" in the general context of the Biblical perspective on the diversity of gifts and the unity of the body. A person, therefore, is fulfilling his highest calling when he discovers his gifts and talents, and employs them to God's glory. The "highest of all service" is "to recover men from the snare of Satan and bind them to God" (6T, p. 339). This statement does not mean that He wants all of us to be pastors, evangelists, or denominational employees in the narrow sense of the word, but it does imply that He calls all of us to be workers with Him (Ed, p. 264). D. Elton Trueblood's discussion of the idea of Christian vocation reinforced this viewpoint. "The Christian philosophy of vocation is one in which we are convinced that our daily work is a holy enterprise. The Christian conviction is that to become a housewife is as much a holy undertaking as to become a pastor, that to enter the ministry of business is as much a sacred calling as to enter the ministry of theology." This is implied, he noted, in the doctrine of the priesthood of the believer.[9]

Every person has a summons to work for God in one way or another. "Not all can fill the same place," wrote Ellen White, "but for all there is a place and a work." —8T, p. 16. Man's true vocation is to serve his fellowman. His job or profession is merely the channel for his service. What specific social role a person should fill is determined by his aptitudes and capabilities (Ed, pp. 233, 267). Many people fail in life while others get hung up on the Peter Principle because they aspire to fill a social role for which they are neither called nor equipped (ibid., p. 267). They are not fulfilling their Christian vocation to the best of their ability because they are in the wrong profession. Laurence J. Peter touched upon this problem when he wrote that "most real improvement in the quality of life is the result of dedicated individuals performing their jobs with art and skill. Much individual discontent, as well as the defects in products and services, is the result of eyes turned upward to higher-level jobs rather than forward to the task at hand." [10]

"Up" and "Down" Versus "Calling"

One way to escape such discontent is for each of us to change his mind-set from the destructive myth of up and down to the truth of God's gifts. Such a mental transformation will be a liberating experience, since it is the truth that makes us free. Its acceptance will make it easier for Christians to change roles in a "downward" direction without guilt or self-denigration. After all, moving "down" may actually be moving "up" in terms of our happiness, achievement, and social impact. Nothing is more frustrating than being a round peg trying to fit into a square hole, or being afraid to be honest because of the myth of up and down after realizing that we have reached our level of incompetence. If I were the devil I would push that myth with all my effort, since it seems to produce both individual and social discontent and inefficiency.

A transformation of our minds from the myth of up and down to the conception of calling and vocation will not only help us beat the Peter Principle but it might also enable us to get a handle on "Parkinson's Law." "Parkinson's Law" holds that the increase of administrative positions within a bureaucracy proceeds from the inner nature of bureaucracy itself rather than from additional responsibilities and increases in the volume of work. The law rests on two axioms: First, that an official's status increases (he moves "up") as he multiplies subordinates; and second, that officials make work for each other.[11] These two motivating factors obviously interrelate and compound the situation.

Many Christians are concerned with the multiplication of administrative positions within the educational system, the government, and the church. I contend that a rejection of the myth of up and down would have a definite effect upon the bureaucratic problem highlighted by Parkinson. This would, in turn, free more people to serve on the front lines, where the victories must eventually be won.

A Biblical concept of leadership must also enter into the picture in Christian institutions. In the world at large a leader is a "superior" to those who work for him. Christ revolutionized this scheme of things and rocked the up-and-down myth when He claimed that the true function of leadership is service (Matt.

20:25-28; 23:1-12). Jesus specifically warned against a hierarchical up-and-down mentality when He noted that God is our leader and that we are all "brethren" (chap. 23:8). Pauline terminology equates the concept with the idea that we are all members of the body of the church, which has one head—Jesus Christ (Eph. 5:23).

The Bible makes it clear that there does exist a true activity of administration (1 Cor. 12:28). It, however, is a function rather than a level of human value within a hierarchy. The function of administration (and leadership) is service. In this view, we might see the role and purpose of a school principal as one of coordination and facilitation. The principal is not "above" the teachers. Neither is he "below" them. Ideally the role of the principal would be filled by one who is a teacher among teachers, a master teacher, one who truly understands teaching and the needs of students. We might view him as a leading teacher-principal— one who has not lost touch with the challenges and problems of the classroom. His function would be to provide an atmosphere conducive to teaching and learning. He would be his teachers' greatest helper in his role of facilitator and coordinator. The teachers are not to serve him, but he is to help them, and both teachers and principal are to meet the needs of the students and their parents. The Christian principal will never forget that the real action of the school takes place at the point where the students encounter the teacher. Administration, though important, is not the center of the educational endeavor.

What has been said about the servant-leadership role in education also holds true in the formal structure of the church. We must never fail to realize that most of the crucial action takes place in the local church and not in the "higher" realms. This ought to say something about the deployment of the church's talent. If the battle is not won in the field, it will not be won at all.

Confronting the myth of up and down is one of the most crucial issues facing the church and its educational system today. The real problem for the Christian is not worrying about "up" and "down" or striving for a "higher" position, but discovering his talents and using them for the glory of God and the benefit of his fellows. After all, "life's true aim is not to secure the greatest possible gain" for ourselves, "but to honor" our Maker by doing our "part of the world's work, and lending a helpful hand to those weaker or more ignorant" (Ed, pp. 221, 222). We should also keep in mind that "the Lord does not reward the large amount of labor. He does not regard the greatness[12] of the work so much as the fidelity with which it is done. The good and faithful servant is rewarded."—CT, p. 513.

Goodness and faithfulness are evaluated in terms of the development and use of our personal talents (Matt. 25:14-30), and not by a faulty striving to move ourselves upward in the mythological hierarchy of "up" and "down."

8 Myths About Human Nature

*T*oday," wrote G. C. Berkouwer, "more than at any time, the question 'What is man?' is at the center of theological and philosophical concern."[1] Although made more than twenty years ago, his statement is still valid not only in theology and philosophy but also in the realm of social and educational thought.

In chapter 4 we noted D. Elton Trueblood's assertion that "until we are clear on what man is we shall not be clear about much else,"[2] and Ellen White's view that an understanding of the nature of man and his current predicament is essential if we hope to comprehend the work of education (Ed, pp. 14, 15). People, however, are hopelessly divided upon both humanity's nature and significance. We see this in how they approach education and every other social endeavor.

This chapter will treat two basic anthropological myths, one centering upon the concept that man is either totally good or completely evil and the other focusing on the "animalness" of man. A clear understanding of both myths will help teachers, parents, and other educators to relate better to both children and current educational and social theories in the world at large.

Theological, psychological, and educational literature has spanned the entire spectrum on the nature of man. At one pole we find those stressing man's animalness and lack of morality. Thomas Hobbes, a philosopher, wrote that the life of man is "solitary, poor, nasty, brutish, and short"; Desmond Morris, a biologist, described man as essentially "a naked ape"; and B. F. Skinner, a leading behavioral psychologist, has claimed that man has neither freedom nor dignity. Theologians, as is well known, have not hesitated to expound upon the evil nature of man and the total depravity of human nature. Jonathan Edwards, for example, pictured man as being quite similar to a loathsome insect being held over the pit of hell by an angry God. In addition, in case we haven't gotten the message from the scholars and thinkers, we can also find the seamy side of human nature emphasized in the daily news.

A second polar stand in Western thought has focused on the goodness and dignity of man—that he is a "god," or is at least developing into one. The eighteenth-century Enlightenment, for example, had much to say about the infinite perfectibility of mankind. Nineteenth-century Americans picked up this theme, combined it with the millennial dreams of Protestant Christianity, and postulated an imminent heaven on earth through social improvement. Such views of man's goodness fueled the social reform movement of the nineteenth century. By midcentury such writers as Ralph Waldo Emerson were proclaiming that "within man is the soul of the whole." Earlier Jean Jacques Rousseau had promoted the theme of man's goodness in his influential *Emile* (1762). Theories based on the dignity-goodness pole of the human nature spectrum are popular in current psychology and education through the writings of such men as Carl Rogers and his colleagues among the humanistic psychologists and those desiring "open education." The general idea underlying such movements is that if we leave children "free" enough, their goodness will naturally come to the surface.

Man Is Neither "Good" nor "Evil"

The large amount of religious and educational literature and the great number of programs developed upon beliefs in the innate goodness or evilness of man have not made either position true. The fact is that man is neither good nor evil—he is both. Blaise Pascal caught the picture when he noted that "man is neither angel nor brute."[3] Pascal showed this same insight when he wrote that "it is dangerous to make man see too clearly his equality with the brutes without showing him his greatness. It is also dangerous to make him see his greatness too clearly, apart from his vileness. It is still more dangerous to leave him in ignorance of both. . . . Man must not think that he is on a level either with the brutes or with the angels, nor must he be ignorant of both sides of his nature; but he must know both."[4]

The strength of the extreme views of human nature is that they have both captured a part of the truth. Man does have a spark of good in him, but a tendency to choose the bad also plagues him. Paul in Romans 7 vividly pictured this fact of life as he described his personal internal conflict. The struggle that takes place in our daily lives also reflects it.

One of the most serious human problems in the twentieth century is that man has lost his identity. He no longer has the ability to ask, "Who am I?" and answer it in a meaningful way. Yet, noted Abraham Heschel, his every impulse is to continue to advance the question, along with others such as "What am I here for?" and "What is at stake in my existence?" [5] Modern life, maintained Heschel, makes it plausible for contemporary man to see himself in the image of a machine—" 'an ingenious assembly of portable plumbing' " or " 'a machine into which we put what we call food and produce what we call thought.' " [6] Such an image, however, does not ring true, because, unlike the "other machines" and his "hairier cousins," man still persistently asks, "Who am I?" "Man's final conquest," wrote C. S. Lewis, "has proved to be the abolition of man." [7]

Yet man won't stay abolished. He keeps asking meaningful questions. His identity crisis is a crushing problem, and from it stem all the rest of the problems of human existence.

Unaided, man will continue to search in vain for his identity. He will fail because human nature, when viewed on the empirical level of daily life, is a hopeless confusion of glory and wretchedness, of sublimity and depravity, of good and evil.

The first chapters of Genesis plainly state the answer to the human identity dilemma. Man was created in the image of God (Gen. 1:26, 27). Scripture pictures the race at its creation as being loving, trustworthy, rational, and righteous. Yet it does not take a great deal of insight to realize that man is no longer completely lovely, good, responsible, rational, or righteous. Man has changed, and the transformation has resulted from the Fall, outlined in Genesis 3. His attempt to place himself at the center of his world resulted in a loss of identity, in alienation, and in death. Without God man is lost.

It is important to note that the Fall did not totally destroy the image of God in man (chap. 9:6; 1 Cor. 11:7; James 3:9). Man can still have hope. Francis Schaeffer highlighted this point when he wrote that "man still stands in the image of God—twisted, broken, abnormal, but still the image-bearer of God." Fallen man has not lost his "mannishness." [8] A residue of the image continued to exist in him after the Fall. Every man, through the Holy Spirit, has a spark of the divine nature within him. Christ is the "Light, which lighteth every man that cometh into the world" (John 1:9, K.J.V.).

Ellen White, in commenting upon this passage, wrote that "a perception of right, *a desire for goodness, exists in every heart.* But against these principles there is struggling an antagonistic power. The result of the eating of the tree of knowledge of good and evil is manifest in every man's experience. *There is in his nature a bent to evil, a force which, unaided, he cannot resist. To withstand this force, to attain that ideal which in his inmost soul he accepts as alone worthy, he can find help in but one power. That power is Christ.* Co-operation with that power is man's greatest need. In all educational effort should not this co-operation be the highest aim?"—Ed, p. 29. (Italics supplied.)

The Bible and the writings of Ellen White indicate that man is neither totally good nor completely evil, but rather that he is a seething mixture of both. Schaeffer has remarked that "man's achievements demonstrate that he is not junk, though the ends to which he often puts them show how lost he is." [9] A controversy rages within human nature, as it does in the world at large, between the forces of good and evil. Man finds himself torn between his desire for goodness and an inclination toward evil, and he is often drawn toward the good even though his natural propensities lead him to choose the evil. We cannot understand his potential for both good and evil apart from the Fall. The Biblical revelation of his original position in relation to God and the subsequent loss of that position explain his potential for both good and evil. Now man lives in an abnormal world in which he is divided against himself and separated from God. Fallen man is in active rebellion against the Creator. The most delusive part of his current situation is his ignorance of his true condition and his possibilities for unaided betterment. The Bible presents fallen man as a deceived rebel (Jer. 17:9) incapable of finding God on his own.

Fortunately, God does not leave lost man to his own helplessness. God has taken the initiative to help him out of his plight and to renew and restore him to the fullness of His image (Col. 3:10). For this reason Christ came into the world. The work of Christ was and is to reverse the effects of the Fall by making it possible for man to become at one (in harmony) with God, with others, with his deceptive self, and with the natural creation. The essence of salvation is to restore the relationships broken at the Fall and to return God to His rightful place at the center of the individual human life. Some people respond positively to God's initiative, while others reject it. As a result, two humanities emerged after man's introduction to sin—those still in revolt and those who have accepted Christ as Lord and Saviour. No man, however, is morally neutral (Matt. 12:30). Every individual has placed either God or himself at the center of his life. Those in the former category have solved their identity crisis and their problem of personal meaning, while those in the latter group must continue to grope in their lostness.

Redemptive education focuses upon the lostness of individuals. It never loses sight of the fact that the life of every person is a scene of active conflict between the powers of good and the forces of evil. Each student's life is continually the scene of a dynamic struggle between Christ and Satan.

We have noted that people are neither completely good nor totally evil. It is true of Christians as well as non-Christians. Even though the born-again Christian has made a decision to live the "good" life, that does not make it an accomplished fact. C. S. Lewis' Screwtape noted this in his insightful letters when he wrote to his devilish apprentice Wormwood soon after Wormwood's patient suffered a conversion to Christianity. At that time Screwtape encouraged Wormwood not to despair, since "all the *habits* of the patient, both mental and bodily, are still in our favour." [10] The transformation of attitudes and hearts is the work of an instant, but the transformation of habit patterns is the task of a lifetime.

Realizing that the life of each student is the scene of an ongoing struggle between Christ and Satan is a preliminary step in redemptive education. After the introduction of young people to Jesus as Saviour, education within the home, school, and church has a vital role to play in the process of habit transformation (i.e., sanctification or character development). In accomplishing this task, the Christian educator seeks to develop the good in each child through the aid of the Holy Spirit. It takes patience, caring, and sanctified imagination on the teacher's part.

A challenge to Christian educators is to see beyond where their students are now in their lives to where they can be with God's help. Heschel noted that one of the outstanding facts about man "is the superiority of the possibilities of his being over the actuality of his being. . . . Man must be understood as a complex of opportunities as well as a bundle of facts." [11] Ellen White wrote that Christ, "looking upon men in their suffering and degradation, . . . perceived ground for hope where appeared only despair and ruin" (Ed, p. 79). "In every human being, however fallen, He beheld a son of God, one who might be restored to the privilege of his divine relationship. . . . In *every* human being He discerned *infinite possibilities*. He saw men as they might be, transfigured by His grace." — *Ibid.*, pp. 79, 80. (Italics supplied.) Here is the challenge of Christian education: to see the *infinite* potential in every one of our children, students, and acquaintances. Such vision in itself takes an act of grace on our imagination. After all, every teacher has had students who didn't look like very promising prospects. And what about Peter, James, John, and the other disciples and their continual bickering about who was the greatest? Christ saw their true potential beneath the surface.

Such visualizing, encouraging, and developing of the potential for good in each individual is a vital task of Christian education. It was a central theme in Christ's ministry. Of His relation with individuals, Mrs. White wrote: "Looking upon them with hope, He inspired hope. Meeting them with confidence, He inspired trust. Revealing in Himself man's true ideal, He awakened, for its attainment, both desire and faith. In His presence souls despised and fallen realized that they still were men, and they longed to prove themselves worthy of His regard. In many a heart that seemed dead to all things holy, were awakened new impulses. To many a despairing one there opened the possibility of a new life." — *Ibid.*, p. 80.

Here is the heart of the art of Christian teaching and redemptive education. It is up to us whether we shall inspire hope or hopelessness in those with whom we have significant daily contact. We cannot escape the responsibility of our relationships. Through them we affect each other's self-image and sense of personal worth. In turn, this partly determines whether our acquaintances will see their own potential as devilish or Godlike. Such perception tends to create a self-fulfilling prophecy. What individuals see in themselves they will tend to become, for better or worse.

On this theme Ellen White indicates that an important task for teachers is "to arouse hope and aspiration in the youth, to help them to realize the possibilities lying before them" (CT, p. 498). "The good that a teacher will do his students will be proportionate to his belief in them. And let the teacher remember that it is the most unfortunate, those who have a disagreeable temperament, who are rough, stubborn, sullen, that most need love, compassion, and help. Those who most try our patience most need our love."— *Ibid.*, p. 267.

Christian education can achieve its goals more fully when educators clearly realize that individuals are neither totally good nor completely evil and that each student has the potential to develop either way. Such a recognition removes education from the humdrum of daily routine and places it in the universal panorama of the great controversy as a spectacle to the universe (1 Cor. 4:9).

Man as an Animal

A second crucial issue concerning human nature in education

is the animalness of man. Many Christians have been somewhat confused on this point. Some, in reaction to the Darwinian-Hux-leian revolution, have automatically rejected as myth any idea that man is an animal. Others, profoundly influenced by the accomplishments of the behavioral scientists and the cause-and-effect relationships apparent in God's natural law, find it hard to believe that man could be anything but an animal. Closely related to the whole question is whether a man is free or determined. These issues are crucial to Christian education and Christian life because of the impact of behavioral science on instructional theory and public mind control.

It seems, if we move beyond an emotional response to Darwinism, hard to deny the fact that man is an animal. We share much with the animal world, from structural likeness in our physical bodies to our digestive and respiratory processes. Furthermore, we participate in many of the same activities. Both people and dogs, for example, enjoy riding in automobiles, eating good food, and having their heads rubbed affectionately. It is impossible to deny the fact that we share a great deal with our canine (and other animal) friends.

The point that we need to emphasize, however, is not that man is an animal, but that he is more than an animal. Here is where the rub comes into human understanding. What is this "something more"? Heschel has noted that "the animality of man we can grasp with a fair degree of clarity. The perplexity begins when we attempt to make clear what is meant by the humanity of man." [12]

E. F. Schumacher, a social philosopher, has pointed out that humans share much with the mineral realm, since both people and minerals consist of matter; that humans have more in common with the plant world than the mineral realm, since both plants and people have life in addition to a mineral base; and that humans have even more yet in common with the animal world, since both people and animals have consciousness as well as life and a mineral base. But, observed Schumacher, only humans have reflective self-awareness. Animals undoubtedly think, he claimed, but man's uniqueness is his awareness of his own thinking. Schumacher pointed out that we can learn a lot about man by studying him at the mineral, plant, and animal levels—"in fact, everything can be learned about him except that which makes him human." [13]

The Bible further explicates man's uniqueness. Not only was he created in God's image, but God singled him out at Creation as being the one creature on earth that is responsible and accountable

(Gen. 1:28). In one sense man was within creation, but in another sense he was above the natural order. Man was to have "dominion" over the rest of the created beings. Only man had the holy calling of the stewardship of God's creation laid upon him. And only man acts as God's vice-regent, prophet, and priest upon the earth. He has endowed only man with the ability to live the extended life of the mind through internal thought and external verbalization, and given him the capability of transcending his world and his own being through both consciousness and self-consciousness. Thus, only man, of all earthly creatures, can truly worship and develop a personal relationship with his Creator, because only man has been made in God's likeness.

The Christian educator can never forget the fact that man is an animal with the possibilities inherent in animal life. Likewise, he can never neglect the truth that man is more than an animal and has more than animalistic potential. Keeping both aspects of human nature in mind, claimed Reinhold Niebuhr, is not an easy task. "How difficult it is," he suggested, "to do justice to both the uniqueness of man and his affinities with the world of nature below him is proved by the almost unvarying tendency of those philosophies, which describe and emphasize the rational faculties of man or his capacity for self-transcendence to forget his relation to nature and to identify him, prematurely and unqualifiedly, with the divine and the eternal; and of naturalistic philosophies to obscure the uniqueness of man." [14]

A problem closely related to man's animal nature is the issue of whether human life is free or determined. It seems to be quite evident from extensive experimentation that reinforcement contingencies involving rewards and punishments determine animal life. In other words, animals do not have freedom of choice, but are conditioned and controlled by their needs and their environment. We can train an animal to do anything within the range of its abilities. The question that has divided theologians, philosophers, and educators is "Can man be trained to do anything?" The answer is a definite Yes if a man lives at the animal level. A person who operates at the level of his appetites and passions is functioning on the animal level, and, like the animals, reinforcement contingencies can control him. The saying that "every man has his price" is not an idle jest. It is based on experience and observation. The unfortunate fact is that apparently most men do live most of the time on the level of their animal propensities. This fact underlies the apparent validity of behaviorism's claim that man is not free and that a person's behavior can be shaped to any desired pattern if the controller has enough time and enough knowledge of that individual and his environment.

The crucial point in the whole issue, however, is that man can rise above the animal level of existence because he is related in a unique way to God and has received the power to transcend his own consciousness through self-awareness. Being in the image of God, humanity can reason from cause to effect and make responsible choices and spiritual decisions. According to the Bible, man has genuine freedom of choice and can therefore make moral decisions through the use of his rationality as it is aided by special revelation and the guidance of the Holy Spirit.

Man's freedom of choice, however, is not absolute in the sense that he is autonomous and can live without God. But it is genuine in the sense that individuals can choose Jesus Christ as Lord and live by His principles, or choose Satan as master and be subject to the law of sin and death (Rom. 6:12-23). C. S. Lewis has remarked that God has made free will possible because, even though it makes evil possible, it also is the only thing that "makes possible any love or goodness or joy worth having." [15]

The big question for the Christian is whether his animal attributes or his "higher" nature will control his life. Ellen White has written that "it rests with us individually to decide whether our lives shall be controlled by the mind or by the body."—Ed, p. 202. This issue is central in Christian education and the Christian life. For a human being to let his appetites or bodily desires rule him is to be less than human from the Biblical perspective.

Our discussion brings us to the concept of behaviorism and its applicability in Christian education and other aspects of Christian endeavor. Behaviorism is a philosophy of the science of human behavior that assumes that human beings are merely animals[16] who learn in the same way as other animals. The concept is particularly important in education, since many current educational methodologies and ideas employ behavioral premises.

Behavioral techniques have undeniable power and, in some cases, utility. The advertising industry and the propaganda bureaus of modern governments are probably the most obvious examples of the power of behaviorism in contemporary society. One of their major objects is mind control, and beyond mind control, the shaping of individual lives and actions. One of the primary tasks of the advertising industry, for example, is to convince people to buy things they don't really need or want. We can gauge the success and strength of advertising's application of behavioral techniques by the fact that it continues to be lavishly funded as one of America's largest businesses in a society that has relatively few genuine needs but possesses outstanding production capabilities. Advertisers play upon the appetites, desires, and vanity of the public, and the public responds. It was no accident that John B. Watson, acknowledged founder of behaviorism, ended his scholarly career in mid-life and entered the world of advertising.

The power of behavioral methods is undeniable. What is less understood are the limits of behaviorism. One of its basic assumptions is that man, being an animal, will respond to stimuli in the same manner as Pavlov's dogs and Skinner's rats and pigeons. Thus, given enough time and knowledge of an individual, claim the behaviorists, one can determine that person's choices through reinforcements playing on pain and pleasure. Such a belief is just as true as the assumption that man is an animal. So far as man is an animal (or lives on the animal level), we can condition and control his choices. The important point is, however, that he has the potential (often unrealized) to rise above the animal level and above the power of behavioral techniques. He has the capability of transcending the animal level and the powerful effects of behavioral techniques through a willingness to live on the uniquely human level in the likeness of God and to accept the power of the Holy Spirit in his life.

David G. Myers, a Christian psychologist, spoke to this issue when he pointed out that "humanity's unique achievement is its ability to control the environment for its own purposes." [17] This comes as a result of God's charge to Adam to "subdue" the natural creation and to "have dominion" over it (Gen. 1:28). Paul, in a similar vein, has told us, "Don't let the world around you squeeze you into its own mould" (Rom. 12:2, Phillips), as the environment does to the lower forms of life. Even though individuals can never fully escape the effects of their environment, they can rise above environmental forces. Man has the potential to make choices individually and initiate actions at a level beyond the boundaries of behavioral conditioning. Human beings therefore have, within the context of the great controversy, a degree of freedom not available to animals.[18]

It seems that behaviorism and behavioral techniques have utility in Christian education to the same extent that the insight that man is an animal is true. Behaviorism has certainly contributed to our understanding of human development, individual learning, and social interaction through making explicit some of the natural law relationships built into human nature by God.

Behaviorism has also been beneficial in enabling us to create more effective learning situations. After all, it is better to utilize reinforcement principles consciously and knowingly than to have them operating haphazardly in our ignorance. Christian educators should utilize behavioral techniques whenever they are helpful, while at the same time realizing that they are most effective in shaping human beings in those tasks that are closest to the animal level of mechanical activity.

On the other hand, the dangers inherent in behaviorism are threefold. One is the failure to realize its limitations in regard to those aspects of education above the animal level. A second is the fact that society or individuals can use this powerful body of techniques for immoral ends. Coupled with the modern media, the prospects of behavioral technology for mind control are frightening. A third danger is that the scientific validity of behaviorism in its experimentation with animals has led to its becoming a scientific faith among many. Donald MacKay, a specialist in brain physiology, has distinguished between positive and negative behaviorism. Positive behaviorism is behaviorism as a scientific method, while the negative aspect sets behaviorism up as a metaphysical doctrine that claims that human freedom and dignity are prescientific relics and that we can discover all important aspects of reality through the senses.[19] The Christian has an obligation to accept the positive contributions of behaviorism, even though he rejects the negative aspects.

The Christian answer to the dangers inherent in behaviorism is to realize that ultimate truth is rooted in God's scriptural revelation rather than in the limited world of human experience. This fact helps us to recognize the limits of behaviorism and provides the ethical framework for implementing a technique arising from natural law.

A Christian approach to the animalness of man must develop "thinkers" in its educational system rather than mere responders to and reflectors of the powerful forces at work to control people's lives (Ed, p. 17). As this is done the Christian school, home, and church must consciously help people create approaches for discovering and analyzing the underlying principles of the issues they face. These educational institutions must also lead young people into the process of reasoning from cause to effect. Developing such traits is an important part of restoring God's image in man. We must inspire our students to live above the animal level through moral choice.

In conclusion, we have noted that man has the potential to be either good or evil, and that he is both animal and at the same time more than an animal. An individual can choose to exist at the subhuman level—mineral through death, vegetable through paralyzing accident, or animal through living on the level of his appetites and passions. Few elect to live at the mineral or vegetable stages, but many opt the animal level. The great truth of the gospel is that each person can become fully human through a personal relationship with God through Jesus Christ. This fact is a central pillar in an education that finds its primary purpose in helping individuals come into a restored relationship with God, that sees every person as a child of God, and that helps each one develop his highest potential. Ellen White forcefully stated the possibilities inherent in every person when she wrote: "Higher than the highest human thought can reach is God's ideal for His children. Godliness—Godlikeness—is the goal to be reached."—*Ibid.*, p. 18. To aid in the transformation of this ideal from potentiality to actuality is the function of Christian education in the home, school, and church.

9 The Myth of the Ignorant Christian

*T*he idea that spirituality, humility, and other Christian virtues are related to ignorance is deeply entrenched in some segments of Christian society. Such groups often correlate the intellectual life with pride, self-sufficiency, and worldliness. The origin of evil in the Garden of Eden has prompted some people to entertain such a line of thought. Eve, after all, made her mistake when she ate of the tree of "knowledge" (Gen. 2:17; 3:1-7). Here, so the interpretation goes, was the beginning of "worldly knowledge."

A second Biblical source for equating ignorance with Christian virtue has been the lives of Christ's disciples. The Bible indicates that they were uneducated. The "best" of them, according to the myth, were in fact "ignorant fishermen." Of course, we observe one interesting exception to their general ignorance—Judas Iscariot. The subsequent careers of the disciples seem to prove two things for many people: First, lack of formal learning has a close relationship to godliness; and second, eating from the tree of knowledge had the same effect on Judas that it had on Adam and Eve. The conclusion that follows from such reasoning is that ignorance is a good thing—especially ignorance of the knowledge of this world.

An internal tension has always existed in Christianity between a religion of the mind and one of the heart, between the emotions and the intellect. The Christian community has perennially fought over whether it should subordinate emotion to intellect or vice versa. Richard Hofstadter has demonstrated that the emotional and anti-intellectual aspects of Christianity became predominant in the American churches because of the dissenting inheritance of American immigrants and the continued presence of a frontier that tended to depreciate book knowledge.[1] American religion was, to a large extent, a reaction against formal churches and an educated clergy. Baptists and Methodists particularly defended the idea of an unlearned ministry. Billy Sunday, the popular evangelist, represented such a view when he proclaimed that "thousands of college graduates are going as fast as they can straight to hell. If I had a million dollars I'd give $999,999 to the church and $1 to education." [2] In America, religion became a matter of the heart rather than of the head. In itself this might have been healthy enough had it not led to a depreciation of the head.

American society's anti-intellectual attitude naturally influenced early Adventism, a sect closely related to the frontier and to both the Baptists and Methodists in its point of origin. Some later Adventists also headed in this direction by carefully selecting statements from the writings of Ellen White, such as those related to a speedy preparation (see FE, pp. 334-367). Ellen White also wrote that in the last days God will take men from the plow and vineyard and send them forth to give the Adventist message to the world. They are "the very men and women who cause us discouragement. In them He sees qualifications that will enable them to take a place in His vineyard." And they will preach through the power of the Holy Spirit (7T, p. 271). "God can and will use those who have not had a thorough education in the schools of men. A doubt of His power to do this is manifest unbelief." Such doubt closes up the way of the Holy Spirit and leaves many willing Christians in idleness (9T, p. 259). Again she remarked: "It is not true that brilliant young men always make the greatest success. How often men of talent and education have been placed in positions of trust, and have proved failures. . . . They walked in the sparks (their bright flashes of thought) of their own kindling. They did not depend on the wisdom which God alone can give."—FE, p. 193. When the final message to a fallen world goes with "greatest power," she said, the Lord will employ "humble instruments. . . . The laborers will be qualified rather by the unction of His Spirit than by the training of literary institutions."—GC, p. 606. Finally, several statements indicate that "success will be proportionate to the degree of consecration and self-sacrifice in which . . . work is done, rather than to either natural or acquired endowments."—CT, p. 538.

In summary, these passages from Ellen White, along with the historical facts and Biblical interpretations previously mentioned, have all tended to support the myth of the ignorant Christian. Like all myths, however, it is built on a selection of the facts rather than a balanced view of the whole. The truth is, as we shall see, that ignorance is not an element of godliness. God, who created our minds and intellects, naturally expects us to employ the gifts He has given us.

Learning and Christianity

Early Adventists were firmly in the current of the anti-intellectual thrust of American Protestantism. We should never forget that it was thirty years after the great Disappointment before Adventists developed their first college and secondary school, and that fifty years had elapsed after 1844 before they established more than a handful of elementary schools. Formal education was the last major institutional endeavor of the Adventist Church. Publishing houses, sanitariums, and church organization all preceded the development of a system of schooling. This fact seems hard to believe in the light of subsequent Adventist education, but it reflects something about the ideas and values of early Adventism.

A letter written to James White by W. H. Ball in 1862 reflects the educational outlook of many early Adventists. Ball asked: "Is it right and consistent for us who believe with all our hearts in the immediate coming of the Lord, to seek to give our children an education?" White's reply is a classic, and it set the tone for what we find in the attitude of later Adventism toward formal learning. "The fact that Christ is very soon coming," he wrote, "is no reason why the mind should not be improved. A well-disciplined and informed mind can best receive and cherish the sublime truths of the Second Advent." [3]

His wife sounded the same note in 1872 when she wrote that "*ignorance will not increase the humility or spirituality of any professed follower of Christ. The truths of the divine word can be best appreciated by an intellectual Christian.* Christ can be best glorified by those who serve Him intelligently."—FE, p. 45. (Italics supplied.)

A close examination of Scripture brings the same picture to the forefront. God did not condemn Eve, for example, because she sought knowledge, but because she sought the knowledge of evil and placed her wisdom above the wisdom of God. He had been adding to the knowledge of Adam and Eve day by day, and this mind-expanding experience was to continue throughout eternity (Ed, pp. 15, 20-22). In God's plan all knowledge was available to them with the exception of the knowledge of sin and its results, but even it was an open option (Gen. 3:1-7).

The disciples, likewise, may have been unschooled, but they were not unlearned or ignorant. When Christ chose them they may have been unlettered and from the ranks of the common people, but they were to receive one of the best educations ever given to men at the personal hand of history's greatest Teacher. We are told that Christ would have selected His disciples from the ranks of the noble and educated, but they apparently would not do His work. As a result, He chose humble men who had both native ability and a teachable spirit (CT, pp. 511, 512; Ed, p. 85). God and man have different views of ignorance. The human standpoint regarded John, James, and Peter as ignorant because they had not attended the schools of the rabbis. Even this, however, was an advantage because they did not have to unlearn a large amount of falsehood before beginning their "real education" at the hands of the Master. "Jesus," penned Ellen White, "did not despise education. The highest culture of the mind, *if sanctified* through the love and the fear of God, receives His fullest approval."—FE, p. 47. (Italics supplied.)

The Lord, we should further note, did not always use unschooled men. Some of the greatest Biblical heroes and those who have penned the largest and, in many ways, the most penetrating sections of both the Old and New Testaments had excellent educations by the highest standards of our world. Think of Moses, the dominating figure of the Old Testament, who received an education in the courts of Egypt; of Daniel, who sat under the world's greatest teachers at the "University of Babylon"; and of Paul, the New Testament figure second only to Christ, who had the highest education available in the Jewish sector of the Roman Empire. Paul could span the great gulf between the Jewish and Gentile worlds because of his understanding of both. It was a task the disciples lacked the qualifications to accomplish.

God was able to use Moses, Daniel, and Paul in the mighty ways He did because of their education, not in spite of it. It is true that God had additional lessons to teach to at least Paul and Moses through a course of study in the wilderness, but that was because of a lack of balance in their original training and their need for an understanding of the divine perspective as well as for greater humility and tenderness as leaders of God's church. The point is that God is not any more able to use one-sided intellectualism than one-sided ignorance. In His educational ideal God seeks to develop well-rounded individuals who have balance among their mental, physical, spiritual, and social attributes. The labor of such persons is of great value to God because humility and the motive of service blend with their achievements.

Perhaps the greatest argument on behalf of intellectual Christians appears in the nature of God Himself. God is omniscient—He knows all there is to know. He does not despise knowledge. In short, God is intellectual, and man should be also since he is created in God's image. It is therefore incumbent, noted

Arthur Holmes, for Christians to develop the intellectual potential that God has given them. Learning, he admitted, brings with it the temptation of intellectual pride. "But the cure for intellectual pride is not ignorance, any more than the cure for sexual license is celibacy. To prize ignorance, when God gives us the capacity and opportunity for understanding, is a sin." [4] The human mind is a part of God's creation, and it is man's responsibility to develop it, a point implicit in both Christ's teaching of the talents and Paul's doctrine of the gifts (Matt. 25:14-30; Rom. 12:3-8).

The Bible, unless one reads it superficially, does not leave us with the view that ignorance is holiness. To the contrary, Peter indicated that growth in knowledge is a part of sanctification (2 Peter 1:5-7), and Solomon noted that gaining that wisdom which guides and evaluates the use of knowledge is of utmost importance (Prov. 4:7). True wisdom in the Bible, however, is never separated from its source in God (e.g., chap. 1:7). Paul, in writing to the Corinthians, had occasion to contrast the wisdom of God with the "wisdom of the world" (1 Cor. 1:20-22). Holmes has rightly remarked that the "wisdom of the world" is not human knowledge as such, nor a knowledge about the natural world, but rather the rejection of the plan of salvation as revealed in the Bible. Such "wisdom" is foolish because it "excludes God's saving work in Christ and tries to know God independently of the cross." [5] The Bible never depreciates either the love of wisdom or the pursuit of truth because of the simple fact, as we shall note in the next chapter, that God is the source of all genuine truth and wisdom, wherever we may find it.

Ellen White has taken the same position as that of Scripture. Her injunctions make it explicit that the Christian should seek high attainments in literary and scientific knowledge as well as that knowledge more closely related to the Bible and religion in the narrow sense of the term. She spoke directly to the myth of the ignorant Christian when she wrote that "dullness and ignorance are no virtue."—FE, p. 316. In a more positive vein she penned the following words: "Above all other people upon the earth, the man whose mind is enlightened by the opening of the word of God to his understanding, will feel that he must give himself to greater diligence in the perusal of the word of God, and to a diligent study of the sciences, for his hope and calling are greater than any other."—Ibid., pp. 243, 244. Again: "All who engage in the acquisition of knowledge should strive to reach the highest round of the ladder. Let students advance as fast and as far as they can; let the field of their study be as broad as their powers can compass; but let them make God their wisdom."—CT, p. 394; see also FE, pp. 82, 213. Likewise, a religious education "will not lead to a cheapening of the literary attainments" (FE, p. 118).

We observed earlier that "God can and will use those who have not had a thorough education in the schools of men."—CT, p. 511. The point that we must now make is that He is able to make broader use of those who have both dedication and learning rather than just dedication by itself. Dedication is the more important of the two elements, since God can work through an unlettered but dedicated person, while He is unable to use either educated or unlettered individuals fully if they have not surrendered to the power of the Holy Spirit (FE, p. 346). But education coupled with dedication and self-surrender widens the sphere of what God can do with us. In *Fundamentals of Christian Education* we read that "ignorance is not acceptable to God, and is unfavorable for the doing of His work. . . . But God works for people in spite of their ignorance. Those who have had no opportunity for acquiring knowledge, or who have had opportunity and have failed to improve it, . . . can be useful in the service of the Lord through the operation of His Holy Spirit. *But those who have education, and who consecrate themselves to the service of God, can do service in a greater variety of ways, and can accomplish a much more extensive work in bringing souls to the knowledge of the truth than can those who are uneducated.*"— Page 369; see also pages 108, 109, 255, 256; CT, p. 42. (Italics supplied.) For these reasons, among others, Ellen White wrote that God wanted Battle Creek College to "reach a higher standard of intellectual and moral culture than any other institution of the kind in our land" (4T, p. 425).

It is important to recognize that ignorance is not the only knowledge myth with which the Christian must contend. At the other pole stands another that has plagued the church—the myth of intellectualism.

Antithesis: The Myth of Intellectualism

Intellectualism is not any more a panacea than ignorance, even though many Christians have chosen to play that game. Ellen White threw out a rather cautious note when she remarked that "knowledge will *not necessarily* dwarf Christian growth."—3T, p. 223. (Italics supplied.) More explicitly, she wrote that mental culture may be gained at the same time "the heart is becoming an easy prey to deception."—CT, p. 425. Christians must be aware of both the nature of the pitfalls in the acquisition of knowledge and the way around them.

Knowledge (even knowledge about God) detracts from the Christian life when it turns into an end in itself rather than a means to an end. For the Christian, as God's responsible servant, life includes more than the satisfaction of merely knowing. Christian knowing is always an instrument for living in a healthy relationship to both God and our fellow beings. Anything that becomes an end in itself, except for God, is an idol. Knowledge—even good knowledge—that we turn into an end in itself becomes that escape from reality that is the antithesis of Biblical Christianity, which seeks to bring individuals face to face with the reality of both their condition before God and their responsibility to enrich the lives of others through the use of their talents. Another result of seeing knowledge as an end rather than a means is that it leads to pride, vanity, self-sufficiency, and bigotry. Finally, the Christian should never forget that knowledge is not neutral. It becomes a power for good or evil depending upon the use to which we put it. People who have separated it from the principles of God's love have found a seemingly unending variety of destructive uses for such knowledge.

A wide gulf exists between the Christian intellectual and the Christian "hung up" on intellectualism. We will now examine some of the attributes of Christian knowledge. First, and perhaps most important, we must see it in its overall relationship to the Christian life. Knowledge and intellectual attainment are important, but they are not the most important aspects of the Christian life. Mrs. White has written that "true education does not ignore the value of scientific knowledge or literary acquisitions; but above information it values power; above power, goodness; above intellectual acquirements, character. The world does not so much need men of great intellect as of noble character. It needs men in whom ability is controlled by steadfast principle."—Ed, p. 225. She also wrote that "heart education is of more importance than the education gained from books" (8T, p. 311) and that "knowledge . . . is a power for good only when united with true piety. It must be vitalized by the Spirit of God in order to serve the noblest purposes."—CT, p. 38. In short, an essential characteristic of the culture of the Christian mind is that it be "sanctified through the love and the fear of God" (FE, p. 47). The Christian always sees knowledge and the value of intellectual attainments in relation to both God and the total context of Christian character development. What does it profit a man if he gains all knowledge and knows all things and yet loses his soul? While it is true that God is most interested in the individual's spiritual culture (7T, p. 281), it is also true that spiritual and intellectual culture are not mutually exclusive, even though one has prior importance. The Christian can have both, and those who do have spiritual culture will continue to develop intellectual culture in both the present world and in the hereafter.

A second attribute of Christian knowledge and intellectual development is that it does not exist separate from Christian purpose. Ellen White wrote that "it is right for the youth to feel that they must reach the highest development of their natural powers. We would not restrict the education to which God has set no limit. But our attainments will avail nothing if not put to use for the honor of God and the good of humanity. *Unless our knowledge is a stepping-stone to the accomplishment of the highest purposes, it is worthless.*"—FE, p. 541; see also CT, p. 505; MYP, p. 173. (Italics supplied.) The Christian can never isolate his intellectual and literary accomplishments from the imperative to witness the gospel to his fellowman. Richard Niebuhr, in critiquing the desire of some Christians to escape from their social and witnessing responsibilities, has remarked: "The conservation, selection, and conversion of cultural achievements is not only a fact; it is also a morally inescapable requirement. . . . If he [the Christian] is to confess Jesus before men, he must do so by means of words and ideas derived from culture."[6] In this process, noted Niebuhr, it will be necessary to translate the meaning of cultural concepts and ideas into the terms of the Christian worldview.

Niebuhr's perception is a crucial insight that many Adventists have not yet faced. If we hope to spread the message to those outside the Christian community we cannot expect them to be much impressed with the superiority of our ideas if they perceive our ignorance of what they consider the "best" of the larger culture. The autobiography of M. L. Andreasen, who became one of Adventism's foremost authors and educators earlier in this century, highlights a case in point. Andreasen made some interesting remarks about his first meeting with an Adventist minister. He noted that the preacher was virtually ignorant outside of the doctrines of the church and prophetic history. "Of literature in general he did not know much, nor of history outside of his particular interest. . . . I had been much impressed by his learning in fields of which I knew nothing. But when I discovered the field he covered was very narrow, I recovered my balance."[7] Fortunately, Andreasen was able to see beyond the pastor's limitations. But, we might ask, how many others might have looked upon such ignorance as an excuse to neglect conviction?

The Christian has the responsibility, in such encounters, to build the bridge from the culture of this world to the wider culture of God's kingdom. That does not mean that we need to become "experts" in every field of human knowledge or make the mistake of arguing from a non-Christian perspective. But it does imply that Christians should be culturally literate and should be able to present the gospel in relation to the scientific and literary background of the people with whom they are seeking to communicate. However, Christianity, not current culture, will set the framework of our thinking. The gospel imperative is to reach men where they are and then to lift them to higher ground. To do this we must at least understand "where they are," even though we have chosen not to live there because we have found a better way.

A careful reading of Ellen White demonstrates that she never separated the acquisition of knowledge from its Christian purposes. Writing to two young men, she said: "You have thought that it was of the highest importance to obtain an education in the sciences. There is no virtue in ignorance, and knowledge will not necessarily dwarf Christian growth; but if you seek for it from principle, having the right object before you, and feeling your obligation to God to use your faculties to do good to others and promote His glory, knowledge will aid you to accomplish this end. . . . The object for which you are obtaining an education should not be lost sight of for a moment. It should be to so develop and direct your faculties that you may be more useful, and bless others to the extent of your ability."—3T, pp. 223, 224. Several years later she commented that "the teachers in our colleges may do a high, noble, holy work in educating the youth that they may reach the highest standard in intellectual acquirements. *There is no danger of their soaring too high, if balanced by the sanctification of the Holy Spirit.*"—MS 23, 1889. (Italics supplied.)

Lack of space forces us to touch upon several other aspects of Christian knowledge only briefly. First, Christian knowing is never separate from Christian action. Knowing, in the fullest Biblical sense, is applying perceived knowledge to one's daily life. Christian knowing is experiential. Second, we can never isolate Christian knowledge from feelings, emotions, or commitment. It is always related to the whole man. Third, Christian knowledge must always be coupled with understanding. When the Holy Spirit directed Philip to the Ethiopian eunuch in the desert he asked, " 'Do you understand what you are reading?' " (Acts 8:30). The important thing was not the reading, but whether he understood. Christian education must go beyond blind imitation, mindless conformity, and mechanical knowing. Last, we can never divorce Christian knowing from faith in the God of revelation. Mankind of itself is impossibly lost, and all human knowledge has bogged down in hopeless philosophical circles.[8] The most significant event in earth's history is that God has broken through to man with the revelation of the written and living Word so that human beings can have certainty in their understanding of both personal and universal meaning.

A Lesson From Adventist History

It is unfortunate that Seventh-day Adventists have not always kept in view the purpose of both knowledge and education. In 1895 Ellen White penned a stiff testimony aimed at Battle Creek College entitled "Speedy Preparation for the Work" (FE, pp. 334-367). Among other things it indicated that the college was leaning too heavily on book knowledge, subverting the spiritual aspects of education, viewing education and knowledge from the human perspective, keeping young men and women too long in school without practical experience, dampening missionary impulses, and seeking for a "perfect education" through more extensive study than was needed for the times.

Some of her readers apparently thought that Mrs. White meant to lower the standards in the sciences and to downplay the whole area of learning generally. Such extremist views stimulated her to clarify her position one month later in two important essays entitled "The Essential Education" (ibid., pp. 368-372) and "Diligent and Thorough Education" (ibid., pp. 373-380). In the two articles she noted that she had not implied a superficial education and that she certainly did not want the standards lowered in the education given at Battle Creek. What she was seeking was the uplifting of the spiritual and the uniting of the "natural and the spiritual" in the various studies. She stressed the point that the Bible should receive its proper role in education and that we should see every other subject within the context of the Biblical worldview. In effect, she was stating that Adventist education needed to be brought into line with both its foundation and its goals if it was to be meaningful.

In the battle that took place between Adventist education as it existed in the nineteenth century and true Christian education as it should be, Mrs. White never denigrated education itself. She never downplayed sanctified learning, but she did indicate that students might be getting too much schooling—especially when it was divorced from practical Christian living and when it became an end in itself.

We now come to the issue of how much education a Christian should have if he is to operate effectively in the social order. The answer is that it all depends on the educational level and the needs of the larger culture that forms the milieu of the church. In the late nineteenth century when the average person was doing well to have an eighth-grade education, Ellen White did not see much need for programs that spent up to seven years studying the pagan classics in the original languages. This, in part, was the essence of her thrust in "Speedy Preparation." That she would not put the same stress on "speedy" today we find indicated by her 1891 statement that "in the future there will be more pressing need of men and women of literary qualifications than there has been in the past."—*Ibid.*, p. 192.

That future has arrived. The church now exists in a world where the "average" education of people in industrialized nations is on the college level. In the United States roughly 50 percent of the upcoming generation will attend college, and the amount of preparation for the labor market is continuing to increase. The Adventist Church in such a context cannot afford to develop an ignorant constituency if it is serious about its gospel imperative. On the other hand, neither can it afford to repeat the mistakes of Battle Creek College by separating the spiritual and the scriptural from the literary and scientific. The church's educational institutions should rather help young people view the totality of curricular offerings from the perspective of Christian meaning. It is this task, along with the mandate to develop the "Christian mind," that Christian educational institutions must accomplish if they are to justify their existence.

PART III

MYTHS ABOUT CURRICULUM AND METHODS

10 The Myth of the Sacred and the Secular

Dichotomy and Beyond

*C*hristian discussion is riddled with expressions that point to a rift in reality. For example, we often talk of the here as opposed to the hereafter, natural in contrast to supernatural, reason as against revelation, science as divorced from religion, law as opposed to grace, body as separate from soul, and secular as distinct from sacred. A. Victor Murray highlighted such common usage when he wrote that "the phrase 'religious education' is almost self-contradictory, for it seems to join together two opposites which all experience has put asunder. It is held that education proceeds by enquiry, criticism and experiment; religion is a matter of faith, obedience and tradition. Education concerns the intellect; the root of religion is feeling. Education has to do with the world here and now; religion has its vital interest in the unseen world of spirit. Education requires teaching; religion is 'caught, not taught.' " [1]

From the Biblical perspective such dichotomous expressions are the language of a pervasive myth that has eaten the heart out of daily Christian living by providing a rationale for people to separate their "in church" attitudes and demeanor from the way they think and act the rest of the week in the "real" world. Such dichotomies have also, in many ways, destroyed the vitality of Christian education by segregating the "religious" elements from the "important" things one needs to know to make it in life and by designating certain people (Bible teachers and principals) as spiritual leaders as opposed to those other teachers who have "less weighty" responsibilities in the realm of the mundane. The myth of the sacred and the secular (along with the other false dichotomies) is one of the most destructive misconceptions facing Christianity and Christian education today.

All of these dichotomies are false from the Christian point of view. *Here* and *hereafter*, for example, are two words describing one progressive existence rather than two separate existences. Jesus made this explicit when He said that he who believes has already entered eternal life (John 6:47). Death for Him was merely a temporary interruption in one continuous life (verses 39, 40). Ellen White stated it beautifully when she wrote that "the life on earth is the beginning of the life in heaven."—Ed, p. 307.

The idea of the "natural" being distinct from the "supernatural" is also misleading. We most often use the term *natural* to discuss those aspects of the universe that we can explain in terms of physical and chemical laws, while *supernatural* we generally employ to refer to the realm existing above and beyond the realm of sense experience—"the belief that behind the world of ordinary, everyday experience is the world of the spiritual or divine." [2] Once again, such a dichotomy is a product of man—particularly modern man, who has categorically chosen to disbelieve anything beyond the reach of his senses and the scientific instruments he has developed to extend them.

The Bible, contrary to the myth, shows a continuity between the "supernatural" and our everyday world. It demonstrates that God is at work both in the realm of human understanding and also beyond the limited human sphere. Ellen White, in debunking the myth of the radical distinction between the natural and the supernatural, noted that natural law is under the "continual and direct agency of God" (8T, p. 259) and that the daily production of food through the laws of growth is just as miraculous (supernatural) as was the feeding of the five thousand by Jesus (Ed, pp. 107, 108). In the same vein, Jack Provonsha, of Loma Linda University, has written that "there is a sense in which everything is supernatural. . . . But there is also a sense in which everything is natural—natural, that is, to God." Provonsha also made the provocative suggestion that we might dispense with such words as *supernatural* and think in terms of God's acts as being "usual and unusual—the one the mark of His dependability" as He upholds the operation of natural law and the other signifying the miraculous. [3]

As popularly defined, *secular* implies those things that relate to this world as opposed to the church and religious affairs. *Sacred*, on the other hand, is that which is religious or that which belongs to a god or a deity. The dichotomy of the sacred and the secular disintegrates, however, when we realize that "the earth is the Lord's and the fulness thereof, the world and those who dwell therein" (Ps. 24:1). Everything has an ultimate relationship to God because He is both Creator and Sustainer. In one sense, every shrub is a burning bush, and all ground is holy. As Elton Trueblood has noted, God is the God of both the altar and the laboratory. If He is

God only of the altar as opposed to the laboratory or factory, "He is not worthy of our worship, and prayer is idle." [4] The fact is, however, that God is " 'Lord of heaven and earth' " (Matt. 11:25). He is Lord of both factory and church. Christianity is not a compartmentalized faith. The way a Christian does his work, therefore, is just as important to God as the way he worships.

These three illustrations should be sufficient to indicate the shallowness of the popular dichotomies. Other of the dichotomies I listed above we will highlight in subsequent chapters, but my point should be sufficiently clear: Nothing on earth or in the universe is separate from God. Everything is religious in the broad sense of the term. Perhaps we might best think of the above-listed pairs of words as extreme points on a continuous scale, while others we might view in terms of complementary relationships. The words themselves may be useful and should not be discarded. My point is that we must begin to use them with more Christian understanding and with the knowledge that they are never separate from their counterparts. I might, for example, still choose to use the word secular to express a worldview that leaves God out of its reckoning, but from the Christian perspective it is clear that secularism is still a religious choice. It is a religious decision against God rather than one that has nothing to do with Him. Carl Henry caught this meaning when he noted that secularism is evident when a society "acts as if there were no God." [5] Decisions either for or against God are both religious in nature. Individuals can never escape the Creator and Sustainer, even though they may pretend to live in a world without God. Christians may still choose to use the word secular because of the necessities of human communication, but they understand that nothing is secular in the sense that it is outside of religion. Everything has religious implications because everything is related to God's creative and sustaining activities.

Christians, likewise, might choose to employ the term supernatural to represent that which is beyond the realm of human understanding. But at the same time they must remember that no essential distinction exists between the supernatural and the natural. It is a well-known fact that as human knowledge of the natural world increases, man's concept of the sphere of the supernatural decreases in size,[6] a process that apparently will continue throughout eternity (Ed, pp. 301-309). Again, I find some usefulness in the terms here and hereafter even though I know they express a continous rather than a dichotomous experience. As human beings, it is essential for us to categorize and classify things by descriptive terms. Beyond our outward use of words, however, lies the deeper Christian understanding of some fundamental unities on the conceptual level.

All Men Live by Faith

We have noted that all of life has religious implications. Closely related is the point that all men are essentially religious in the sense that they live by faith, even though they may disclaim that fact with the greatest zeal and sincerity. In *Issues and Alternatives in Educational Philosophy* I pointed out that the helplessness of the human race is indicated by the fact that "it is not possible to make statements about reality without first having a theory for arriving at truth and, on the other hand, a theory of truth cannot be developed without first having a concept of reality." Human beings find themselves caught in the "web of circularity. . . . Nothing can be known for certain in the sense of final and ultimate proof that is open and acceptable to all men. Every person—the skeptic and the agnostic, the scientist and the businessman, the Hindu and the Christian—lives by a faith." Each of us must individually make a "faith-choice" and a commitment to a way of life. All men live by faith in the basic beliefs they have chosen.[7]

This fact does not come as much of a shock to the Christian, but it disturbs the average "secular" individual who has scientific "proof" for his beliefs. What such a person fails to realize is that science rests upon a set of unprovable assumptions that humanity must accept by faith. Thus, "naturalistic" science, when isolated, is in effect a religious alternative to Christianity. As such, it has its own beliefs concerning origins, human and universal significance, and human destiny and salvation (often salvation through progress). What many people do not recognize is that modern science, as we know it, consists of three parts: (1) a method for discovering facts about a segment of reality, (2) the facts discovered, and (3) a view of ultimate reality that gives meaning to those facts. Science as method is valid in the sense that it can discover regularities in the physical world. But when science becomes a view of reality it has exited the realm of proven facts and entered the realm of metaphysics and religion and stands on the same faith basis as any other system of belief. Harvard's George Buttrick touched upon this fact when he wrote that "secularism is not objectivity, but a faith after its own kind." [8]

People cannot escape religious choice. A choice against God is still a religious decision. One cannot avoid individual responsibility to relate to Christ by pretending that He doesn't exist, any more than he can evade the effects of a bullet by the same thought process. Religious reality encompasses all aspects of our lives. Neither can a person escape placing faith in something, since life becomes meaningless without an aim larger than our individual selves. J. E. Barnhart hit the nail on the head when he wrote that "the unbeliever is also a believer." [9] Marxism, for example, despite its antireligious attitude, has all the attributes of a formal religion, with its sacred writings, prophets, and holy places. We might say the same about "civil religion" in the United States, which sets forth the Constitution and the Declaration of Independence as its basic documents, has rituals surrounding such "holi-days" as Thanksgiving and Independence Day, and has shrines such as the Lincoln Memorial, which "is visited by Americans in a spirit similar to that which animates the Jew who stands before the Western Wall" and has a religious experience. [10] Even much modern art, in essence, is making a statement about the meaning of life in a meaningless world. Belief in meaninglessness thus becomes a faith that meaninglessness is at the base of human existence. Meaninglessness, therefore, becomes a criterion for ordering life's priorities and activities. In short, all men have chosen to believe in something, and their faith-choice entails a religious commitment that colors their actions and provides a framework for their thoughts. Man cannot evade the religious aspect of his nature, because God created him in His image.

What we have said of life in general can also apply to education. Ellen White has written that "by some, education is placed next to religion, but true education is religion."—CT, p. 108. It does no injustice to the facts to expand upon this quotation and say that all education is religion. The difference is that true education is true religion, while false education is false religion. We cannot escape the religious aspects of education. Just because a school system does not actively teach the centrality of the Creator-God does not mean that it is making a nonreligious statement. On the contrary, the neglect of God in the curriculum is a definite religious statement that either He does not exist or that He is not important, since His realm is in the church rather than in the world of daily life. *All education is therefore religious by its very nature.* Education cannot buy the myth of the sacred and the secular just because it chooses to do so. John Henry Newman perceived this point when he stated that "it is easy enough to divide knowledge into human and divine, secular and religious, and to lay down that we will address ourselves to the one without interfering with the other; but it is impossible in fact." [11] The myth of the sacred and the secular is false in terms of both entire educational systems and of the various subject matters within each system. From God's perspective there are no secular schools or secular topics, because all truth is God's truth.

All Truth Is God's Truth

"The basic Biblical distinction," penned Arthur Holmes, "is not between sacred and secular but between God and his creation."[12] On the one side stands God as the source of all that is, while on the other stands the result of His work. Christian education has its foundation on the overwhelming preeminent facts that God exists and that He has revealed Himself to finite man on a level that human beings can comprehend. It is the oneness of God (Deut. 6:4; Eph. 4:4-6) that undergirds Christian concepts of reality and truth. God does not contradict Himself, and He has not created a disjointed, schizophrenic world that contains several sets of conflicting truths.

Frank E. Gaebelein has suggested that the basic postulate underlying the Christian view of truth is that *"all truth is God's truth."* [13] A failure to comprehend this point has led many to develop the false dichotomy between the secular and the religious that implies that the religious has to do with God while the secular is divorced from Him. Such a faulty perspective regards the study of science, history, and mathematics as basically secular, while that of the Bible, church history, and ethics as religious. But that is not the Biblical point of view. The Bible portrays God as the creator of the objects of science and math as well as the director of historical events. In essence there are no such things as "secular" aspects of the curriculum. All truth in the Christian curriculum, whether it deals with nature, man, society, or the arts, must be seen in proper relation to Jesus Christ as Creator and Redeemer. Christ was the Creator of all things—not just those that people have chosen to call religious (John 1:1-3; Col. 1:16). As a result, all truth, if it is indeed truth, is God's, no matter where we find it.

That fact does not imply that the Bible discusses all truth. Scripture does not explain nuclear physics, for example. This does not mean that nuclear physics has no connection with natural laws or has no moral and ethical implications as its applications affect the lives of mankind. On the contrary, noted Ellen White, "the laws of nature are the laws of God—as truly divine as are the precepts of the Decalogue."—Ed, p. 196. It is the "pretended friends of education" who seek "to divorce religion from the sciences" in our schools (FE, pp. 135, 136).

Mrs. White was quite clear on the fact that all truth has its source in God. "The world has had its great teachers, men of giant intellect and extensive research. . . . We can trace the line of the world's teachers as far back as human records extend; but the Light was before them. . . . The world's great thinkers reflect the rays of the Sun of Righteousness. Every gleam of thought, every flash of the intellect, is from the Light of the world."—Ed, pp. 13, 14. Even authors who deny Christ have received, indirectly, great truth from God, who is " the Source of *all* light" (CT, p. 378; italics supplied). We must never forget that even Satan had his education in heaven, and that it is his studied practice to mix God's truth with his own error so as to confuse and deceive (ibid.).

The Bible contains the clearest and most comprehensive revelation of truth that man has. Scripture draws aside the curtain between our daily world and that beyond our senses, enabling us to see the true significance of individual lives, historic events, and the dynamics of God's activity in an otherwise inexplicable and contradictory world. God's Word helps people understand the problem of evil, deterioration, and pain in a world that gives evidence of being created for higher purposes. In short, it is in the Bible that people find the pattern of God's truth that helps them fit together the bits and pieces of their daily knowledge into a meaningful whole. The Scriptures present a total worldview that provides the context for all that we know and all that happens to us. Richard H. Bube, Stanford professor of materials science, remarked that "no interpretation of ultimate significance can be made without the Biblical revelation. Lacking the perspective it gives us, the things of the world are disconnected objects only, the events of the world are mere unrelated coincidences, and life is only a frustrating attempt to derive ultimate significance from insignificant trivialities." [14]

Biblical revelation holds the strategic position in human knowledge systems. Man's nonrealization and/or rejection of this fact is a major source of his continuing lostness. Having thrown away the pattern of truth, he cannot make sense out of his world. He has spurned the divine insight that would enable him to understand an apparently senseless existence. The modern world faces a paradox. On the one hand are those who proclaim that life is meaningless. They reflect their frustration in existentialism, certain modern art forms, and hedonistic lifestyles. On the other hand, large segments of the intellectual community cling to meaningfulness as found in nature. This is the basis of modern science, which, by and large, having discarded the pattern of God's truth, now struggles with the impossible task of trying to fit known facts into the false pattern of evolutionary materialism. It is one of the contradictions of our knowledge-rich age that modern man finds himself hopelessly divided on whether reality is meaningful or meaningless, with the arts largely heading in one direction and the sciences in another. Both groups have captured certain aspects of truth, but both have failed to realize its full significance because they have thrown out and/or mythologized the Bible as God's authoritative revelation.

Because of its "revealing" contents about the shape of ultimate reality, the Bible becomes, for the Christian, the contextual framework and the yardstick by which he evaluates all other sources of knowledge. This is in direct opposition to modern Western mentality, which measures all knowledge by its correspondence with the findings and theories of science. The Christian is therefore an epistemological radical because of his faith in a transcendent revelation from an omniscient Being.

The world of nature also displays valid knowledge (Ps. 19:1-4; Rom. 1:20). Theologians have defined knowledge derived from the world of nature and human experience as a general revelation of God's truth as opposed to the special revelation found in the Scriptures. Rightly understood, both special and general revelation give the same message because they have the same author. "The book of nature and the written word," noted Ellen White, "shed light upon each other."—Ed, p. 128. But people soon find that nature gives a confusing picture. It demonstrates not only love and life but also hate and death. The natural world, as seen by fallible humans, presents a garbled and seemingly contradictory portrayal of ultimate reality because the Fall has affected the whole of creation (Rom. 8:22). "To man's unaided reason," Mrs. White reminded us, "nature's teaching cannot but be contradictory and disappointing. Only in the light of revelation can it be read aright."—*Ibid.*, p. 134.

In other words, we can understand nature, daily experience, and the findings of science fully only within the all-important context of the pattern of God's truth. The same holds true for knowledge claiming to be from intuition or authorities in a given field. Outright rejection is not the Biblical answer. The Christian, on the contrary, has the responsibility to "test" purported knowledge from all sources by the standard of the Biblical view of reality[15] and to "hold fast what is good" (1 Thess. 5:21; Isa. 8:20).

We might make similar remarks about man's rationality. Human rationality has its roots in the fact that man was created in the image of a rational God. But man's rationality is not a source of truth as much as it is a mode of apprehending and evaluating it. Bernard Ramm has correctly remarked that "it is the truth apprehended which is authoritative, not reason." [16] The rational aspect of Christian knowing is an essential element in the acquisition of truth because it helps us understand the disclosures of special and general revelation, and it enables us to extend that knowledge into the unknown. Human reasoning, however, can be deceitful, and it may lead away from truth. Therefore, we must check its findings against the revealed pattern of God's Word.

All truth, we have noted, is God's, whether we discover it through scientific experiment, daily experience, correct reasoning, an intuitive hunch, or studying the Bible. We might view the total body of man's knowledge as a dynamic and interlocking mosaic in which each knowledge source helps clarify the others and in which all knowledge is seen within the broad outlines of the Biblical worldview. Gaebelein has pointed out that "nothing true is outside the scope of Christianity." [17] Everything that exists finds its roots in the Godhead.

If God is the fountain of truth, we might ask, why is human knowledge so limited and faulty? Michael Christensen indicated the reason when he wrote that "the divine light is obscured by the medium through which it shines." [18] Man is unable to escape from his finite limitations. Now "we see through a glass, darkly" and "know in part" (1 Cor. 13:12, K.J.V.). The divine imperative is not, however, for people to remain in a static state of ignorance, but for them to continue to grow in knowledge. An essential aspect of such growth is the development of the Christian mind.

The Christian Mind

Harry Blamires, in his insightful book *The Christian Mind*, has highlighted the fact that modern Christians have retained "a Christian ethic, a Christian practice, and a Christian spirituality," but they no longer possess a Christian mind. In other words, most modern Christians see religion in its moral, worship, and spiritual aspects, while having succumbed to secularism as thinking beings. They have rejected the Christian worldview—"the view which sets all earthly issues within the context of the eternal, the view which relates all human problems—social, political, cultural—to the doctrinal foundations of the Christian faith, the view which sees all things here below in terms of God's supremacy and earth's transitoriness, in terms of heaven and hell." Blamires pointed out that except for a very narrow field mainly concerned with personal conduct, most Christians think within a frame of reference constructed by the non-Christian mind. In addition, they utilize a set of intellectual criteria that reflect non-Christian evaluations.[19]

A related problem, noted Blamires, is that people often fail to make the distinction between thinking Christianly and thinking about Christian matters. "To think secularly is to think within a frame of reference bounded by the limits of our life on earth. . . . You can think Christianly or you can think secularly about the most sacred things. . . . Likewise you can think Christianly about the most mundane things." [20] It should be obvious that both of the issues raised by Blamires stem from the myth of a division between the sacred and secular.

The challenge confronting the Christian church and its educational system is to develop the Christian mind so that Christians will think Christianly about everything in their lives and every aspect of their existence. The Christian mind is rooted in the eternal perspective, and, therefore, it has a totally different frame of reference than the non-Christian mind. Christianity and the non-Christian world have different philosophic views about the nature of truth, ultimate reality, the destiny of man, and what is good, beautiful, and valuable. The Sermon on the Mount is one of the world's most revolutionary documents because a worldview that is Christian in the fullest sense of the word supports it. "To think 'Christianly,' " claimed Holmes, "is to think 'world-viewishly.' This means we locate each field of inquiry within a Christian understanding of life as a whole, and that we interpret what we know in that larger context." [21]

The basic framework of beliefs about reality that provides the context for thinking Christianly consists of the following elements: (1) the existence of the living God, the Creator-God; (2) the creation by God of a perfect world and universe; (3) man's creation in the image of God; (4) the "invention" of sin by Lucifer, who forgot his own creatureliness and sought to put himself in the place of God; (5) the spread of sin to the earth by Lucifer, and the Fall of man, which resulted in his loss of God's image; (6) the inability of man, without divine aid, to change his own nature, overcome his inherent sinfulness, or restore the lost image of God; (7) the initiative of God for man's salvation and his restoration to his original state through the incarnation, life, death, and resurrection of Jesus Christ; (8) the activity of the Holy Spirit in the plan of restoring God's image in fallen man and His work in the calling out of the community of believers, the church; (9) the return of Christ at the end of earthly history; and (10) the eventual restoration of our world and its faithful inhabitants to its Edenic condition. Even a cursory glance at this list indicates the radicalness of the Christian worldview compared to that of the larger culture.

One of the frightening things about Christianity for many historic cultures, noted Richard Niebuhr, is that Christianity in its truest sense is all-pervasive. Christianity is not just an idea of God and a code of ethics. It reaches into all areas of life, from art to politics and business. As a result, it threatens non-Christian cultures. "A Christian," wrote Niebuhr, "is ordinarily defined as 'one who believes in Jesus Christ' or as 'a follower of Jesus Christ.' He might more adequately be described as one who counts himself as belonging to that community of men for whom Jesus Christ—his life, words, deeds, and destiny—is of supreme importance as the key to the understanding of themselves and their world, the main source of the knowledge of God and man, good and evil, the constant companion of the conscience, and the expected deliverer from evil." [22]

The Christian faith is all-pervasive in both the Christian life and in Christian education. Its uniqueness is that it supplies a different interpretation because of its unique worldview. Ellen White spoke to the point when she noted that "every topic has a new significance" when we view it in the light of the Biblical worldview (Ed, p. 125).

Christian education must see beyond the atomism of the contemporary world, which is so intent on compartmentalizing knowledge and activity that it fails to see the larger whole. Modern culture, along with modern education, is seemingly obsessed with ever-extending specialization. Specialization may be a worthy goal in many cases, but never when achieved at the expense of removing specialized functions and knowledge from their meaningful context. The role of Christian education is to develop Christian persons able to think Christianly about every topic in every social situation. Specialization may follow after this, but to develop specialists without developing Christians who think Christianly may mean that we are turning out mindless technicians—automatons who perform their function well but do not have a unified Christian view of reality as a base for action and decision-making. Certainly one of the major goals of Christian education would be fulfilled, wrote Holmes, if each of its graduates could claim: " 'I learned what it is to see and think and act like the human person God made me to be.' " [23] One of the natural outcomes of teaching people to think Christianly will be the shattering of the myth of the distinction between the sacred and the secular. Everything will be seen in its relation to God.

Developing the Christian mind and teaching individuals to think Christianly is obviously linked to the role of the Bible in education. We now turn to that topic.

11 The Myth of the Bible as Omniscient Textbook

*O*ne of the educational principles Ellen White most strongly urged was the primary position of the Bible in Christian schools. In 1888, for example, she wrote: "If used as a textbook in our schools, it [the Bible] will be found far more effective than any other book in the world, in guiding wisely in the affairs of this life, as well as in aiding the soul up the ladder of progress which reaches to heaven."—FE, p. 131. She also said that the students' attention "should be called, not to the assertions of men, but to the word of God. Above all other books, the word of God must be our study, the great textbook, the basis of all education."—6T, p. 131. Again, she stated that "the Bible should not be brought into our schools to be sandwiched in between infidelity. The Bible must be made the groundwork and subject matter of education. . . . It should be used as the word of the living God, and esteemed as first, and last, and best in everything."—FE, p. 474. Such statements form the basis for one of the more persistent myths in certain Adventist educational circles—that the Bible should be the textbook in every subject.

Adventist History and the Bible as the Only Textbook

Up through the mid 1890s neither the Bible nor the Biblical worldview had found a central role in Adventist education. Adventist educators largely organized their curriculum from the standpoint of the Greek and Latin classics, but Ellen White, W. W. Prescott (educational secretary of the General Conference and president of Battle Creek College), and others pushed hard to correct the problem. In Mrs. White's writing on the topic of the role of the Bible in education we observe an ever-ascending crescendo from 1872 up through the late 1890s.

In the spring of 1897 the reform element, led by Edward A. Sutherland, Percy T. Magan, A. T. Jones, and John Harvey Kellogg, gained control of Battle Creek College. The group's goal was to transform the college. One prong of their attack consisted of placing the Bible at the center of instruction. Jones and Sutherland, in fact, both taught that the Bible should be the "textbook in every line of study." [1] They apparently believed that they were following Mrs. White in this matter. The controversy stimulated on the topic was hot and heavy in Adventist circles, even forming a subject for floor discussion at the General Conference session of 1899. Meanwhile, a myth had been born that is still alive among some Adventist educational reformers. [2]

Between 1897 and 1900 the church experienced a great deal of confusion over what the claim that the Bible should be the textbook in every line of study actually meant. Early on, Sutherland apparently believed that the ideal would be to use the Bible as the only book. One of his more promising graduates, a Miss Ellis, took the idea to Australia in 1898, where she sought to practice it. According to Ellen White, Miss Ellis made a mess out of things. Furthermore, she noted, Sutherland had a tendency to go to extremes, was making a mistake, and needed "to put on the brake." "In the church schools to be established," she wrote, "I cannot recommend no textbooks whatever." Instead, she advocated that "books should be prepared as soon as possible to lead minds to a study of the Bible." [3]

Once taken, however, extreme positions do not die easily. The issue of what it meant to make the Bible "the foundation of our educational work" continued to agitate Adventist leaders. At the 1899 General Conference session, for example, C. C. Lewis pressed the reformers on what they had in mind. He wanted to know if they meant that teachers should use no other books. Prescott rose and stated that he would explain how to teach physical geography from the Bible. Lewis interrupted: "Take the multiplication table." Prescott declined. In the end, Prescott admitted that "if, as I went on with the Bible, I found the need of any other book, I would use it. But I would not use it until I found the need of it." J. H. Haughey immediately spoke up: "You would find the need." Prescott confessed: "I think so." [4]

By October, 1899, Jones had arrived at an interesting distinction between the "textbook" (the Bible) from which the teacher takes the "text" for the study of the topic at hand, and the "studybook," which sheds light on the meaning of the Biblical texts that form the foundation for every line of study. With such a distinction he could continue to maintain that the Bible should be the only textbook. [5] Sutherland, on the other hand, was not quite so adamant in his stand or as consistent in his use of the word textbook. By April, 1899, he had come to grips with the recommendations of Ellen

White concerning his extremism on the matter and openly advocated the preparation of Biblically oriented denominational "text-books." [6]

The issue of the place of the Bible in education perplexed the reformers. By the turn of the century, however, many of them were beginning to gain significant insights as to how to make the Bible "the foundation of our educational work." Both Jones and Sutherland, for example, had begun to realize that it was the theoretical framework of educational systems that provided the key, rather than the use of the Bible as the only book. Both recognized that facts and items of knowledge were interpreted within a conceptual context. What they now sought to do was to use the Bible to provide a Christian context for education rather than rely on a context based upon the pagan classics or evolutionary materialism.[7] Sutherland acknowledged that this implied a restructuring of the curriculum so that the Bible became an integral part of the entire curriculum rather than just an addition to a course of study or a substitution for the classics. He wrote: "This does not mean the substitution of a class in Bible or sacred history for the former classics. As the classic literature has been the basis of all instruction in our schools since the Middle Ages, a reformation necessitates a decided breaking down of the old system, and the adoption of a new system built upon an entirely different foundation—a system in which the Word of God shall be the basis of all education." [8]

By the turn of the century Sutherland, Marion E. Cady, and others were busy creating Christian "textbooks" to supplement Bible study and aid in viewing other school subjects from the Biblical perspective. But the myth was not dead. In June, 1902, E. J. Waggoner, of 1888 fame, set out to reform the reformers, Sutherland and Magan, with his "new order." According to Waggoner, who wanted a controlling hand at Emmanuel Missionary College, "there had never yet been such a thing as a Bible school" among Adventists. His idea was that "there must be no other book than the Bible" employed in such a school, and that if his program was implemented, "every branch of learning would be carried as far as any teacher would be able to carry it" through the use of the Bible as the only book.[9]

Waggoner never got the chance to put his "new order" into practice. Fanaticism on the topic was dead, even though the myth has lived on. The real challenge to Adventists by the turn of the century was to create a program in which the Bible could "be made the groundwork and subject matter of education" (FE, p. 474).

The Role of the Bible in Education

The Problem: Discovering the Pattern of Curricular Unity

Adventists were not the only ones in educational turmoil at the turn of the century. The classics were on their deathbed in both public and private education, while the Christian worldview that had given some meaning to the course of study in American education was losing its hold nearly everywhere in American schooling. Frederick Rudolph, a prominent historian of American higher education, has characterized the period from 1875 to 1914 as one of "curricular disarray." [10]

A major challenge for education of all stripes in the twentieth century has been to find the pattern that holds the curriculum together and gives it unity and meaningfulness. Alfred North Whitehead has claimed that curricula generally suffer from the lack of an integrating principle. Instead of a single unity, "we offer children—algebra, from which nothing follows; geometry, from which nothing follows; science, from which nothing follows; history, from which nothing follows; a couple of languages, never mastered; and lastly, most dreary of all, literature, represented by plays of Shakespeare, with philological notes and short analyses of plot and character to be in substance committed to memory. Can such a list be said to represent life, as it is known in the midst of living it? The best that can be said of it is that it is a rapid table of contents which a deity might run over in his mind while he was thinking of creating a world, and has not yet determined how to put it together." [11] In a similar vein, Columbia University's Philip Phenix has noted that "it is not easy to sustain a sense of the whole. ... Students and teachers alike are prone to take the curriculum as they find it, as a traditional sequence of separate elements, without ever inquiring into the *comprehensive pattern* within which the constituent parts are located." [12]

The crux of the problem, however, has not been to recognize the need for some overall pattern in which to fit the various subjects of the curriculum together in such a way that they make sense, but to discover that pattern. The authors of Harvard's influential report on general education remarked in 1945 that "the search continues and must continue for some overall logic, some strong, not easily broken frame within which both college and school may fulfill their at once diversifying and uniting tasks." [13] We live in a world that has fragmented knowledge to the place where it is extremely difficult to see how individual realms of expertise relate to the whole of either a particular subject or of life.

During the past century many have attempted to discover the framework that gives meaning to individual subjects in the course of study. Herbert Spencer's probing question "What Knowledge is of Most Worth?" received wide attention in the late nineteenth century. His widely accepted answer was "Science" in every area of human endeavor.[14] Other educators answered that the knowledge of most worth was to be found in the needs of society or vocationalism. Such needs, they suggested, should form the organizing principle and the selection criteria for curriculum development. Ellen White repeatedly answered Spencer's question in her own writings. To her an understanding of the Bible was the essential study that was of "most worth" (e.g., CT, pp. 11-24, 427; FE, pp. 368-380).

Discovering the knowledge that is most essential, however, is a totally different problem from understanding how a course of study can be developed from that insight. All too often the thought has been to add Bible courses to the curriculum along with providing chapel services and missionary programs. As worthy as such additions are, they do not necessarily make a school Christian. Mrs. White, in commenting on Adventist schools in their attempt to insert Bible courses and Christian thoughts into the curriculum without reorienting the entire course of studies, complained that *"human productions have been used as most essential and the word of God has been studied simply to give flavor to other studies."*—FE, p. 395. (Italics supplied.) In a similar vein is her statement that "the Bible should not be brought into our schools to be sandwiched in between infidelity."—*Ibid.*, p. 474. Philosopher Gordon Clark referred to such innovations as "a pagan education with a chocolate coating of Christianity." [15] Such an approach is not of itself Christian.

The problem is not one of injecting Christian elements into an existing curriculum, but rather the Christianization of the entire school program. All too often the curriculum of the Christian school has been "a patchwork of naturalistic ideas mixed with Biblical truth." This has led, claimed Frank E. Gaebelein, to a form of "scholastic schizophrenia in which a highly orthodox theology coexists uneasily with a teaching of nonreligious subjects that differs little from that in secular institutions." [16] The challenge confronting the developer of the curriculum in a Christian school is to move beyond a view focused on the bits and pieces, and into a position that clearly and purposefully integrates the details of knowledge into the Biblical framework. Only this will make a truly Christian education.

The Solution: The Integration of All Knowledge

It should be obvious even to the casual reader that the Bible is not a source of information about everything. It deals mainly with the "big issues": the meaning of life and death, where the world came from and what its future will be, the origin of sin and God's plan for dealing with it, and the like. Scripture has as its purpose to make man "wise unto salvation through faith which is in Christ Jesus" and to provide doctrine, reproof, correction, and "instruction in righteousness: that the man of God may be perfect" (2 Tim. 3:15-17, K.J.V.). The Bible was never intended to be an exhaustive source of knowledge or a "divine encyclopedia." It leaves many questions unanswered. On the other hand, in speaking to the most basic questions of finite beings, it provides a perspective, worldview, and context in which to explore unanswered questions and to arrive at unified answers.

We could not possibly use the Bible as a textbook for every topic in the curriculum, since it doesn't even discuss many subjects. Scripture does not explain modern real estate contracts, for example, but the study and practice of real estate has an intimate connection with the Bible's ethical and moral principles. The important point is that no topic is outside the worldview of the Bible. "The teaching authority of Scripture," penned Arthur Holmes, "commits the believer at certain focal points and so provides an *interpretive framework,* an overall glimpse of how everything relates to God." [17]

The concept of an interpretive framework needs constant emphasis in Christian education. The Bible is not the whole of knowledge, but it does provide a frame of reference within which we may study and interpret all topics. Whether that framework is the view of evolutionary naturalism, the pagan classics, the Biblical worldview, or any other perspective makes a great deal of difference. A Christian school is Christian only when it teaches all subjects from the perspective of God's Word.

Elton Trueblood, in discussing the marks of a Christian college, noted that "the important question is not, Do you offer a course in religion? Such a course might be offered by any institution. The relevant question is, Does your religious profession make a difference? . . . A mere department of religion may be relatively insignificant. The teaching of the Bible is good, but it is only a beginning. What is far more important is the penetration of the central Christian convictions into the teaching of all subjects." [18]

Gaebelein was driving at the same point when he wrote that there exists "a vast difference between education in which devotional exercises and the study of Scripture have a place, and education in which the Christianity of the Bible is the matrix of the whole program or, to change the figure, the bed in which the river of teaching and learning flows." [19]

An educational system that maintains a split between the secular and the religious can justify adding on religious attributes to a basically secular curriculum. It may even go so far as to treat the Bible as the "first among equals" in terms of importance. But the school whose constituency and teachers hold that "all truth is God's truth" will find themselves bound by that very belief to develop a curricular model in which the Biblical worldview permeates every aspect of the curriculum.

It was this insight that Ellen White sought to implement in the 1890s. She advocated that Adventist schools remove the Greek and Roman classics from the center of the curriculum, since they did not "present the proper foundation for true education" (FE, p. 381). In their place she uplifted the Bible, which "is the foundation of all true knowledge" (ibid., p. 393). Part of the genius of Christ's teaching ministry was that He had "rescued truth from its obscurity, and set it in its proper framework" (CT, p. 29). Mrs. White, in her day, was attempting the same task. This was and is a primary concern for Adventist education in every generation, since Christian education cannot take place in the context of secular humanism or any other "ism." Christian education is Christian only when it sees all truth from a Christian perspective.

According to Mrs. White, "the science of redemption is the science of all sciences," and the Bible is "the Book of books."—Ed, p. 126; CT, p. 442. Only an understanding of this "science" and this "Book" makes everything else meaningful in the fullest sense. *Viewed in the light of "the grand central thought" of the Bible, "every topic has a new significance."*—Ed, p. 125. (Italics supplied.) Every student, noted Ellen White, should gain a knowledge of the Bible's "grand central theme, of God's original purpose for the world, of the rise of the great controversy, and of the work of redemption. He should understand the nature of the two principles that are contending for supremacy, and should learn to trace their working through the records of history and prophecy, to the great consummation. *He should see how this controversy enters into every phase of human experience;* how in every act of life he himself reveals the one or the other of the two antagonistic motives; and how, whether he will or not, he is even now deciding upon which side of the controversy he will be found."—Ibid., p. 190. (Italics supplied.)

The conflict between good and evil has left no area of existence untouched. On the negative side we see the controversy in the deterioration of the world of nature, in war and suffering in the realm of history and the social sciences, and in man's concern with his own lostness in the humanities. On the positive side we find evidence of it in the wonder of a natural order that seems to be purposefully organized, in man's ability to care for his fellows in social life, and in his deep visions and desires for wholeness and meaningfulness. "Why," every individual at last has to ask himself, "is there evil in a world that seems so good? Why is there death and sorrow in an existence that is so delicately engineered for life? How is it possible that mathematical orderliness is all-pervasive in the world of nature?"

The questions go on and on, but earthbound man is helpless as he seeks to discover the ultimate answers. It is true that he can discover bits and pieces of "truth" and build theories concerning their meaning, but only in God's cosmic breakthrough to man in his smallness and lostness is that ultimate meaning provided.

God's special revelation contains the answers to mankind's "big questions." It is this revelation, therefore, that must provide both the foundation and the context for every human study. Every topic within the curriculum, and even human life itself, takes on new meaning in the light of God's Word. It is imperative, therefore, that Christian schools teach every subject from the Biblical perspective.

Gaebelein, in his classic treatment of the issue, has suggested that what we need is the "integration" of every aspect of the school program with the Biblical worldview. Integration "means 'the bringing together of the parts into the whole.' " [20] The Bible, he suggests, provides the pattern within which every other aspect of both the formal course of studies and the informal curriculum find their meaning. Hastings Rashdall, in his monumental study of medieval universities, caught the same picture when he noted the centrality of religious study. Religious study was the "architectonic science whose office it was to receive the results of all other sciences and combine them into an organic whole." [21] That this is the rightful place of religion in education, claimed Henry P. Van Dusen in his Rockwell lectures, is not because the churches say so or because it is dictated by tradition, but *because of the nature of reality.*" [22] God is the being whose existence brings unity and meaning to the universe. Likewise, it is His revelation that provides unity and meaning to the curriculum.

In the most common curricular design, Bible or religion is just one topic among many, as illustrated by Figure 2. In this model every topic is studied according to its own logic, and each is regarded as being basically independent of the others. The history or literature teacher is not concerned with religion, and the religion teacher does not involve himself with history or literature since each is teaching in his specialty. Each subject has its own well-defined territory and "traditional" approach. This model is not generally concerned with the relationship between the fields of study, let alone their "ultimate meaning." In such a model, religion is one topic among many.

Religion	History	Mathematics	Literature	Science	Et Cetera

Figure 2. Curriculum Model: Self-contained Subject Matter Areas

Adventist reformers, in seeking to escape from the above model, early went to the extreme of making the Bible and religion into the whole curriculum, as illustrated by Figure 3. We have treated its shortcomings earlier in this chapter and need not discuss it further.

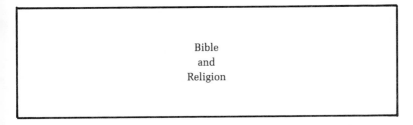

Bible
and
Religion

Figure 3. Curriculum Model: The Bible as the Whole

A third model we might define as the foundational and contextual model (see Figure 4, next page). It implies that the Bible and its worldview provide a foundation and a context for all human knowledge, and that its overall meaning enters into every area of the curriculum and adds significance to each topic. An integration model, it indicates that we must approach every subject in the light of the Biblical perspective if we are to understand it in its fullest meaning. The broken lines in Figure 4 signify that there are no hard and fast divisions between the various subjects, let alone a false dichotomy between the sacred and the secular. The two-headed arrows indicate not only the fact that the Bible helps us understand every topic in the curriculum but also that the study of history, science, and so on also sheds light on the meaning of Scripture. God has revealed Himself through the Bible in a special revelation and through the world of nature in a general revelation. We can grasp the significance of the latter only in the light of the former, but both shed light on each other, since all truth has its origin in God (Ed, p. 128). Every topic in the curriculum impacts upon every other, and all become the most meaningful when integrated within the Biblical context.

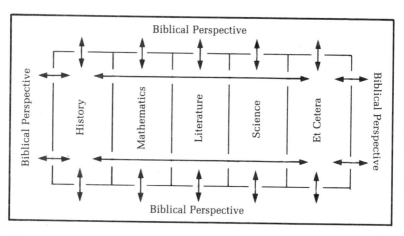

Figure 4. Curriculum Model: The Bible as Foundational and Contextual

The Radical Curriculum

The point that Christian educators must recognize is that *the teaching of any subject in a Christian school is not a modification of the approach used in non-Christian schools. It is rather a radical reorientation of that topic within the philosophic framework of Christianity.* For example, the Christian school views history in terms of the Biblical message of God seeking to work out His purpose in human affairs as events move toward their prophetic end. The Bible provides the interpretive framework for the events between the fall of man and the second coming of Jesus. The Christian teacher does not treat Scripture as a comprehensive history of the world, but recognizes it as an account that centers on the history of salvation. In addition, there are points of intersection between general history and the Bible in terms of prophecy and archeology. The Christian historian realizes, however, that the specific points are limited and that the major function of the Bible in history teaching is to provide a context for understanding.

We might say the same of the life, physical, and social sciences, or physical education or agriculture in the curriculum of a Christian school. The Bible provides the framework of a troubled world, while the academic disciplines bring forth the bits and pieces of knowledge. Scripture supplies the pattern that gives meaning to the otherwise meaningless details uncovered by the scholar. It is from this perspective that we can view the Bible as the focal point of integration for all of our knowledges. Chapters 12 and 13 will provide a more complete illustration of the principles of integration in the field of literary study.

In discussing the topic of developing correlations between Christian concepts and the subject matter of the various fields of study, Gaebelein pointed out some necessary cautions in curricular integration. A major pitfall, as he saw it, is the danger "of a false integration through forced correlations that are not truly indigenous to the subject in question. Such lugging in of stilted correlations, even though motivated by Christian zeal, is liable to do more harm than good through giving the impression that integration of specific subjects with God's truth is a put-up job.

"What may be needed is a more relaxed attack upon the problem and a clearer realization of the limits under which we are working. Here a suggestion of Emil Brunner is useful. Speaking of the distortion brought into our thinking through sin, he sees it at its greatest in such areas as theology, philosophy, and literature, because these are nearest man's relation to God and have thus been most radically altered through the Fall. They therefore stand most in need of correction, and in them correlation with Christianity is at its highest. But as we move from the humanities to the sciences and mathematics, the disturbance through sin diminishes almost to the vanishing point. Thus the Christian teacher of the more objective subjects, mathematics in particular, ought not to seek for the detailed and systematic correlations that his colleagues in psychology, literature, or history might validly make." [23]

Gaebelein does not mean that there are no points of contact between such a topic as mathematics and Christianity, but rather that they are fewer.[24] The Christian teacher will still utilize them, but he will not seek to force integration in an unnatural way.

From one point of view the integration of mathematics and the physical sciences with Christian belief is even more important than that of literature and the social sciences with Christianity. Because of their uncritical understanding, many students regard these fields as "objective," neutral, and functional, having no philosophical presuppositions, biases about reality, or cosmological implications. In reality, the study of mathematics and the "hard" sciences is totally embedded in bias and assumption. For example, mathematics, like Christianity, rests upon unprovable postulates. Beyond this, assumptions such as the orderliness of the universe and the validity of empirical observation are presuppositions that undergird science, but many modern people in both Western and Eastern cultures reject them. It is essential that we make students aware of such assumptions because they often take them as fact. The average student raised in an age that has placed its uncritical faith in science and mathematics rather than in the Creator of scientific and mathematical reality is not even aware of them.

Christian teachers in all subject matter areas should creatively utilize the natural points of integration between their topic and their religion. Mathematics, for example, certainly has contact points with the Christian faith when it deals with such areas as infinity and the existence of numerical regularity in other parts of daily life, from music to crystallography to astronomy. The world of mathematical precision is God's world, and mathematics is not outside the pattern of His truth.

In addition to the natural points of integration, teachers in every field have opportunity to integrate their faith with their academic specialty on the personality level as they relate, in the spirit of Jesus, to their students and answer their questions in regard to the subject matter at hand, religious meaning, and personal difficulties.

Some Concluding Remarks

In conclusion, we should consider three points. First, if we want to grasp integration's positive implications better, we should note what it is not. Gene Garrick has written that "it is vital to realize that integration does not mean point-by-point reconciliation of each discipline with Bible statements or doctrines, nor merely bringing in verses which relate to the unit being studied, . . .

nor moralizing or exhorting in the course of the study. All of those have their place in Christian teaching. But integration means the uniting of parts into a whole. Therefore, integrating life and studies with the Bible means discovering their foundational relationship of unity as God's truth given for the purpose of revealing God and enabling man to do His will and glorify Him. This requires much study of both the subject and the Bible and careful thought about how to impart the truth or lead students to this discovery." [25]

Second, Holmes has remarked that "integration is concerned not so much with attack and defense as with the positive contributions of human learning to an understanding of the faith and to the development of a Christian worldview, and with the positive contribution of the Christian faith to all the arts and sciences." He also observed that we should not see integration as an achievement "but as an intellectual activity that goes on as long as we keep learning anything at all." [26] As we teach our students how to integrate within the Christian perspective, we will be contributing to one of the goals of Christian education—the development of the Christian mind.

Last, it is of the utmost importance that Christian educators and their constituencies realize that the Christian worldview must dominate the Christian curriculum if Christian schools are to be Christian in actuality rather than merely in name. This is especially crucial today, since Christian education is becoming increasingly expensive. The Christian educator must ask himself this probing question: If I, as a Christian teacher, am teaching the same material in the same way that it is presented in a public institution, then what right do I have to take the hard-earned money of my constituents? The answer is both obvious and frightening. Christian education that does not provide a Christian understanding of the arts, sciences, humanities, and the world of work is not Christian. One major aim of Christian education must be to help students think Christianly.

The call is not for Christian educators to discard all teaching materials except the Bible, but for Christian teachers to help students see and think about the meaning of every topic from the Biblical perspective. Chapters 12 and 13, after examining some popular myths, will attempt to illustrate how we might do so in the area of literary study.

12 Literary Myths

*T*he Adventist subculture has an abundance of literary myths. The next two chapters will examine four of the most important ones: (1) the myth of the true and the false, (2) the myth of the good and the evil, (3) the myth that Ellen White had a clearly framed and explicitly stated philosophy on literature, and (4) the myth that literary study is not important for Christians. In discussing them, I intend to move beyond the negative to a positive position on the role of literary study in Seventh-day Adventist schools.

The Myth of the True and the False

Many Adventists define the central literary issue as the question of fiction. Thus, the line that separates proper from improper reading material divides that which has actually happened from that which human minds have made up in story form. A superficial reading of Ellen White provides what seems, at first glance, to be excellent support for such a position. For example, one of her strongest statements on fiction appears in *The Ministry of Healing*. "Even fiction," she penned, "which contains no suggestion of impurity, and which may be intended to teach excellent principles, is harmful. It encourages the habit of hasty and superficial reading merely for the story. Thus it tends to destroy the power of connected and vigorous thought; it unfits the soul to contemplate the great problems of duty and destiny. . . . It is often urged that in order to win the youth from sensational or worthless literature, we should supply them with a better class of fiction. . . . The only safety for the inebriate, and the only safeguard for the temperate man, is total abstinence. For the lover of fiction the same holds true. Total abstinence is his only safety."—MH, pp. 445, 446. The quotation does not leave much doubt. Reading "fiction" is wrong for Christians.

The issue becomes somewhat complicated, however, when we begin to inquire into the question of what Ellen White meant by fiction. Dictionaries consistently define it as imaginative happenings that have never taken place in space-time history. Therefore, we may contrast fiction with factual events that have occurred in history.

The topic's complexity surfaces when we discover that Ellen White used and recommended what we call fiction. For example, she spoke of her regard for John Bunyan's *Pilgrim's Progress* (GC, p. 252), and she even included some "nonfactual" (fictional) pieces in her four-volume compilation of *Sabbath Readings for the Home Circle*.[1] Beyond this, she read the Bible, which contains fiction by twentieth-century definitions. The parable of the rich man and Lazarus (Luke 16:19-31) and the story of the trees who "went forth to anoint a king over them" (Judges 9:8-15) are samples of Biblical fiction. A parable is fiction, since it is an imaginative story. If we should read no "fiction" or not have it on the shelves of our school libraries, then we should throw out our Bibles, since they contain "fiction."

On the other hand, Mrs. White also condemned the reading of historical works that uplift "enormities," "cruelties," and "licentious practices" (7T, p. 165), despite the fact that such works do report events that actually occurred. Certainly this type of reading includes much of the "true news" that comes to us in the daily paper and certain popularized books on historical topics. Whether the events an author relates in his work actually happened does not seem to be Ellen White's criterion for determining the suitability of a piece of literature for Christians.

At this point we should note that the whole topic is a dangerous one. By even examining the issue, we may easily be misunderstood. Some people's first reaction might be that we are seeking to explain away the truth or to provide a rationalization for doing that which we have been warned against. A more healthy reaction would be to ascertain if the previously cited information is factual. If so, then we must face it responsibly and honestly rather than ignore it. Christians have nothing to fear from the truth—after all, it is the truth, rather than tradition and honest misunderstandings, that makes us free (John 8:32).

It seems quite clear that Mrs. White did not use the word *fiction* with the same meaning that most of her readers give to it today. Either one must admit this point or take the alternative position that she blatantly contradicted herself. If she did use a different definition, then we must discover what it is by searching her writings to see how she employed the word. In 1971 the General Conference Department of Education hosted a meeting to accomplish, in part, this task. The thirty-four-member committee included editors, general conference officers, educators from all levels, and members of the White Estate. "From an intensive examination of her references to fiction," they concluded, "it appears that Ellen G. White used the term *fiction* to apply to works with the following characteristics: (1) It is addictive. (2) It may be sentimental, or sensational, erotic, profane, or trashy. (3) It is escapist, causing the reader to revert to a dream world and to be less able to cope with the problems of everyday life. (4) It unfits the mind for serious study, and devotional life. (5) It is time-consuming and valueless." [2]

In short, Mrs. White saw fiction in qualitative terms rather than as something that was not factual in the sense that it never happened in space-time history. Once we examine all the facts the conclusion is inescapable.

Both Max Phillips, an Adventist editor, and Paul T. Gibbs, a longtime English teacher in Adventist colleges, have pointed out that we might avoid part of the confusion if we made a distinction between "truth" and "fact." *Pilgrim's Progress*, the parable of the rich man and Lazarus, and some of the stories in *Sabbath Readings for the Home Circle* present truth but not fact. [3] Good reading, from this perspective, is that which uplifts truth rather than error.

It should be obvious that the conclusions stated above do not open the floodgates to all types of reading. They simply mean, noted Phillips, "that not all nonfactual literature is harmful to read."

It is pertinent at this point to observe that W. C. White, Ellen White's assistant and closest son, had early come to grips with this problem. Writing to the editor of the *Review* in 1921, he remarked: "Mother has been emphatic in her condemnation of fiction, and when pressed to define what she referred to as fiction, she has always spoken of those works of fiction which lead the mind away from God. With these things in mind, I suppose we may understand her condemnation of fiction to refer to those works of fiction which lead the mind away from heavenly things." [4]

Pioneer Adventist educator Alma E. McKibbin raised an interesting point when she wrote that truth may be expressed in "verse, prose, story, drama, allegory, or any other form of literature. The same is true of error. It may be expressed in any literary form." The question, she asserted, is not a matter of literary form, but rather "What does it teach?" Whether the events narrated in a story actually occurred should never decide the question of whether a story is good or bad. Most things that have actually occurred in our sinful world have been bad. Likewise, "some things wholly imaginative have been very good, so good indeed that they have been the means of grace to many." In conclusion, she wrote, "Every word written or spoken by man in whatever literary form he may be moved to express himself, if it be truth, is helpful and beneficial." [5]

This conclusion is perceptive, but since not all truth is good, it merely raises another issue. In actual fact, much truth is evil. How are we to integrate this Christian insight into literary study? Here we encounter the myth of the good and the evil.

The Myth of the Good and the Evil

A few years ago I had much simpler answers concerning the criteria for literature selection than I do today. In my good old days I found that Philippians 4:8 provided the only standard I needed. "Finally, brethren," wrote Paul, "whatever is true, whatever is honorable, whatever is just, whatever is pure, whatever is lovely, whatever is gracious, if there is any excellence, if there is anything worthy of praise, think about these things."

A surface understanding of this text sufficed quite well until one day, as I was explaining my application of it in class, a perceptive student asked me if I had ever read the Old Testament. His question was a bombshell to my complacency—it exploded my pat answer. The problem is that the Old Testament presents stories that are sordid in the extreme. In fact, it even adds details about sin that are seemingly unnecessary for understanding the account. A case in point is Judges 19-21, which is the evil tale of the basest passions of man in terms of sexual immorality and mass murder. Or what can we say about the story of David and Bathsheba, or about the genealogy of Matthew 1, which lists only four women besides Mary—three with sinful backgrounds and one who happened to be a Gentile? Why select Tamar, Rahab, and Bathsheba instead of the many virtuous female ancestors of the Lord? It is furthermore interesting to note that Matthew 1 does not even name Bathsheba. Instead, it refers to her as the wife of Uriah the Hittite. By this one seemingly unnecessary stroke, Matthew calls to our remembrance not only the whole tale of adultery by Israel's prophet and king but also the incident of David's premeditated murder of one of his most faithful servants and the innocent men serving under his command.

Such stories lead us to inquire: What does Philippians mean by such words as *true, honorable, just, pure, lovely, gracious, excellent,* and *worthy of praise*? The simple proof-text answers seem to evaporate when we consider all the facts. Perhaps the best way to work through our dilemma is to examine how the Bible itself treats evil and evil stories.

First, Scripture never seeks to avoid the seamy side of life. It deals with both the good and the evil, and it puts both in proper perspective. For literature to emphasize only the good and beautiful is less than Biblical. Such a practice would be romantic rather than true to life in the sense that the Bible is true to life.

Francis Schaeffer has pointed out that one can divide the Christian worldview into a major and a minor theme.[6] The minor theme deals with the abnormality of a world in revolt, with the fact that man has rebelled, become separated from God, and has come to see his own meaninglessness. It portrays the defeated and sinful side of human nature. The major theme is the opposite of the minor. It uplifts the fact that God exists, that all is not lost, and that life is not absurd. Man has significance because he is made in God's image.

If literature exclusively emphasizes the major theme, it is both un-Biblical and unreal. By its shallowness and lack of insight into real-life problems we would have to reject it as genuine literature in the Biblical sense. On the other hand, it is equally un-Biblical for literature to emphasize exclusively man's lostness, degradation, and abnormality. The Bible deals with both the major and the minor themes. It is a highly realistic, true-to-life book that does not hesitate to show man in all his degeneration. It does not, however, exhibit man's foulness as an end in itself. As former *Adventist Review* editor Kenneth Wood has noted, the Bible exhibits no "lip-smacking" over the sin described.[7] Rather, it depicts sin, evil, and ugliness to point up man's desperate need of a Saviour and the efficacy of God's grace in the sinner's life. Scripture treats the relationship of the beautiful and the ugly realistically so that the Christian can, with the eyes of faith, come to hate the ugly because he has come to know the God who is beauty, truth, and goodness.

In selecting literature for both personal reading and for the classroom, Christians are not interested in how close they can come to what might be defined as objectionable. Their goal is to select the very best literature to accomplish their aim in the light of Christian belief. The selection of appropriate literary works, however, is only half of the Christian teacher's responsibility. The other half is the interpretation of these works in the context of a Christian worldview. Both selection and interpretation are important as Christians seek to integrate the religious viewpoint with a particular aspect of the curriculum.

While the Bible does not avoid stories portraying evil, it places such stories in an *interpretive framework* that gives insight into the nature of man, the results of sin, and the struggle between the forces of good and evil. Scripture often uses such stories to show, first, the degradation that stems from sinful lives, and second, God's willingness and ability to save. With this in mind Matthew wrote, after the genealogy of chapter 1, that Jesus came to save His people from their sins (Matt. 1:21). Here is the keynote of Matthew's Gospel. God's ability to save is seen in terms of who "His people" are—Rahab, Tamar, the wife of Uriah the Hittite, and Ruth the Moabitess. God is able to save these kinds of sinners. In a similar vein, the Bible does not relate the story of the multiple sin of David and Bathsheba to fascinate the sinful mind. Rather, it couches the story in terms of the tragic results of that sin in the lives and deaths of David's children and the events that eventually led to his repentance (2 Sam. 11:1-18:33), his penitential prayer (Psalm 51), and the assurance of God's saving power. In like manner the story of Judges 19-21 gives insight into the nature of sinful man left on his own. The major lesson of the book of Judges is that man is not naturally good and that without the divinely appointed institution of government life would soon degenerate into a chaotic existence (Judges 21:25; cf. chaps. 17:6; 18:1; 19:1).

The interpretive function of literary instruction has generally been approached in two different ways, which we may illustrate by Drawings A and B (Figure 5). Drawing A represents a classroom approach that places the major stress on the literary qualities of the material and that uses the Bible or ideas from the Bible from time to time as asides. This point of view studies literature largely as it is studied in non-Christian institutions, with the Biblical insight as an added enrichment.

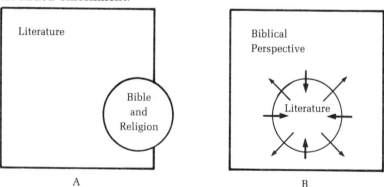

A   B

Figure 5. The Contextual Role of the Biblical Perspective

On the other hand, Drawing B depicts the study of literature in the context of the Biblical perspective and what that means in terms of man's universal and personal dilemma. It views literature from the distinctive vantage point of Christianity and the context of the abnormality of the present world and of God's activity in that world. From this position the study of literature in a Christian institution can be richer than in non-Christian institutions, since non-Christians are handicapped by a lack of the all-important (in terms of insight and interpretation) Biblical view of sin and salvation. This does not mean that such literary elements as plot and style are unimportant, but rather that they are not, within the context of Christianity, the most important aspects of literary study.

Note also that in Drawing B the arrows indicate a two-way transaction between the Biblical perspective and literary study. Not only does the Biblical worldview help us interpret literature but literary insights also help us better understand religious experience within the context of religious truth.

In retrospect, it appears that what Philippians 4:8 means by such adjectives as *good, true,* and *honest*—in the context of the Bible as literature—is that we should put the problems of sinful humanity in the context of the great controversy as revealed by God. "Every topic," including literature, "has a new significance" when viewed in the light of the Bible's "grand central theme" (Ed, p. 125). The extremes that ignore evil at one end of the spectrum and glorify it at the other are neither true nor honest and certainly leave no room for a viable concept of justice. The challenge for the Christian is to approach literary study in such a way that it leads both himself and the youth to see the reality of man and his world as it actually is—sinful and suffering, but not beyond hope and the redeeming grace of a caring God.

The responsibility of the literature teacher in a Christian school is to help the young to learn to read critically and interpretively, so that they can perceive the meaning of what they study in terms of the great struggle between the forces of good and evil. Literary study is not merely a relaxing diversion into the realm of art. T. S. Eliot has observed that what we read affects "the whole of what we are. . . . Though we may read literature merely for pleasure, of 'entertainment' or of 'aesthetic enjoyment,' this reading never affects simply a sort of special sense: it affects our moral and religious existence." [8] There is no such thing as artistic neutrality. Those items in life that appear to be neutral are in effect harmful in the sense that their impact is diversionary and they lead us away from the great issues of life in the conflict between Christ and Satan. Anything that keeps us from facing the problem of our condition before God and from confronting ourselves in the light of Christ as Saviour is a tactical victory for the forces of evil. The function of literary study in a Christian school is not to help us become "learned" in the great authors of the past and present, but to assist us, through some of their writings, to view the issues at stake in the cosmic controversy with more clarity and sensitivity.

Paul T. Gibbs spoke perceptively when he remarked to a convention of Adventist teachers that the major issue is less *what* we read than *how* we read.[9] Ellen White made the same point in writing to a family in which the children were "hooked" on storybooks, to their religious and moral detriment. *"Some of the books you read contain excellent principles, but you read only to get the story. If you would gather from the books you read that which would help you in the formation of your character, your reading would do you some good.* But as you take up your books and peruse page after page of them, *do you ask yourself, What is my object in reading?* Am I seeking to gain substantial knowledge? You cannot build a right character by bringing to the foundation wood, hay, and stubble."—AH, p. 417. (Italics supplied.)

One inference from her advice is that the same material may have either a good or bad effect on the reader, depending on his purpose in reading. A Christian approach to reading is a responsible one that leads a person to read with the purpose of gaining insight into the issues of life and destiny. It is not an escape from reality, but a confrontation with it through the insights imbedded in serious literary work. Joyce Rochat, of Andrews University, has observed that "genuine art . . . is concerned with bringing to the reader some new idea, some deepened insight that will change his attitudes and values, or at least [enable him] to see old ones in a new light." "Pop literature," on the other hand, "gives him nothing permanent. . . . Pop literature, in fact, is a kind of narcotic and the habitual indulgence of it deadens the faculties of apprehension and sensitivity. Highly charged as it is with sentimentalism or sensationalism that constantly call for over-response on the part of the reader, pop literature plants the reader in a fantasy world and subjects him to a kind of psychic illness." [10]

Christian education must help the student move beyond the story to the meaning of its insights for daily life. The function of literary study in a Christian institution, wrote Virginia Graybill, is to aid the student to learn how to "think" about the issues of life—his identity and purpose, the presence of good and evil, justice and forgiveness, the beautiful and the ugly, sexuality and spirituality, ambition and humility, joy and suffering, purity and guilt, and so on.[11] C. S. Lewis made a similar point when he wrote that " 'one of the minor rewards of conversion is to be able at last to see the real point of all the literature we were brought up to read with the point left out.' "[12]

In short, the essential thing in literary study is not the passing on of a body of knowledge, but the development of a skill—the ability to think critically and to interpret literary insights within the Biblical worldview. By "critical" I do not mean finding fault, but rather the quality of thought characterized by careful analysis. In this sense it is imperative that young people learn, both at home and at school, to evaluate all of their reading "critically." We must approach even the Bible and the writings of Ellen White with critical awareness and critical insight if we are to gain their fullest meaning. Part of the function of literary study should be to help us develop this skill. The alternative is mindless absorption.

The Christian reader must ask not only "Is this worth reading?" but "What is its meaning for my life in terms of the great controversy between Christ and Satan?" and "What does this say about man and his predicament?" We should also teach young people to apply this critical awareness to other areas of communication such as television and music—media forms that sometimes fall into the same category as Mrs. White's description of fiction—media forms that are often superficial, sensational, erotic, addictive, and the like.

Beyond interpretation, a Christian approach to literary study should help young people to develop both taste and discrimination based on Christian principles. Chapter 13, after discussing some further misconceptions, will highlight the positive role of literary study for Christians.

13 More Literary Myths

The Myth That Ellen White Developed a Clearly Framed and Explicitly Stated Philosophy of Literary Study

*A*n unspoken assumption seems to exist among Adventists that Ellen White's writings set forth a well-rounded philosophy on literary study. Some even suggest that we find it by examining the topic with the aid of the *Comprehensive Index* to her writings. These are myths. Most of Mrs. White's statements on literature, outside of Biblical literature, were aimed at abuses and harmful practices rather than at forming a balanced exposition. In other words, most of her comments refer to harmful aspects rather than to the true place of literary study in Christian education.

Ellen White claimed, as we will observe in the second section of this chapter, that literary study is important, but she never fully developed the implications of that claim in a positive manner. We could and should treat this problem extensively, but space is limited. My presentation, therefore, will restrict itself to a listing and short discussion of the contextual categories into which most of Ellen White's statements fall. Most of them were reactions to specific historic situations in Adventism. The following treatment is suggestive rather than comprehensive. It is my contention that we will be in a position to determine the proper role of literary study in Adventist education only after we understand Ellen White's approach to the topic. Then we will still face the challenge of developing a well-rounded philosophy of literary study based on inspired principles. That task lies beyond the scope of the present study, although this chapter and the previous one do provide an introduction to some possible solutions.

In the following discussion I do not propose to recommend any specific works. Rather, my aim is to point out the negative or corrective function of most of Ellen White's statements on literary study. The final section will outline some positive criteria for the selection of literature.

One of the most important contextual factors affecting Ellen White's views about literature was the place of the classics in the education of her day. In nineteenth-century secondary and higher education, the Greek and Latin classics, read in the original languages, held the center of the curricular stage. The study of the "heathen authors" occupied the bulk of the students' time. Such a non-Christian framework of mythology, pagan ethics, and "great thoughts" provided the worldview in which Adventist education couched its curriculum. The classics dominated the Bachelor of Arts program at Battle Creek College (and other Adventist institutions up through the late 1890s). To earn a Bachelor of Arts degree, students at Battle Creek had to spend up to seven years in such study. Ellen White's early writings on education did not have much to say on this problem, but by 1891 she had declared all-out war on the ancient classics. By that time it was apparent to her that Adventists could never provide a truly Christian education unless the Bible and the Biblical worldview replaced the classics and the classical worldview as the heart of the curriculum. In her battle against the Greek and Roman authors, Ellen White fought a well-entrenched enemy. She therefore had to use forceful language both to uproot them and to establish the place of the Bible. We must understand many of her statements on literature in the context of this major struggle. She did not oppose literary study, but rejected the heavy emphasis on a knowledge of classical authors as the basis of true education—a widely held educational doctrine among Adventist educators. This curricular struggle had great conse-quence for the church's educational development, since no course of study can have two intellectual frameworks. Either Biblical Christianity or non-Christian literature would hold the center stage. One or the other would have to give way. According to Mrs. White, it would have to be classical literature that yielded, since the Bible provided "essential knowledge" and the "proper framework" for Christian understanding (FE, pp. 187, 184; cf. p. 467).[1]

A second context for Ellen White's statements on literature was the growth of the pulp-book industry that had been rapidly expanding since the 1850s. The dime novel and serialized "storypapers" (often called newspapers) flooded the American market, and many Adventists spent their time and money on these soap operas in print. Critics of the day characterized this popular fiction by such adjectives as cheap, sensational, plot-oriented, worthless, and so on. Many of the authors wrote a novel in less than a week. The plot often focused on cheap romance, Indian slaughter, and "the bad, bad outlaw." Mass production, rather than quality, was the name of the game. Prentiss Ingraham, for example, managed to write about one thousand dime novels—121 on the exploits of Buffalo Bill—even though he did not get started until mid-life. John Wood found, in his study of late-nineteenth-century fiction, that the most successful dime novels were eventually printed in beautifully embossed and gilded bindings and people considered them "high-class" fiction. Religious writers, meanwhile, were busy creating a "better class" of fictional dime novels with the same attributes. The Reverend Joseph Holt Ingraham (the father of Prentiss) authored the immensely popular *Prince of the House of David* and other stories that his son referred to as "dime novels of the Bible."[2] Thus Ellen White and her Adventist contemporaries could condemn "religious novels" and "religious fiction,"[3] even though she recommended the reading of *Pilgrim's Progress*. Quality rather than factuality was the concern.

Many of Ellen White's references to fiction and novels refer to such low-class literature. Under the title of "Mental Inebriates," for example, she wrote how troubled she was to see, in Adventist homes, "periodicals and newspapers containing continued stories that leave no impress of good upon the mind. . . . These dear youth need . . . to put into their character building the very best material." But "the mind is feasted upon sensational stories. They live in an unreal world, and are unfitted for the practical duties of life."—FE, p. 162.

A third context for Ellen White statements on literature involves the activities of Adventist publishing houses. In both Michigan and California they had overexpanded. In order to keep their presses busy, they were doing commercial work (e.g., advertising and check printing) and publishing non-Christian books that were, in effect, "loading the guns of the enemy" (7T, p. 167). In discussing the problem, Mrs. White wrote of historical works of atrocities that hold "satanic fascination" for the human mind and soul-destroying theories found in books advocating spiritualism, hypnotism, and other questionable subjects. God, she claimed, could not bless printing establishments built to spread the gospel when they became entangled with such literature (ibid., pp. 161-168). Her rebuke has obvious implications for schools and private reading in addition to its meaning for the church's publishing program.

A fourth context that we should be aware of, if we are to understand Mrs. White's approach to literature, involved the pantheistic theories of John Harvey Kellogg and his associates that threatened the theology of the Adventist Church near the turn of the century. The remarks about speculative literature dealing with human philosophy and science found in *The Ministry of Healing* (1905), *Education* (1903), and volume eight of *Testimonies for the Church* (1904) need to be read in the light of that crisis.

Another context in which Ellen White addressed the subject of literature was the misuse of religious journals to advertise and/or "glorify" authors. How would you react if you found a picture of Shakespeare's (or any other "secular" writer's) birthplace on the front cover of the *Signs of the Times,* accompanied by an article praising him, while claiming that he died soon after a feast at which he "drank too hard"?[4] Or how would you relate to Dudley Canright's recommendation in the *Review and Herald* (the semiofficial organ of the church) of *Uncle Tom's Cabin* and *Robinson Crusoe* along with the Bible and nine other books as the twelve books of most value to Christian families? The implication, claimed Canright, was that "no children in this age can be regarded as passably intelligent unless they have read" these books. They are, he remarked, the "best" books he could recommend.[5]

If you were the church's prophetic guide, how would you react to such articles in magazines founded to uplift Jesus Christ? Mrs. White promptly replied to them in a responsible manner, pointing out the wrong impression left by such inappropriate editorial inclusions. Paul T. Gibbs caught the point when he wrote that even "if it be granted that Shakespeare is good for some things, it still would not be classified as spiritual food, as evangelistic material." Gibbs was also on target when he noted that it is one thing to criticize the eulogization of Shakespeare in a church paper, while it is another to forbid a knowledge of his writings. Writers should not be eulogized anywhere, but "one can no more ignore Shakespeare in the world of literature than he can ignore the Mississippi River in the geography of North America or George Washington in U.S. history."[6] Of course, if literary ignorance is the goal, then a lack of knowledge of the great writers is justified. This, however, was not Ellen White's position.

The Myth That Literary Study
Is Not Important

Early in my Christian life I became quite convinced, through a selective reading of Ellen White, that literary study was not important if one knew the Bible. In college I even refused to take the required literature course. Later, as I continued to read and study, I came to see that I had made a one-sided interpretation of the issue. The one-sidedness was undoubtedly a result of my failure to understand that the major proportion of Mrs. White's statements on literary study were aimed at literary abuses and that they did not set forth her position in its positive aspects. A careful study of her writings, however, indicates that her primary concern was neither positive nor negative statements about literary study, but that Adventists place the Bible and its worldview at the center of Christian education and the Christian life. Once she had made this point, she seemed quite willing to grant the importance of literary study.

Far from condemning the study of literature, Mrs. White sought to place it within its proper framework. A careful reading of the following quotations will help us understand her balanced position. "*While religion,*" she penned, "*should be the prevailing element in every school, it will not lead to a cheapening of the literary attainments.* It will make all true Christians feel their need of thorough knowledge, that they may make the best use of the faculties bestowed upon them. While growing in grace and in knowledge of our Lord Jesus Christ, they will seek constantly to put to the stretch their powers of mind, that they may become intelligent Christians."—CT, p. 504. (Italics supplied.) "While the pursuit of knowledge in art, in literature, and in trades should not be discouraged, the student should *first* secure an experimental knowledge of God and His will."—Ibid., p. 19. (Italics supplied.) "True education does not ignore the value of scientific knowledge or literary acquirements," even though character development is more important (Ed, p. 225). "We are neglecting our salvation if we give authors who have but a confused idea of what religion means, the most conspicuous place and devoted respect, and make the Bible secondary."—FE, p. 404. The real issue that Mrs. White attacked was not the inclusion of literary study, but the placement of the study of authors at the center of the educational process, while relegating the Word of God to a secondary position (CT, pp. 423, 424, 443, 444). Finally, we read that "while religious principle is held paramount, every advance step taken in the acquirement of knowledge or in the culture of the intellect is a step toward the assimilation of the human with the Divine, the finite with the Infinite."—Ibid., p. 52.

The Bible also reflects a positive position toward the literary and cultural education of some of its greatest heroes. Moses, for example, had a thorough training in the schools of the Egyptians (Acts 7:22), as well as in the wilderness, where he learned God's ways more fully. Ellen White wrote that "the education that Moses had received in Egypt was a help to him in many respects."—MH, p. 474. It was a part of God's providence that he should understand the world as well as the Lord. His broad intellectual grasp added to his usefulness in God's cause.

Daniel, likewise, refused the king's meat, but not the king's learning (Daniel 1, 2). On the king's examination he showed up far superior in Babylonian knowledge than the Babylonians themselves. Remember that many of the wise men of Babylon were "magicians and enchanters" (chap. 1:20), "sorcerers" (chap. 2:2), and "astrologers" (verse 27). This may give us some idea of Daniel's reading when God gave him "learning and skill in all *letters* and wisdom" (chap. 1:17). Apparently the faithful Daniel felt he needed to know the cultural background of the people among whom and for whom he was to work.

Paul also had a familiarity with both the Judeo-Christian religion and pagan cultures. As a result, God could use him more broadly than the twelve disciples once he got his priorities straight. He was able to meet the educated people of his day because he showed "himself familiar with their works of art, their *literature*, and their religion" (AA, p. 237; italics supplied; cf. Ed, p. 67).

One implication of this is that a Christian should have some familiarity with, but not necessarily a mastery of, the culture of those whom he hopes to reach. The Koran, for example, has some false ideas about religion. If you were going as a missionary to a Moslem country, however, you should read the Koran so that you could better understand the thinking of the people you were trying to help. Likewise, if you hope to be a Christian witness among osteopaths, you will be more successful if you have done some reading in the area. Your ignorance certainly won't impress them. Such situations, noted Gibbs, are rather unlikely situations for most of us. On the other hand, most modern American Christians hope to live and witness for their faith among English-speaking Americans. They, therefore, need some knowledge of their cultural background.[7]

We certainly don't want to find ourselves in the position of the first Adventist preacher M. L. Andreasen came across—one who was ignorant about most formal knowledge outside of the Bible.[8] The Lord can use sharp tools better than dull ones. Jesus sent us to be missionaries *in* the world, but He warned us not to be *of* the world. It is one thing to be familiar with culture, while it is quite another thing to place culture at the center of our being. That place we should reserve for God alone.

Adventists have tended to undervalue the role of literary study in the curriculum. I have personally come full circle, from the place where once I would not "contaminate" myself with a literature class, to the position where I now see it as one of the most potentially effective educational tools for the teaching of religious values and truths.

Literature is a powerful tool in the Christian curriculum for at least two reasons. First, serious literature faces and seeks to answer mankind's greatest questions. It reveals man's basic desires, wishes, and frustrations, and develops insight into the human experience. Beyond aesthetic sensitivity, the study of literature leads to inductive insights in such areas as psychology, philosophy, history, theology, and sociology. Significant literary works provide data on such topics as the nature of man, sin, and the meaning and purpose of human existence. Perry LeFevre spoke to this point when he wrote that "the issues of religion are never merely peripheral in literature. There is implicit, if not explicit, in every work of art a vision of life and of man which that work expresses." [9] It is this vision that the Christian teacher should help the student understand and evaluate in terms of the Biblical worldview. Frank Gaebelein has correctly pointed out that the overlap, and thus the opportunity for integration, is great in literature because the "common ground between Christianity and literature is . . . as comprehensive as life itself. Both are concerned with the springs of human character; both have to do with the outward manifestation of that character in human action." [10]

There is no "secular" literature. Donald Whittle, remarking on *Lord of the Flies* and other books, noted that they "are not 'nice books,' but they are religious books because they are concerned with the problem of evil and the nature of man." [11] Nathan A. Scott has written that much modern literature (and other art forms by extension) does not express the wholeness and hope of the Christian worldview. It rather points to a world and to lives that are fractured, broken, isolated, and meaningless. The world's art forms reflect its predicament. Thus, even works that echo the extreme lostness and hopelessness of modern man fit into the Christian interpretative perspective because man without God is lost and hopeless indeed. Some modern writers, by their very despair, point to the need for the hope that we can find only in Christ. Their great sense of deficiency exposes mankind's need of the Saviour. [12]

Seen within the framework of Christian interpretation, all art forms take on a new meaning. If some modern art forms appear meaningless, it is because they reflect the meaninglessness deep in the soul of their creators. In their own way, the very prevalence of the despairing arts points the Christian to the nature of his modern task. Like the Athenians of old, modern people in their alienation are in desperate need of the "unknown god" (Acts 17:23). Christianity and its doctrine of "the last things" holds the only hope.

We can therefore view literary study as a form of religious study, since it helps us see into the philosophic and religious perspective of large segments of modern culture. While not all literature explicitly asserts a philosophy, most of it does exhibit a philosophic stance.[13] Thus, even literature and art expressing a non-Christian message have meaning for those with a Christian perspective. Such literature helps the Christian understand the world he must reach with the message of Christ. In addition, the Christian can praise God for the hope that he already possesses.

One function of literary study is to arouse our sensitivity to realities in daily life. Its role, claimed Sallie TeSelle, is "one of awakening our faculties of perception and of revising our usual way of looking at things." It disrupts our stereotypes of life and gives us " 'new sight.' "[14] John Waller, addressing the 1968 meeting of Adventist English teachers, refined this point somewhat when he remarked that "the Adventist scholar won't look in literature for any absolute truth, but if he knows how to use his tools he *can* find supplementary truth, truth about how men have reacted to being men."[15] The sensitivity of serious literature is thus one avenue to understanding who man is, his variety of responses to God, and his greatest needs, hopes, and fears. From such a perspective, one can see the Bible as the greatest collection of literature—a literature that reveals the ultimate issues of life and provides a context for the study of all other literature.

A second reason that literature is a powerful tool in the Christian curriculum is that beyond providing a philosophical perspective, it delivers that perspective in a package that elicits an emotional response from the reader. Literature (along with other art forms) is tied to the world of intellectual understanding, but beyond this it soars into the realm of feeling and emotion. The aesthetic experience enables people to transcend the limits imposed by purely rational thought and the weaknesses of human language. A picture, song, or story can create an impression in a person that we could never convey through logical argument. Christ relied on this dynamic when He created word pictures in His parables. James Londis, in his perceptive article "God Loves Stories," highlighted the fact that God used stories because they confront us with the power and drama lacking in theoretical and analytical discourse. They provide personal experiences that one cannot always grasp intellectually.[16]

Literature demands a response from the whole person, not merely his brain. In reading a well-written story, a person cries and laughs, feels hunger and fullness, experiences fear and courage, and so on. Quality literature does not allow us to view the issues of life with detachment. It moves us beyond the objective to the subjective. It helps us "feel" the issues at hand. Thus David, in the grips of his sin, felt himself stirred to utter the bald truth by Nathan's imaginative story concerning the stolen ewe lamb. He might not have made the same response had Nathan merely confronted him with the facts (2 Sam. 12:1-15). "Imaginative literature," wrote Michael Christensen, "functions to bring us into contact with universal realities. It creates thoughts in us, arouses emotions, desires, and hopes we did not know we had, and allows us to *taste* what is real." He noted that C. S. Lewis recognized the truth that religious experience is difficult, if not impossible, to conceptualize. "Language can only *point* to that which cannot be adequately communicated." [17] Here is the reason why God used stories in both the Old and New Testaments to bridge the gap between ultimate truth and the weakness of human language and imagination. Christ, in fact, was a master artist in this way of communicating truth.

Literary study, therefore, holds a position of centrality in curricular structures because it is both an avenue for conveying religious philosophy and because it does it in the most meaningful manner.

Some Concluding Remarks

Christian education should help every student understand at least two aspects of literary study—responsible selection and critical interpretation. It is important that young people learn how to act responsibly in both tasks, since they will soon be beyond the reach of parents and teachers.

As for selection, we need to help students realize that the basic question is not "How close can I come to that which is questionable and still remain orthodox?" but "What literature will be the *very best* agent to lead to the development of genuine Christian insights and values?" The problem is not a dearth of good literature, but selecting the best.

Obviously, the selection process has dangers—especially since we are prone to favor our human weaknesses. Ellen White pointed out many of the dangers. A representative statement, found in the seventh volume of the *Testimonies*, speaks of love stories and frivolous, exciting tales that may have religious sentiments. She claimed that their superficial sentiments may merely be Satan clothed in angel robes to deceive and allure more effectively. She then warned that "the mind is affected in a great degree by that upon which it feeds. The readers of frivolous, exciting tales become unfitted for the duties lying before them. They live an unreal life, and have no desire to search the Scriptures. . . . The mind is enfeebled and loses its power to contemplate the great problems of duty and destiny." The youth, she continued, "are exposed to the greatest peril from improper reading. Satan is constantly leading both the young and those of mature age to be charmed with worthless stories. Could a large share of the books published be consumed, a plague would be stayed that is doing a fearful work in weakening the mind and corrupting the heart. None are so confirmed in right principles as to be secure from temptation. All this trashy reading should be resolutely discarded."—7T, pp. 165, 166. Her counsel applies with equal force to the other media, including music and television—the equivalent of dime-novel fiction in the late twentieth century. The selection of literature is a weighty responsibility, and we should not take the above cautions lightly.

While cautions are important, so are positive criteria for literature selection. In 1971 the General Conference Department of Education, after much study and discussion, published a useful list of general criteria for literature in Adventist schools that is also a helpful guide in choosing personal reading material. It is an error merely to impose literary selections on young people in a manner that does not enlist their intelligence in the decision process. Christian education should help students develop, understand, and implement a personal set of criteria for media that will be useful throughout their life. The Department of Education's list of criteria provides a starting point for class discussion (or discussion between parents and their children) regarding a rational Christian basis for the choice of reading matter.

According to the report of the Department of Education, "literature assigned in Seventh-day Adventist schools should: A. Be serious art. It will lead to significant insight into the nature of man in society and will be compatible with Seventh-day Adventist values. B. Avoid sensationalism (the exploitation of sex or violence) and maudlin sentimentality (the exploitation of softer feelings to the detriment of a sane and level view of life). C. Not be characterized by profanity or other crude and offensive language. D. Avoid elements that give the appearance of making evil desirable or goodness appear trivial. E. Avoid simplified, excitingly suspenseful, or plot-dominated stories that encourage hasty and superficial reading. F. Be adapted to the maturity level of the group or individual." [18]

Beyond responsible selection stands the need for students to learn to evaluate critically that which they read, view, or hear. Gene Garrick, of the Tabernacle Church of Norfolk, has perceptively noted that *"though the school must shelter to some extent, we must be careful not to keep the student from learning to think critically. The Christian school is the ideal place to tackle some problem areas and help the students think through the non-Christian precepts and implications as judged by the Bible."* [19] It is better, for example, for students to face some explicit issues in religion, ethics, and science in school, where they have some guidance, than after graduation, when they are on their own.

Part of the function of Christian education is to help young people think actively (Ed, p. 17). Harry M. Tippett observed, in an address to Adventist English teachers, that while it is fine and good to study "the social life of beetles, bugs, and bees," we "too often shut our eyes to our manifest responsibility in guiding these youth in reading that will help them relate themselves intelligently to the great social problems of human life with which each graduate must wrestle soon after he receives his beribboned diploma." [20] It is important to introduce young people to the fine arts, but it is just as important to help them move beyond a consideration of them as ends in themselves to an understanding of their meaning for daily living. Students need to be educated to think actively about what they see, feel, and hear. We need to teach them to see beneath the surface plot in what they read and experience.

Reuben Hilde, while associate secretary of the General Conference Department of Education, met the problem of responsible reading head-on when he wrote that most books on our library shelves contain some error in science, social views, philosophy, life standards, human relations, and so on. Pulling them off the library shelves, suggested Hilde, is not the answer. We must rather "teach students to be thinkers. They must learn to distinguish between the true and the spurious. . . . I am not suggesting that error must be taught that truth might be recognized. I am saying, however, that at some time or another all learners will be confronted by a decision; in its simplest form the question will be, 'Is it true or false?' The student must have the tools, the mental and spiritual equipment, and the fortitude to make the correct decision regardless of the setting or circumstances. . . . The solution is not in emptying the library of books but in filling the life with God's principles." [21]

Christian education must provide students with a Biblical-Christian framework for thinking and for evaluating all that they encounter. Literary study takes on deeper meaning within such a framework. If young people are able to internalize Christian principles of selection and interpretation in literary study because they are an explicit part of the curriculum, then they will be able to apply the same guidelines to their daily lives in such areas as music and television. The issues faced in the literature class are universal, and the opportunities for Christian development through literary study are challenging.

14 Religious Instruction Myths

What do Seventh-day Adventists hope to achieve through religious instruction in their schools and colleges? Are we fulfilling those goals? Have we consciously thought about our aims? If so, are our instructional programs structured to reach the desired destination? Such questions are crucial because they stand at the heart of Adventist education's reason for being.

We find at least two myths rooted in the area of religious instruction. They are not always stated explicitly, but one or the other of them is often implicit in the way we talk and operate in the classroom. The first is the myth that the function of religion classes is to teach theology. The second myth is a reaction to the first. It basically suggests that the presentation of theological knowledge is a rather unimportant aspect of religious instruction. This chapter will examine both myths and then move beyond them to propose a set of goals appropriate for religious instruction in Adventist schools.

The present chapter is closely related to chapter 4, which dealt with educational purposes, and to chapter 9, which examined the myth of anti-intellectualism and its antithesis. It will pass over lightly material discussed in those two chapters.

The Myth That the Goal of Religious Instruction Is to Teach Theology

The manner in which Adventist schools sometimes approach religious instruction and Biblical studies tends to highlight a problem that often exists in practice even after we have recognized it as a fallacy in thought. Adventists at all educational levels have too often taught religion on the intellectual plane. The fallacious reasoning underlying this mistake rests upon the false assumption that the teaching of theology is equivalent to the teaching of religion.

For the purpose of our discussion, *theology* will refer to

academic and cognitive knowledge about God and religious ideas, while *religion* (a word with many definitions) will designate the experiential-relational aspects of Christian living. Perhaps the following quotations will help us see the distinction more clearly. Perry LeFevre has written that "religion is the *commitment* to that which sustains, nourishes, and creates the good in human life. Theology is the intellectual interpretation of that to which man commits himself. . . . Religion is the trust; theology is the intellectual interpretation of that upon which we rest our trust."[1] William Temple made a similar point in his Gifford lectures. "The heart of Religion is not an opinion about God, such as Philosophy [or theology] might reach as the conclusion of its argument; it is a personal relationship with God." Again: "Philosophy seeks knowledge for the sake of understanding, while Religion seeks knowledge for the sake of worship."[2] Elton Trueblood echoed this concept when he wrote that "the essence of philosophy [and theology] is to *think*; the essence of religion is to *dedicate*."[3]

While the two concepts are related, one does not necessarily imply the other. Theology, or knowledge about God and the Bible, may not lead to religious experience. Pascal grasped this truth when he remarked that "the knowledge of God is very far from the love of Him."[4] Theological knowledge that falls short of practice and positive relationships with the object of that knowledge is, in one sense, meaningless. After all, some of the world's greatest infidels and atheists have known the content of their Bibles extremely well. Even Satan himself has an excellent knowledge of God—he is a cognitive believer (James 2:19).

Ellen White drove home the dangers inherent in mere knowledge (including religious knowledge) when she wrote that "students must be impressed with the fact that *knowledge alone may be*, in the hands of the enemy of all good, *a power to destroy them*. It was a very intellectual being, one who occupied a high position among the angelic throng, that finally became a rebel; and many a mind of superior intellectual attainments is now being led captive by his power. The sanctified knowledge which God imparts is of the right quality, and will tell to His glory."—4T, p. 422. (Italics supplied.) Along the same line, Francis Schaeffer perceptively remarked that serious theological study may actually be the means of shutting us off from God rather than opening doors to Him. Such a thing takes place when the pursuit of theological and doctrinal knowledge becomes our end in religious study.[5]

Reuben Hilde, of Loma Linda University, put his finger on the problem when he claimed that "one of the stark realities we face in

Seventh-day Adventist education is that in too many cases the education provided in our schools has not appreciably changed young people." He noted that many stay in the church, but that "this is not particularly satisfying. . . . When a Christian school doesn't bring about transformation of lives, the purpose of that school comes close to being absurd." The central problem, he claimed, is that much learning enters the mind that has never gone through the heart. "To put it bluntly, a person can graduate from being a stupid sinner to [being] an intelligent sinner." [6]

So far we have highlighted the negative: the dangers of an unbalanced emphasis on theological knowledge in religious teaching. Perhaps the best way to get a handle on the positive aspects of religious instruction is to review what we hope to achieve through such instruction. H. E. Carnack has summarized the threefold aim of religious instruction in three short phrases: (1) "Bring the pupil to Christ," (2) "Build him up in Christ," and (3) "Send him forth to work for Christ." [7] Thus the ultimate goal of religious instruction is the same as the ultimate aim of Christian education in general—to lead young people beyond understanding to relationship, and beyond relationship to service.

Bible knowledge is not an end in itself. Rather, instruction in the Bible and Christian truth is a means to an end. The important thing is that the encounter with Biblical truth has an effect on the life of both teacher and student. Trueblood observed that "those who promote religion are never satisfied with imparting information *about* religion; they are concerned, instead, that people *be* religious." The heart of such religious experience, he noted, is a commitment that includes "courageous involvement." [8] Arthur Holmes reinforced this point. Faith, he suggested, is man's response to God. It is more than assent to intellectual truth, even though that is involved to a certain extent. "Credal assent is not enough. . . . Religious faith includes trust, openness, consent, and commitment, as well as assent. It is the response of the whole person to the revelation of God's grace that transforms his life." [9] Faith, in part, is the application of what we know to our daily existence. The Christian ideal is not scholarly detachment, but energetic involvement in the issues of life.

Mrs. White has treated the above thoughts repeatedly in her writings. One of her major educational themes was that higher education is not mere intellectual knowing, but *"experimental knowledge* of the plan of salvation" (CT, pp. 11, 434, italics supplied; cf. pp. 45, 455). The believer experiences such knowledge in his character rather than just in his mind *(ibid.,* p. 37). "An intellectual religion will not satisfy the soul. *Intellectual training must not be neglected, but it is not sufficient.* Students must be taught that they are in this world to do service for God. They must be taught to place the will on the side of God's will."—*Ibid.*, p. 540. (Italics supplied.) Again, she wrote that "accepting new theories does not bring new life to the soul. Even an acquaintance with facts and theories important in themselves is of little value unless put to a practical use."—8T, p. 316; cf. CT, p. 97.

In Christianity a major gulf exists between knowing about the truth and knowing the truth, just as there is a difference between knowing about Christ and knowing Christ as one's personal Saviour. The Bible is not concerned with abstract truth. We must not confuse knowledge with saving knowledge. The first is a mere intellectual understanding of truth, which we can achieve through the teaching of theology. The latter involves the application of God's truth to our lives and is inherent in what I have called *religion.*

A first reaction to the above argument by teachers of Bible classes in Adventist schools might be "So what? We have known this all along." Undoubtedly this is true for the great majority of religion teachers at the elementary, secondary, and college levels. Nearly all teachers of Biblical subjects are committed, in theory at least, to the proposition that what a person believes should affect the way he lives. It is only natural to conclude that religious instruction ought to be concerned with both intellectual truth and behavioral goals. Unfortunately, noted Wheaton College's Robert Webber, many teachers "of Bible and theology forget to emphasize the lifestyle resulting from the formation of Christian ideas and remain content to perpetuate the scholasticism of their graduate studies on the helpless victims in their classroom."[10] In other words, they tend to focus on doctrine as doctrine and on Bible study as Bible study, while failing to bridge the gap between knowledge and experience. In too many cases the Bible teacher faces the danger of succumbing to the temptation to live on two levels—one of theory, where verbal expression cannot be separated from practice, and another in the everyday world of the classroom, where the separation does take place. Not all teachers of Bible courses fall into this pit, yet certainly many more believe they have succeeded in avoiding it than actually do. The acid test, however, might be the perceptions of the students rather than those of the teacher.

An extremely real problem here is that it is infinitely easier to develop a course of religious instruction that passes on information than to prepare one that brings a student into a personal confrontation and/or relationship with the living God. The latter, however, is the ideal that we must seek to accomplish despite its difficulties. The very least we should do is to attempt to develop curricula and instructional techniques that aim at the more vital realm beyond the transmission of knowledge. Lois E. LeBar spoke to the issue: "Because evangelicals have such a high view of Scripture, we sometimes get our pupils related to the written Word without getting them through to the Living Word. We strive to get them to understand doctrines, memorize, complete their workbooks without dealing personally with the Living Lord. Words, doctrines, and ideas are stepping-stones to the Person of the Lord—essential means to spiritual reality." [11] We are lost when the means become the end.

One pertinent point here concerns the qualifications of Bible teachers. Too often, in our attempt to be respectable, we have chosen religion instructors on the basis of academic credentials. In one sense that is good, since knowledge is important. But in another sense, noted Harry Blamires, "the idea that because a man is learned, especially in subjects appertaining to religion, he is therefore secure from the seduction of worldliness is a fallacy." [12] No correlation necessarily exists between being a theological expert and spirituality. The real (primary) qualification of a Bible teacher (or any other teacher) is not intellectual but experiential. "The teacher of truth can impart effectively only that which he himself knows by experience."—CT, p. 435.

The ideal, obviously, is to develop Christian Bible teachers who have both scholarly expertise and experiential Christianity. School boards and administrators, however, often face less than the ideal. In such cases, they should select a teacher with an integrated spirituality before one with isolated intellectuality if the school is ever to approximate its goals.

It may require technical experts to teach theology, but only born-again Christians can teach religion. Let us hope that the experts will be born-again Christians, but let us never forget Schaeffer's observation that much modern theology is "just a game." [13] A person may enter the study of theology because he likes the intellectual stimulation rather than because he has a burning desire to help people know Jesus Christ as their personal Lord and Saviour.

In summary, the essence of Christianity is not a body of knowledge to digest, or a Book to study, but a life to live. Spiritual things are spiritually discerned (1 Cor. 2:14). The presence of the

Spirit in the teacher's life is crucial, since education is a redemptive act.

Beyond the "Grocery List" Approach to Religious Instruction

This chapter has treated extensively the myth that the goal of religion classes is to teach theology. The second religious instruction myth—that theological knowledge is a rather unimportant aspect of religious instruction—can be quickly dispatched. Accurate theological knowledge is both necessary and important, since religious experience cannot take place in a cognitive vacuum. Theological knowledge gives direction to religious experience and provides a framework for testing its validity. And accurate theological knowledge is an important component of religious study even if it is not the most important aspect of the religious studies curriculum. Doctrines, Biblical facts, archeological discoveries, correlations of Biblical thought with Greek philosophy, the implications of the fine points of language, and so on, certainly form part of the "stuff" of religious instruction. By themselves, however, they are no more meaningful, helpful, or interesting to the average student than a grocery list that he needs to memorize.

What makes such items of information valuable, interesting, and important is their relation to the meaning of individual student lives in the here and now. The Biblical themes of the nature of God, the nature of man, God's revelation in Scripture, and the issues of sin and redemption are more than mere formulas to believe—they are vital issues in everyday living. The reality of sin, for example, we can approach in the classroom as a broken relationship between man and God that affects every part of human existence in daily life, rather than as a doctrine to understand. After all, the placing of our selves rather than God at the center of our universe ruptures our relationship with God, our fellow beings, our environment, and our own selves, and ushers in the whole of mankind's individual and collective problems. Likewise, we can teach the study of redemption as the restoration of relationships affected by sin—an at-one-ment that not only took place at the cross but has meaning for the quality of individual life today as God seeks to rebuild fractured and alienated lives. All aspects of theological truth have potential meaning for the students in our classes—all of whom are suffering from the weaknesses of the flesh and have a "gut-level" experience with lostness. Robert Webber has argued that we remove theology from life when we teach it exclusively on the intellectual plane. "Because man is more than mere intellect, truth will have no meaning for him if it is unrelated to human experience." We must recognize the poverty of rational analysis and systematization of Bible truth. Isolated "truth" can be both sterile and deadening.[14]

The world's greatest teacher, Jesus Christ, made theological truth vital by relating it to the daily experiences of His hearers. They never had to ask "So what?" to His teaching. To Him, God was the "living God" who affected daily life. In part, this was the secret of His teaching success. He never presented truth as an abstraction, but rather He took the truths of heaven and applied them to the lives of His hearers (Ed, pp. 81, 82).

Ellen White proposed that "the teaching of the Bible should have our freshest thought, our best methods, and our most earnest effort."—CT, p. 181. She further suggested that effective Bible study enlists the interest of the student. The instructor should observe where the pupils' interests lie and then stimulate their study as they "see what the Bible says about these things" (ibid.). Here she directly refers to younger children, but the same principle holds true for academy students and general education students at the college level. If teachers will use such an approach, the Bible will not become a tiresome book to the student. "Under a wise instructor the word will become more and more desirable."—Ibid., p. 171. This takes place when Bible study becomes a meaningful experience rather than a rote exercise—something that the person must endure as a penalty for attending an Adventist school.

The contact points between human experience and Biblical truth are omnipresent. They include, for example, moral dilemmas, the Christian doctrine of sensuality, questions relating to parental or school authority, the meaning of life, and so on. Paul's letters and the other books of the Bible, rather than being systematic expositions of abstract issues, were written to meet real human problems and universal questions. Christian doctrines, likewise, have held dynamic meaning because their formulation took place in concrete situations. People still experience these problems, ask these questions in one form or another, and face similar situations. The study of the Bible, when seen in the context of man's universal dilemmas, is an exciting process. And students can catch such excitement from teachers who have grasped this vision and have moved beyond the formal categories developed to organize their academic disciplines.

In this chapter I have sought to emphasize that the teaching of theological "truth" is a vital concern of the Christian school so long as we formulate that truth within the context of religious experience. In past chapters I stressed the important concept that we must view all truth, since it is God's truth, within the Biblical framework. Here, as we discuss one of the intellectual functions of religious instruction in Adventist schools, I would like to reverse the picture. Not only do we need to integrate other topics in the curriculum with the Biblical worldview but the Bible class provides a unique forum that can pave the way for this integration in the minds of students by highlighting the Christian worldview and what this perspective means to the rest of their education. The Bible class, rather than being an intermission from the brute facts of everyday life and "secular" knowledge, should instead be the place where we study such realities in terms of their ultimate meaning. If this is so, the Bible teacher should be a person with a broad knowledge of the arts and sciences, rather than a mere specialist in the cloistered realm of "religious" studies. In other words, the Bible class, even in its intellectual aspects, can move beyond topics and organizational formats that theologians find interesting or helpful, to the thinking world of the average student who is trying to make sense out of his education and life. Wheaton College, one of the most successful evangelical liberal arts colleges, has developed such an approach to religious studies in its freshman Bible class, which it has entitled "Christ and Culture." [15] Perhaps we have something to learn from our evangelical brethren who have developed some creative programs to meet the religious needs of their students and the goals of their institutions.

The intellectual function of religious instruction is of vital importance to young people. It must not, however, degenerate into a form of indoctrination that attempts to bypass the critical judgment of the student in order to gain the acceptance of a certain point of view. [16] To the contrary, it should help students develop their powers of critical thought, while at the same time providing a Christian philosophy for the evaluation of the bits and pieces of knowledge. Thus, the Bible class has a distinctive role to play in helping young people learn to think Christianly.

Some General Objectives in Religious Study

We can never accomplish the goals of religious instruction through theological understanding. Neither can we reach them through a mindless experience. The Christian life is a unified life, and Christian experience at its best is informed by the intellect. Religious instruction in Adventist schools must aim at larger targets than it sometimes has in the past. This chapter has not suggested that a well-balanced program of religious instruction is easy to develop, nor has it laid out such a program. It has sought, however, to uplift needs and possibilities, and to point out the major pitfalls of traditional emphases. The main contributions of this chapter, hopefully, will be to stimulate continued thought regarding what we hope to accomplish through religious instruction and to help us evaluate whether we are currently using the best possible means to reach those goals.

In 1959 Fort Wayne Bible College developed a helpful list of eight objectives they hoped to achieve in their program of Biblical studies. Their objectives provide food for thought for those concerned with similar issues in Adventist schools. The college's objectives were: First, "to give the student a working knowledge of the Bible as a divine revelation and to give him an understanding of Christian theology." Second, "to lead the student to a full commitment and loyalty to the Christian faith." Third, "to help the student form a Christian worldview." Fourth, "to guide the student in the development of Christian character." Fifth, "to lead the student to an appreciation of the place of the Bible in his growth into spiritual maturity." Sixth, "to deepen and enrich the student's whole personality—intellectually, emotionally, and volitionally: to secure as his supreme motivation the glory of God and the good of men." Seventh, "to help the student derive from Bible studies the principles of critical thinking, whereby he will be able to evaluate concepts and discriminate between truth and error." Eighth, "to create in the student an appreciation for the place of Biblical studies as the integrating factor in the total curriculum, including student life, school administration, and academic studies." [17]

The committee's objectives reflect a great deal of thought. In addition, they do not commit the error of an overly intellectual approach to religious study. Although not exhaustive, they may well serve as guidelines for teaching, learning, and developing a core curriculum of religious studies that would have components to meet each of the objectives.

The Fort Wayne objectives, however, seem to fall short in the area of Christian service. Christian young people, noted Mrs. White, need opportunities for "missionary work—time to become acquainted with the spiritual needs of the families in the community around them" (CT, p. 545; cf. p. 431). This objective may perhaps be the responsibility of the entire school rather than that of the Bible department, but it is an essential part of the religious mission of the Christian school that we neglect at great loss. George Akers and Robert Moon, of Andrews University, have written that "trying to help students develop Christian values without providing opportunity for them to practice these values can be compared to a person alone on a desert island who takes a correspondence course on love."[18] Therefore, we could list opportunities for missionary work as a ninth objective for inclusion in a well-rounded program of religious instruction.

In some ways, providing practical service opportunities of a Christian nature is easier to implement in small elementary schools than in large institutions, but it should be a conscious goal at all levels of education. If we can successfully foster service to others in school, this concept will have a greater chance of being a permanent part of the lifestyle after graduation. Some have held that Seventh-day Adventist programs of religious instruction have been heavy on knowledge and weak on application. If this is true, we need remedy it in either the formal or informal curriculum.

15 The Myth of the Best Method

The Myth Unmasked

*T*he myth of the one best method is much wider than Adventism. It is a misconception that has infected a large portion of the educational profession in the United States and many other countries during the twentieth century. To their misfortune, educators have been obsessed with finding that methodology that will provide the perfect solution for teaching every student. Thus, society has spent hundreds of millions of dollars developing and studying teaching methods in an effort to find the "best" instructional technique.

Over the past century one fad after another has arrived on the educational scene. Teaching machines, teacher aides, a multitude of audiovisual techniques, open classrooms, team teaching, instruction by television, behavioral objectives, competency-based instruction, computer-controlled learning, and a host of other techniques have come forth as "the answer" to the problem of educational methodology. Most of these methods have had a period in which their proponents put them forth as the universal solution. But eventually, educators have come to see each as an aid to good teaching rather than the royal road to success.

All the millions of dollars spent in researching teaching methodology, claimed Arthur Combs, have failed to isolate any method or technique that we can clearly associate with either good or bad teaching. The fact is that good (effective) teachers use widely divergent methods, yet they obtain good results. Three characteristics seem to be common to successful teaching methods: They fit (1) the personality of the teacher, (2) the individuality of the students, and (3) the conditions within which a particular teaching-learning situation occurs. Other than these general factors, no universals in teaching methodologies apply to everybody at all times.[1]

Since good teachers get excellent results using divergent methods, apparently methodology does not make the difference. The solution is found not in the "best method," but in the "best teacher." In turn, as we shall soon see, the quality of the relationship that exists between him and his pupils characterizes the best teacher. Just about any teaching method will work if there is mutual caring and respect between student and teacher. Conversely, no method is effective to its fullest without such a relationship. This does not mean that students will not learn in the absence of a quality relationship. Rather, it suggests that they will do so in spite of the deficit, but will generally learn less than they would have under more positive conditions. On the other hand, this does not reduce the importance of teaching methodology; it only reminds us that it is not the most vital factor. Good methodology can improve the effectiveness of the teaching-learning process when a quality relationship already exists between the pupil and teacher. The important thing is that the relationship provides a foundation for optimum instructional success.

Millicent C. McIntosh, while president of Barnard College, made a similar point when she wrote that "the actual *content* of courses is not so important as the *method* by which it is presented; . . . the material of the curriculum is insignificant in comparison with the quality of those who teach." [2] Content and method are important, but quality teachers are more so. Elton Trueblood has remarked that "if there is any one conclusion on which there is conspicuous agreement in our current philosophy of education it concerns the supreme importance of the good teacher. It is easy to envisage a good college with poor buildings, but it is not possible to envisage a good college with poor teachers." He wrote in another connection that "it is better to have brilliant teaching in shacks than to have sloppy teaching in palaces." The quality of the teacher is more vital than the curriculum, because the able teacher dominates the curriculum. [3]

James Coleman's massive study of American schools (discussed in chapter 5) has empirically supported these observations. Coleman found that the school factors with the greatest influence on achievement (independent of family background) are the teacher's characteristics, not facilities or curriculum. [4] What is true for achievement also applies to the spiritual impact of an educational program. Roger Dudley, in his study of Adventist academy students in the United States, found that *"no other factor was as strongly related to teen-age rejection of religion as was the religious sincerity of their academy teachers."* [5]

Teachers make a difference. The writers of the influential Harvard report, *General Education in a Free Society,* after wrestling for years with the problem of the ideal curriculum, concluded that "everything finally depends on the teacher's quality of mind and spirit." [6]

Given the central role of the teacher in education, it should be obvious that we cannot expect quality education without quality teachers. Likewise, quality Christian education can never occur without Christian teachers. The curriculum and the methods are important, but the teacher is much more fundamental.

The Role of the Christian Teacher

The primary function of the Christian teacher is redemptive, since education and redemption, in their highest sense, are one (Ed, p. 30). Just as Christ, the world's greatest teacher, "came to seek and to save the lost" (Luke 19:10), so the modern Christian teacher is an agent of salvation in God's great plan. He is willing to work in the spirit of Christ to bring his students into harmony with God so that they can be restored to His image through accepting the sacrifice of Jesus and the enabling power of the Holy Spirit. Christian teaching, as we have repeatedly noted, consists of much more than passing on information or stuffing students' heads full of knowledge. In its essence successful teaching is teachers relating to the Master Teacher in such a way that they become effective agents in the great plan of redemption. The Christian teacher must relate to both God and his students if he is to fulfill effectively his "ministry of reconciliation" (2 Cor. 5:18). Since the purpose of Christian education is to lead young people into a saving relationship with Jesus Christ, the role of the Christian teacher is ministerial and pastoral in the fullest sense.

The New Testament clearly specifies teaching as a divine calling (Eph. 4:11; 1 Cor. 12:28; Rom. 12:6-8). Furthermore, the Scriptures do not separate the functions of teaching and pastoring. On the contrary, Paul wrote to Timothy that a bishop (pastor) must be "an apt teacher" (1 Tim. 3:2). In writing to the Ephesians that "some should be apostles, some prophets, some evangelists, some pastors and teachers" (chap. 4:11), Paul used a Greek construction that indicates that the same person holds both the office of pastor and teacher. F. F. Bruce, in commenting on the passage, has remarked that "the two terms 'pastors (shepherds) and teachers' denote one and the same class of men." [7] On the other hand, Scripture lists the other gifts separately. The significance of this point is that we cannot divide these two gifts if they are to remain functional. The pastor must not only care for the souls of his flock but also teach both individuals and the corporate body of the church by precept and example. The teacher, likewise, is not merely an expounder of truth, but one who has an abiding care for the individuals under his tutelage. A Christian teacher is a pastor or minister of the gospel. The difference between the titles of pastor and teacher in modern society arises from the current division of labor. Twentieth-century society may see the Christian teacher as one who does his pastoring in a "school," while the pastor does his teaching in the "larger religious community." We must consciously realize that their function is essentially the same, even though by today's definitions they have charge of different divisions of the Lord's vineyard. Teaching young people is not only a ministerial act but also one of the most effective forms of ministry, since it affects the entire population at a most impressionable age.

The clearest and fullest integration of the gift of teacher-pastor appeared in the ministry of Christ. One of the terms by which people most often addressed Him was *master*. The actual meaning of the word is "teacher." We may see Christ as the best example of teaching in terms of both methodology and meaningful interpersonal relationships. A study of the Gospels from the perspective of Christ as teacher will contribute a great deal to our knowledge of ideal Christian instruction. In addition, such a study will put us in direct touch with the aims and goals of Christian education.

Before we move on in our discussion, it is necessary to comment upon two issues. First, it is important to recognize that the teacher's mastery of subject matter is vital, even though this chapter stresses the personal relationship aspect of the teacher's work. "The question is often asked," wrote Trueblood, "whether a teacher's responsibility is to know his subject or to know his students. This question is essentially unanswerable, being similar to the question of which sex is more necessary for procreation." The good teacher must know both at once. His approach to subject matter is best when he has the needs of his pupils in mind, and his approach to his pupils is most effective when he has some burning truth for their lives. In teaching, the teacher must relate to both the subject and the person at the same time.[8]

The Christian teacher should be an expert in his subject matter. He will, however, see his course content in a different light from the non-Christian teacher, since he interprets it within the Biblical worldview. His concept of sin and its impact upon human lives, for example, will enable him to approach sociology and psychology in a manner beyond the reach of the non-Christian. His vision will also help him recognize and teach the ultimate limitations of political action in a fractured world. The subject matter, in short, takes on a different meaning when viewed from the divine perspective. The Christian teacher knows not only his subject matter but also his students, and he knows both within the context of the Christian worldview. It is an inescapable fact that "the worldview of the teacher, insofar as he is effective, gradually conditions the worldview of the pupil." [9] Most items of Christian knowledge are not different from non-Christian knowledge, but they are packaged in a different philosophical framework. The framework is all-important, since discrete pieces of knowledge take on meaning within an interpretive context. Since no person teaches in a philosophical vacuum, it is essential that the Christian teacher has a Christian philosophy.

A second observation about teaching that we should discuss at this juncture is that Christian teaching is an art rather than a science. Teaching involves human values, which lie outside the range of science, and it touches upon human emotions, which do not lend themselves to systematic analysis and employment. Gilbert Highet, in his classic *Art of Teaching*, has written that "a 'scientifically' brought-up child would be a pitiable monster. A 'scientific' marriage would be only a thin and crippled version of a true marriage. . . . 'Scientific' teaching, even of scientific subjects, will be inadequate as long as both teachers and pupils are human beings. Teaching is not like inducing a chemical reaction: it is much more like painting a picture or making a piece of music. . . . You must throw your heart into it, you must realize that it cannot all be done by formulas, or you will spoil your work, and your pupils, and yourself." [10]

Just as not everyone is a successful artist in the usual sense of the word, so not everyone can be a successful teacher. Some have a calling from God to be teachers (Eph. 4:11; 1 Cor. 12:28). They have the spiritual gift that it takes to succeed as teachers, and they are sensitive to the needs of their pupils. Because they have a divine summons and gift to teach, they approach the task with the flexibility and sensitivity of an artist rather than with mechanical rigidity. While they benefit greatly from systematic instruction in the science of teaching methodology—their art becomes informed by science—they are able to reach the hearts, minds, and spirits of their students effectively because they are skillful artists rather than technicians.

The Heart of Teaching

At the center of the teaching-learning process is the teacher, and at the heart of good teaching is a good relationship between teacher and student. The art of teaching does not have its foundation upon the best method, but upon the best relationship. If this is so, it is important that we understand the characteristics of that relationship. One of the most crucial is the quality of the teacher's *caring.* Ellen White has written that *"if we wish to do good to souls, our success with these souls will be in proportion to their belief in our belief in, and appreciation of, them."*—FE, p. 281. (Italics supplied.) In other words, our effectiveness in working with students is in direct proportion to their perception of our personal caring for them. They will respond to *genuine* care and interest (*ibid.,* p. 55; 4T, p. 423; Ed, p. 231). "The teacher's obligations are weighty and sacred," wrote Mrs. White, "but no part of his work is more important than that of looking after the youth with tender, loving solicitude. Let the teacher once gain the confidence of his students, and he can easily lead . . . them."—CT, p. 503.

Part of the success of Christ's ministry was that people *knew* that He really cared. For example, His presence never repelled children. "His large heart of love could comprehend their trials and necessities, and find happiness in their simple joys."—*Ibid.,* p. 179. Children are quite perceptive. They can tell after talking to us if we are just listening to their "small" joys and concerns to be polite, or if we have genuine interest—if we really care. How many times have we as parents listened to our children, nodded our heads, and then sent them off to play without having the slightest idea what they were trying to communicate? An excellent way to turn children off is to let them feel that we are more concerned with our own "important" thoughts than with them. Expressed and continual caring is the heart of good teaching. Mrs. White has suggested that even though a teacher may have limited literary qualifications, if he really cares for his students, realizes the magnitude of his task, and has a willingness to improve, he will succeed (Ed, p. 279).

Teachers express part of their caring through how they envision the possibilities of their students. In a passage that needs much study and thought, Ellen White wrote of Christ that *"in every human being He discerned infinite possibilities.* He saw men as they might be, transfigured by His grace. . . . Looking upon them with hope, He inspired hope. Meeting them with confidence, He inspired trust. . . . In His presence souls despised and fallen realized that they still were men, and they longed to prove themselves worthy of His regard. In many a heart that seemed dead to all things holy, were awakened new impulses. To many a despairing one there opened the possibility of a new life."—*Ibid.,* p. 80. (Italics supplied; cf. Ed, p. 79.) Her statement contains the challenge of challenges for teachers, parents, and everyone else who works with human beings. To see infinite possibilities in every person, to see hope in the hopeless, takes an infusion of God's grace. But it is the key to good teaching. The alternative is to look upon people with hopelessness and thereby inspire hopelessness.

Psychologist Arthur Combs pointed to several research studies that indicate that we can clearly distinguish good teachers from poor ones on the basis of what they believe about people.[11] In a similar vein, William Glasser, the psychiatrist who developed "reality therapy," believes that failures in both school and life find their roots in two related problems—the failure to love and the failure to achieve self-worth.[12] We get our concept of self-worth from our perceptions of what others think about us. When a child's parents and teachers constantly give him messages that he is stupid, delinquent, and hopeless, they are shaping his sense of self-worth, which he will act out in his daily living.

Fortunately, the self-fulfilling prophecy also works in the positive direction. Earl Pullias and James Young make an excellent point: "When people are asked to describe the teacher that did the most for them, again and again they mention a teacher, often the only one in their experience, who believed in them, who saw their special talents, not only what they were but even more what they wanted to be and *could be*. And they began to learn not only in the area of their special interest but in many others."[13] A teacher is an inspirer of vision.

On the other hand, such an ability to see human potential does not entail a blindness to limitations. Within the Biblical framework, not everyone has every talent, even though each has some. At times students need definite guidance into areas where their personalities and natural gifts will make them most effective.

Another important aspect of student-teacher relationships is that teachers have the opportunity to come close to young people in a manner and to an extent not possible for other adults in modern society. The teacher's greatest gift to his students is his companionship. Companionship is one of the most effective tools in his repertoire of techniques, but it seems to be one of the most neglected and underemphasized components of the ministry of teaching. All too often teachers focus on commanding, dictating, and directing the classroom, while failing to develop significant social relations with students.

Good teaching relationships between students and teachers are most easily established outside the classroom. They generally develop in the field, in the shop, and on the playground as teachers and students learn how to work and play together. Ellen White has written that *"the true teacher can impart to his pupils few gifts so valuable as the gift of his own companionship. . . .* To strengthen the tie of sympathy between teacher and student there are few means that count so much as pleasant association together outside the classroom."—Ed, p. 212; cf. CT, p. 502; FE, p. 116. (Italics supplied.) On another occasion she suggested that if teachers "would gather the children close to them, and show that they love them, and would manifest an interest in all their efforts, and even in their sports, sometimes even being a child among children, they would make the children very happy, and would gain their love and win their confidence. And the children would sooner respect and love . . . [their] authority."—FE, pp. 18, 19.

To a large extent the relationship between teacher and student outside the classroom colors and conditions the one inside it. The teacher or school administrator who takes every opportunity—and even creates opportunities—to socialize, recreate, and work with students will have a definite advantage. He will be able to understand them better and enter into their confidence. They in turn will begin to see such an educator as something besides an authority figure. It will prevent many misunderstandings from occurring and will provide more natural means of communication when difficulties do take place. Entering into social relationships with students is one more way of showing our care for them. As such, it opens the channels through which God's love can flow more fully.[14]

One word of caution is appropriate here. Ellen White said of Christ that "He was highly social, yet He possessed a reserve that discouraged any familiarity."—CT, p. 262. The teacher must never abdicate his special role as leader with his students if he wishes to do them good. Teaching is an art, and part of that art is the ability to be able to enter into social relations with students while at the same time maintaining their respect.

The Selection of Teachers

We have noted that the quality of education does not depend upon teaching methods, curriculum, instructional materials, or nice buildings. It is the caliber of the teacher that primarily determines the level of the education that takes place. The success of Christian education, claimed Gaebelein, stands or falls upon the ability of Christian schools to secure "well-trained teachers who are spiritually alive."[15]

The selection of teachers is therefore of crucial importance.

Ellen White has stressed that "in selecting teachers we should use every precaution, knowing that this is as solemn a matter as the selecting of persons for the ministry. Wise men who can discern character should make the selection; for the very best talent that can be secured is needed to educate and mold the minds of the young, and to carry on successfully the many lines of work that will need to be done by the teacher in our church schools."—6T, p. 200; cf. CT, pp. 150, 151. (Italics supplied.)

If there is any place that we should take care, it is in the choice of the teachers with whom we will place our most valuable possession—our children. That is a point at which the school board should not try to save money. It does cost a few dollars to talk to teachers, and the persons they have given as references, on the phone. And it requires even more to pay prospective teachers' expenses to visit the school and meet with the board before being hired. But such precautions, even though they may consume a few hundred dollars, are well worth the expense when we remember the influence those men and women will have over our children. In the long run it is much more expensive to continue their salaries and expenses for an unsatisfying year or two after we (and they) have made the wrong choice than to spend a moderate amount of money at the outset to ensure the best possible selection.

Also it is important to remember that it is just as crucial for the teacher to be satisfied with the school and its board as it is for the board with the teacher. After all, accepting a teaching position is a major commitment in a person's life, and contented teachers produce better results. Following careful hiring procedures will enhance the possibility of everyone's being happy with the situation.

We should seek the very best teachers for our children. No one wants to hire the least-qualified physician, lawyer, or airplane pilot, even if he is "cheaper." Just as we want the best we can get in such fields, so should it be in the selection of the teacher who has so much to do with the future of our children.

If school board members (and parents) are to function intelligently in the selection of teachers, it is important that they read the writings of Ellen White and books on teaching so that they can understand the essential qualifications of the Christian teacher.[16] It would be even more beneficial if school boards had a nonbusiness meeting from time to time to discuss such issues as the criteria for selecting Christian teachers, as found in the guidelines provided by the Bible and Ellen White.

In conclusion, it is not the best method that stands at the heart of education, but the best teacher. At the heart of good teaching we find a caring relationship between students and teachers. The action in Christian education takes place at the point where the teacher meets the student. Without caring relationships here, no method will be very effective, but with such relationships almost any method will tend to reach students, since they know that their teacher (or parent, pastor, et cetera) really has concern for them. The topic of the caring teacher has a close connection to that of redemptive Christian discipline—a subject to which we now turn.

16 The Myth of the Quiet Classroom

The Myth

*I*magine a parent (or school-board member) walking down the hall with the school principal. As they pass Mrs. Jones's classroom, they hear some quiet talking, a few light giggles, and some shuffling sounds that indicate movement occurring on a regular basis. Next they come to Mr. Smith's room, and to their surprise, they hear nothing—except the teacher's voice. The room is quiet and still. Mr. Smith seems to be in full control of the situation.

What kind of impression, we might ask, would the parent—and perhaps even the principal—have? Most likely the parent would think that Mr. Smith must be an excellent teacher and a first-rate disciplinarian because of the order and quiet in his classroom. On the other hand, this same parent might be tempted to feel that Mrs. Jones was a mediocre teacher.

Interestingly enough, the opposite could be true. It might be that Mrs. Jones's classroom was a little noisy because things were happening—students were learning to work together, they were moving about the room because it was necessary in the learning experience, and they were giggling because they were enjoying what they were accomplishing. On the other hand, it is possible that Mr. Smith is an authoritarian who is able to generate enough fear in his students to keep them absolutely quiet.

Many people equate quiet classrooms with good discipline, and moderately noisy classrooms with poor discipline. The assumptions are false. In saying this, I am not suggesting that moderately noisy classrooms always have good discipline. It is true, however, that discipline has a better chance of developing in a schoolroom not dominated by an authority figure.

Perhaps the better test of good discipline is not how quiet and orderly it is when the teacher is in the room, but what happens when he leaves the room for an indefinite period of time. Under such circumstances, some very quiet classrooms that the presence of an authority figure has held under restraint become very disorderly, while some moderately active classrooms do not change much in the absence of the teacher because the students have been learning to control themselves in the teacher's presence.

In short, a quiet classroom when the teacher is present is not an indication of good discipline. In some cases the very worst type of discipline may be occurring.

On this point, Ellen White has written that "the parent or teacher who . . . trains the child to self-control will be the most useful and permanently successful. To the *superficial observer* his work may not appear to the best advantage; it may not be valued so highly as that of the one who holds the mind and will of the child under absolute authority; but *after years will show the result of the better method of training.*"—Ed, p. 289. (Italics supplied.) Again, she wrote that "teachers who are gratified that they have almost *complete control* of the wills of their scholars, *are not the most successful teachers, although the appearance for the time being may be flattering.*"—FE, p. 18. (Italics supplied.)

We cannot fully evaluate successful discipline in the present. The ultimate test is not how young people act when in the presence of authority figures, since in a few short years they will be beyond the reach of parents and teachers. As Erich Fromm has noted: "The mature person has come to the point where he is his own mother and his own father."[1] Short-term results do not interest the Christian. His real concern is with long-range effects. "After years" will show the results of disciplinary procedures. The aim of Christian discipline is not so much to produce immediate control as it is to develop Christian people who have mastery over their own lives.

The Better Way

At this point it is important to recognize that punishment and discipline are not the same thing. Punishment takes place only after discipline has failed. An authority figure imposes it because a child has not disciplined himself.[2]

Discipline is not something we do to a child, but something we help a child learn to do for himself. One of the most important tasks of adolescence is achieving independence. With this in mind, the words of Mrs. White take on fuller meaning. "The object of discipline," she asserted, "is the training of the child for *self-government.* He should be taught self-reliance and *self-control.* Therefore as soon as he is capable of understanding, his reason should be enlisted on the side of obedience."—Ed, p. 287. (Italics supplied.) John Dewey, America's foremost educational philosopher, amplified the meaning of this concept of discipline. "A person who is trained to consider his actions, to undertake them deliberately, is . . . disciplined. Add to this ability a power to endure in an intelligently chosen course in the face of distraction, confusion, and difficulty, and you have the essence of discipline. Discipline means power at command; mastery of the resources available for carrying through the action undertaken. To know what one is to do and to move to do it promptly and by the use of the requisite means is to be disciplined." [3]

The disciplined person is one who has charge over his life and actions. Others do not have to control him. Ideal Christian discipline is therefore *internal* rather than external. In its mature form it is something we do for ourselves rather than something imposed on us. Discipline as self-control is the Biblical ideal. Solomon has written that "he who rules his spirit" is better "than he who takes a city" (Prov. 16:32). One of the greatest and most important forms of human power is self-control. Christian education must strive toward this end—so that each student will have had opportunities to develop it by the time he leaves his home and school and achieves adult independence.

Discipline as self-control has its roots deep in the Christian concepts of character development, responsibility, and persever-ance. We noted in chapter 4 that character development is one of the major aims of Christian education. Character development and discipline are inextricably entwined. "Strength of character," wrote Ellen White, "consists of two things—power of will and power of self-control."—CT, p. 222. "The will," furthermore, "is the governing power in the nature of man, the power of decision, or choice."—Ed, p. 289. Part of the function of Christian discipline in the home and school is to guide and mold the power of the will as students move toward maturity.

Internal discipline concentrates on developing the child's will through allowing him to make choices and to undergo their results. It is the method we find the father, who realized that love can never be successfully forced upon another moral agent, using with the prodigal son (Luke 15:11-32). Arthur Combs pointed out that "responsibility is learned from *being given* responsibility; it is never learned from having it withheld. . . . Learning to be responsible requires being allowed to make decisions, to observe results, and to deal with the consequences of those decisions. A curriculum designed to teach responsibility needs to provide continuous opportunities for students to engage in such processes. To do so, however, requires taking risks, a terribly frightening prospect for many teachers and administrators."[4]

Even the very problem of allowing others to make mistakes arises from the nature of God and His love. After all, He created a universe in which mistakes are possible when He could have established a foolproof one—but only at the price of creating humans as something less than beings in His image. Beings without genuine choices are automatons rather than free moral agents. God created men and angels in such a way as to make character development a definite possibility. It is important to remember that if individuals do not have the option of making wrong choices, neither do they have the ability to make correct ones. People cannot develop character if they are constantly controlled through being given only one possibility. They are then, in essence, merely complex machines rather than moral agents created in God's image. Love and freedom are risky and dangerous, but they are the way God has chosen to run His universe. These principles are therefore implicit in Christian education.

Christian discipline must therefore take human nature into full recognition. Christian teachers see every student as a person created in God's image. The children under their care must not be just so many objects to control and manipulate. God has purchased each at infinite cost, and He ever seeks to restore His image within them. Parents and teachers have the privilege of being His helpers.[5]

Human beings are "endowed with a power akin to that of the Creator" in that they can reason from cause to effect and act upon their decisions (Ed, p. 17). Through it they develop both will and character. And Christian discipline is a major agent in the process. Animals do not have the same potential for development that humans have. With this in view, Ellen White has written that "the discipline of a human being who has reached the years of intelligence should differ from the training of a dumb animal."—Ed, p. 288. We teach beasts mindless submission—a method that, if employed in the training of children, "makes them little more than automatons. Mind, will, conscience, are under the control of another. It is not God's purpose that any mind should be thus dominated.... While under authority, the children may appear like well-drilled soldiers; but when the control ceases, the character will be found to lack strength and steadfastness."—Ibid. Young people who have never learned to govern themselves do not know how to use their liberty when freed from the restraining influence of parents and teachers (ibid.; cf. FE, pp. 18, 58).

The problem with external discipline is that it breaks down in the absence of the enforcing agency. In a Christian framework the answer to a lack of discipline is not bigger and better "guns" to bring young people under control, but conscious development and application of techniques to build self-control in each child. We gain nothing if by authoritative methodologies we manage to produce quiet, order, and student conformity at the price of intelligent behavior, responsibility, and creativity. Solomon wrote that "a man without self-control is like a city broken into and left without walls" (Prov. 25:28). Internalized control is the ideal at which we must aim.

A Developmental Model of Discipline

One of the goals of Christian education is to enable students to think reflectively for themselves rather than just to respond to the word of an authority figure. It must bring individuals to the place where they can make their own decisions and be responsible for them without others continually coaxing, threatening, directing, and/or forcing them. When he has achieved this goal, and internalized the power to think and act upon that thought, the individual has reached moral maturity. He is both willing and able to direct his own life. But how, might we ask, do we best accomplish this?

One possible model that we can use to illustrate the progressive internalization of discipline appears in Figure 6.[6] It illustrates in a general way the relationship between internal and external control and the weaning process that is the goal of redemptive discipline.

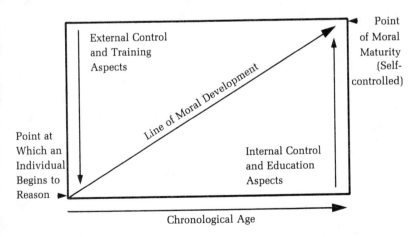

Figure 6. A Developmental Model of Discipline

Infants and extremely young children need a great deal of external control, but the process of individual maturation should lead progressively to more and more self-control and less and less external control, until the individual has reached the point of moral maturity. At that time he is ready to take his place as a responsible person in the adult world. Christian discipline, therefore, is both a positive and a liberating power. It "is *not*," wrote A. S. De Jong, "to keep the child *down* or *to break* him, but to *lift* him *up* or to *heal* him; for that reason discipline may be called upon *to repress only* in order *to set free*, to train children in the exercise of the *freedom* of the children of God." [7] The end product of Christian discipline will be young people who "do right because they believe it is right and not because some authority tells them to." [8]

As we might imagine, the developmental model of discipline is not easy for either parents or teachers to implement. Part of the problem is that levels of moral development and the ability to make responsible decisions do not always correlate with chronological age. A teacher will therefore have to deal with students at several different points on the line of moral development in the same classroom. We should also note that the line of moral development in reality is not straight—it has ups and downs that vary with the individual, the immediate circumstances in his environment, and the skill and dedication of the significant adults in his life. Ellen White recognized the complexity of the task when she wrote that "to develop the minds and hearts of the youth, and not hinder their growth by an unwarranted control of one mind over another, requires tact and understanding."—CT, p. 180. The application of correct discipline is the "most delicate work ever entrusted to mortals" (*ibid.*, p. 264; cf. Ed, p. 292).

Part of the difficulty lies in finding the proper balance between external and internal control that meets the needs of each child. "To direct the child's development," we read in *Education*, "without hindering it by undue control should be the study of both parent and teacher. *Too much management is as bad as too little.*"—Page 288. (Italics supplied.) We face, therefore, two possible errors: (1) releasing to the child decisions for which he is not ready, and (2) withholding from him those decision-making opportunities for which he is ready. [9] The first error creates confusion, while the second leads to unhealthy dependency and the eventual loss of the capacity to make intelligent decisions. Speaking to the second point, Ellen White referred to children who appear well trained while under immediate supervision but are incapable of thinking, acting, or deciding for themselves when left on their own. "Had they been taught to exercise their own judgment *as fast and as far as practicable,* the evil would have been obviated."—FE, p. 58; cf. pp. 16, 17. (Italics supplied.) The crucial task, therefore, is to avoid both extremes in guiding children and youth at each level of their moral development. It is also important for each young person to meet the trials and challenges at one maturity level successfully before moving on to the problems of the next.

Internal Discipline and Rules

One practical area where we can illustrate character development through the internalization of discipline is in the realm of rules. Psychiatrist William Glasser highlighted their place in education when he claimed that "a school cannot function without an effective administration that develops reasonable rules and enforces them. Students should have a voice in making the rules that apply to them; once rules are established, however, students are expected to follow them."[10] James Dobson, in his best-selling *Dare to Discipline,* emphasized the centrality of rules in both the home and school. He questioned the belief of some progressive educators who claim that an environment that places no obligations on its children maximizes self-control. "How foolish," asserted Dobson, "is the assumption that self-discipline is a product of self-indulgence."[11] Rules have an important role to play in the internalization of discipline.

One of Mrs. White's most meaningful statements on rules lists five qualifications they should meet. "Rules should be *few* and *well considered,* and once made they should be *enforced.* Every principle involved in them should be so placed before the student that he will be convinced of its *justice.* Thus he will feel a responsibility to see that the rules which he himself *has helped to frame* are obeyed."—CT, p. 153; cf. Ed, p. 290. (Italics supplied.)

The first qualification of effective rules is that they should be few. It is all too easy for parents and teachers to respond with their rule-making authority to every irritating situation. The result is that they soon have a multitude of rules they find themselves obliged to enforce. The rules and their execution in such circumstances tend to become central, while social, spiritual, and physical development fade into the background. Both adults and children find themselves trapped in a legalistic maze that sets them up for a host of unnecessary confrontations that spawn more (and more) rules. Rules should rest on principles rather than irritating situations if they are not to dominate our lives.

A second requirement is that rules should be well considered. Teachers, students, and parents should be able to see the principle that supports each rule. Without any principle, the rule has no justification. Rules should have their basis in responsible, rational thought rather than irrational whim. Students generally don't rebel against well-considered rules.

Well-meaning parents at times attempt to force ill-considered rules upon the school. For example, I remember the January day that I became principal of a metropolitan junior academy back in the age of the miniskirt. One of the first parents who descended upon me "suggested" that no girl in the school should have a dress any shorter than two inches above the knee. Here was a rigid definition of modesty with the implication that it was my responsibility to go around with my ruler and measure the legs of probable offenders. I explained to the "helpful" parent that this was foolish. After all, two inches above the knee is extremely short on a chubby high school girl who is four feet nine inches tall, while it might appear quite long on one five feet eleven inches. When we called our girls together for a discussion on the dress question, the whole group decided that the principles underlying Christian dress were modesty, cleanliness, and neatness. Each young lady received the responsibility of applying the principles. The group decided that any individual who was not able to apply them would be talked to privately and sent home for a change of clothes if necessary. We had a minimum of conflict on the dress question that year.

An important rule for rules, therefore, is that every rule should be well thought out in terms of its underlying principle(s). Students, parents, and teachers should understand the principle(s). After all, our aim is not to teach mindless rule obedience, but responsible relationship to Christian principles.

A third criterion of good rules is that they be enforced. Glasser pointed out that the failure to enforce rules indicates to children and youth that their parents and teachers don't care enough about them to bother.[12] In the same vein Dobson noted that children often challenge us to see if we really do care enough to make the effort to be firm with them for their own good. He suggested that we should identify the rules well in advance, let no doubt exist as to what constitutes acceptable behavior, punish when the youngster "cold-bloodedly" chooses to challenge known boundaries in a defiant manner, and at all times relate to the child in love, affection, kindness, and understanding. Love and punishment are not antithetical—"one is a function of the other." [13]

According to Ellen White, in developing internal discipline through the enforcement of rules the parent or teacher has a threefold role: first, to lead the young person to recognize his weakness and faults; second, to enlist the child's aid in correcting the problem; and third, to point him to the Source of pardon and power (Ed, p. 291). Glasser has treated the first two points. He suggested that the teacher or parent might avoid telling the child what he did wrong. The better way is to ask him what he is doing and if it is achieving the desired results. To do so involves the child in an analysis of his actions and their results. The child must understand for himself what he has done wrong and why it is unacceptable if he is to achieve growth in responsibility. Then Glasser went on to suggest that we give the child responsibility in working out a better plan so that the problem will not recur. "For example, if a child talks continually and interrupts the class, the teacher might, with the child, work out a new seating arrangement in which the child is away from children who excite him so that he loses control. This simple plan carried out in cooperation with the child helps him to be quiet. *The child has the responsibility, he makes the decision from his own evaluation, and thus he learns responsibility—something to which we give lip service but which we do not teach in school.* We teach thoughtless conformity to school rules and call the conforming child 'responsible.' . . . Responsibility is learned only by evaluating the situation and choosing a path that a person thinks will be more helpful to himself and to others." [14] The Christian teacher or parent, of course, can move beyond Glasser's suggestions by leading the young person to Jesus for forgiveness and power.

Externally imposed punishment becomes an issue when a child refuses to honor his commitments to his school or family. But we can use even punishment as an agent of growth toward self-control. Psychologist Luella Cole has suggested that "punishment should always be constructive and conducive to better self-control. Letting pupils suggest and carry out their own punishment is more likely to develop self-control than the assignment of penalties from above." [15] Teaching a youngster that the punishment should fit the nature of the "crime" whenever possible can be a thought-provoking experience. Such punishment, however, should always take place in conjunction with the guidance of a responsible adult.

The fourth mark of a good rule is that it should be just, and that students should be convinced of its justice. Discard or modify unjust rules. Nothing will more likely stir up rebellion in the hearts of youth than to be treated unjustly in the name of justice. In such circumstances the morally responsible action might actually be to rebel—at least it is the course most intelligent adults would pursue in such a situation. Of course, if they did not have the power to rebel, they would merely let their feelings smolder and comply as minimally as possible with the imposed obligations. Educators and parents certainly do not want to encourage this sort of response. Also, we should realize that we need to alter rules when conditions change.

A fifth characteristic of good rules is that children should help to formulate them. Although this point comes last, it is certainly not least in terms of its import for character development. None of us responds positively to dictatorship: Wives do not like husbands to dominate them, workers react more enthusiastically when they have some part in decision-making, and one cause of the American Revolution was rules imposed without representation. Certainly an educational program that hopes to develop young people for self-government should not attempt to make all the important regulations for them until graduation. Phi Delta Kappa's Commission on Discipline noted that student input in developing rules "is as essential to responsible citizenship in a school as it is in a nation; neither can survive for long if enforcement depends solely on outside forces." [16] Having a part in rule-making helps young people see the reasons for rules and their relationship to the principles that undergird them. Furthermore, Mrs. White correctly recognized that when young people have a part in the decision-making process they quite naturally feel more responsible for the maintenance of mutually agreed-upon rules (CT, p. 153).

Discipline in Perspective

In summary, Christian parents and teachers must never forget the redemptive aim of Christian education. Christian discipline must therefore be salvific rather than punitive—it must aim for the responsible development of the individual. Such responsible development is a part of sanctification, or what educators often call character development. In part, this is a development of the will and the power of self-control. Genuine Christian discipline, like genuine Christian living, involves risks, but it is only through allowing for the possibility of failure that we can develop the good. God has chosen to create us as free moral agents. Christian education must aim at the responsible use of our freedom so that we and our children will develop characters that may safely enter into eternity.

The essence of Christian discipline is the development of self-control. It entails the progressive shifting of control from external authorities to the individual in such a way that young people will be able to fully internalize control over their lives by the end of their home and school experience. Part of the arts of teaching and parenting is to be able to grasp this challenge, to realize the needs and abilities of individual children, and to provide an environment in which such growth can take place. God's aim is to put His laws on our hearts and write them in our minds. When such internalization has transpired, He will truly be our God and we shall be His people (Heb. 10:16; Jer. 31:31-33). Redemptive discipline has the same aim. The goal is to make God's ideals and principles the basis of thought and action in each Christian person. A person should not lead an outwardly Christian life because of external force, threats, or fear, but because Christian education has set forth the Christian way of life in such a manner that its participants have come to see it as "'something better'" than what the non-Christian world has to offer (Ed, p. 296). Because of the crucial nature of the task, Frank E. Gaebelein has referred to discipline as the "acid test" of Christian education.[17] Failure has eternal consequences, while success is fraught with infinite potential.

17 The Myth That Big Is Better

Nearly everyone seems to be under the impression that large schools are better than small schools in terms of their academic and social impact on the lives of young people. This, I must admit, was certainly my belief. I had attended six years of public elementary school in a four-story brick "fort" well supplied with everything from play equipment to administrators. My three years of junior high took place with two thousand other adolescents in a school possessing the latest educational technology. And I spent my high school years in a mammoth institution that taught nearly every possible topic to meet the varied needs of its 2,500 inmates.

Ten years after graduation from high school, however, I found myself in a two-teacher "school" in central Texas—a "school" with a student body of twenty-four—a "school" that operated in two Sabbath-school rooms in the rear of a small church—a "school" with hardly any recreational equipment, teaching helps, or much of anything else. I was totally unprepared, either psychologically or professionally, for the challenge that I faced. (The fact that I had never studied to be a teacher in any kind of a school certainly didn't help.) But I had been hired to teach four grade levels at the same time in the same room. To say the least, the task was mind-boggling.

The situation I faced is not strange to Seventh-day Adventists. During the 1978-1979 school year, 420 of the 1,118 elementary schools in the North American Division were one-teacher institutions. In addition, 292 were two-teacher schools, while 124 had three teachers. Multigrade schools with at least three grades per room are the most common type of elementary school in Adventist education. This has been the case ever since the Adventist elementary school system began in the late 1800s.

As she did so many other things in the church, Ellen White stimulated the Adventist school movement. In Australia, Adventists faced the problem of compulsory education. In such circumstances, she wrote, "schools should be established" by local churches "if there are no more than six children to attend. Work as if you were working for your life to save the children from being drowned in the polluting, corrupting influences of the world."— 6T, p. 199.[1] Adventists in America and other places took her counsel seriously and created hundreds of small elementary schools within a decade. Her urging that families should not move to localities where the church had a large school furthered the small school movement. Rather, each local church should establish its own school (ibid., p. 198). Such admonitions provided the stimulus for Adventism's support of small local church schools. They also guaranteed that small schools would be with the church until the Second Advent, since the denomination is continually entering new territory where it will establish schools that will, in turn, contribute to the vitality, health, and growth of the local congregation.

Most Seventh-day Adventist parents have no real choice except to send their children to small schools if they want them taught from a Christian-Adventist perspective. In such a context, the myth that big is better takes on frightful implications—after all, no parents want to shortchange their children in so vital a thing as formal education. Many parents fear that the "problems" associated with Adventist schools (e.g., small size, multigrade classrooms, low budgets, poor facilities, and so on) will result in an inferior education. These problems, when added to the high cost of Christian education, make them wonder if they shouldn't send their children to the convenient, well-equipped, and free public school.

Parents and church members who finance Adventist education have a right to ask meaningful questions about small schools. Can such schools do the job? Do they prepare children either academically or socially to meet the challenges of modern life?

Before attempting an answer, we should recognize that the issues are many-faceted. On the one hand is the fact that "small" has different connotations for secondary schools than for elementary schools. A small high school, for example, might have an enrollment that would be considered large for an elementary school. On the other hand, even though Adventists might talk about their schools with single-grade classrooms as being large, all Adventist schools are small when compared to the public system. Another factor that we need to understand at the outset is that the most obvious characteristic of the small elementary school is the multigrade classroom. Therefore, this chapter will treat evidence gathered from studies of multigrade classrooms as relevant to the possibilities and problems of small schools.

My remarks will generally be aimed at the small elementary school, but many of the ideas also apply to small academies. A special section, however, will briefly treat the small high school. The thesis of this chapter is that big is not necessarily better—in many cases it is worse. Of course, I am not seeking to demonstrate that small is always better. Both large and small schools have their advantages and disadvantages. But my point is that small schools have the potential to do at least as good an educational job as large schools. A study group sponsored by the North Central Association of Colleges and Secondary Schools has suggested that "the size of a school is not necessarily the determining factor for quality. *There are good large schools and good small schools. The reverse is also true. The quality of the educational program is usually determined by how well a school capitalizes on its strengths and on how well it overcomes its weaknesses.*"[2] This chapter will focus on the advantages of small multigrade schools and some of the ways they can capitalize on their advantages.

Multigrade Schools and Academic Achievement

It is encouraging to realize that schools with multigrade classrooms are not inferior to those with single-grade classrooms in terms of academic achievement. Parents concerned with the ability of a small multigrade school to provide the basic skills (mathematics, reading, and language) needed for subsequent education at all levels will find this fact especially important. One of the most publicized research projects bearing on the topic was the three-year study of multigrade classrooms in the Torrance, California, public schools in the 1950s. J. H. Hull reported that multigrade teaching increased both the spread and speed of learning. He concluded that "in the three skill subjects scored in this experiment—reading, arithmetic, and language—multigrade learning clearly exceeds single-grade learning experiences insofar as can be measured by the standardized test procedures available." In response to the three-year experiment, the Torrance parents requested more multigrade classrooms.[3]

E. Stanley Chace, a Seventh-day Adventist researcher, suggested in the early sixties that perhaps some of the significant gains in achievement in the Torrance study had resulted from experimental effects—the teachers and students performed better because they knew they were in an experimental program and were thus stimulated to do better. Chace sought to control for such bias by using small Adventist schools in which multigrade grouping was not new and exciting. While he found consistently better academic achievement in all areas among students in multigrade classrooms, the difference was not as phenomenal as in the Torrance study. He concluded that "while the data in this particular study do not support the contention that multiple-grade grouping is significantly superior to single-grade grouping, they do support the fact that it is at least equal." [4]

Jerome Thayer studied the test results from the Adventist elementary schools in the Atlantic Union Conference from 1974 through 1978 and came to several conclusions. First, the average achievement level of the nearly eight thousand students tested in the union's elementary schools (all small by public standards) was one month ahead of the national average. These results do not come from superior ability, since the study controlled for that factor. Second, he found only small differences between children from one- and two-teacher Adventist schools and those from larger schools. The differences, surprisingly enough, were most often in favor of the smaller schools. Third, Thayer discovered that the more years students had been in Adventist schools, the higher their achievement levels were. Conversely, the more years enrolled in non-Adventist schools, the lower the achievement. [5]

In a five-year study reported in 1981, Dennis Milburn found little variation between students in multigrade classrooms and those in single-grade classrooms in the development of basic skills, except in the area of vocabulary. Here students in multigrade classrooms were significantly more advanced. He suggested that it might be because teachers in such classrooms tend to speak on a level geared to the comprehension of the older students and thereby boost the vocabulary maturity of the younger students. Also he discovered that the younger children especially benefited from multigrade classrooms. They scored higher on the basic skills than did their age-mates in traditional schools, whereas the older children performed about the same as their counterparts. [6]

Bonny E. Ford, after surveying the major research in multiage groupings in elementary schools between 1961 and 1976, concluded that "most studies find that children in multiage groups show no greater gains in [cognitive] achievement than children" in single-grade groupings. [7] At first glance this conclusion may not look like a plus for small schools, but it should be good news to parents who fear that small, multigrade schools are not up to par in academic achievement. After all, the significant point is that children in multigrade groupings—the mark of small Adventist schools—do at least as well academically as those in larger schools with a single grade per classroom. It is encouraging news to parents concerned with the issue.

Advantages of Small Schools

Advocates have claimed many advantages for small schools. Perhaps one of the most important is flexibility, since it contributes to several other potential advantages. Teachers in small schools largely escape red tape and administrative pettiness. This enables them to implement improved ideas with a minimum of delay. Also it allows teachers to meet the unique needs of their classes, as well as those of individual students, in the most natural manner, since it requires the coordination of the efforts of a smaller number of persons. For example, field trips and use of the playground or a piece of school equipment can fit into the actual flow of the learning experience, rather than having to be adjusted to the plans and needs of several other classrooms.

Closely related to the small school's flexibility are its opportunities for individualization. Since the teacher has fewer students (the average number of students in one-room Adventist schools in the North American Division was twelve in the late 1970s), he has more time for each one. The lower pupil-teacher ratio allows for more careful assessment of the needs, strengths, and weaknesses of each student. The teacher has a better opportunity to see each as a person having unique problems, rather than as just one of thirty-two fourth-graders all working on the same lesson. The possibility for individualization is especially advantageous in classrooms where the teacher has only three or four (or less) at each grade level.

In my own experience as a multigrade teacher, I often found a seventh- or eighth-grade student who was helped more by the fifth-grade math lesson than by his own, while some of the fifth-graders benefited more from the discussion of eighth-grade social studies than they did from doing their graded lesson. Each student had needs and interests often not linked to the graded materials. In a multigrade classroom a teacher has the possibility of allowing a child to read with students in higher grades, while, for example, the same child does math with the lower grades. One can more easily gear the work to individual needs. Along this line, Milburn found that "multi-age grouping . . . enables youngsters to work at different developmental levels without obvious remediation or 'going back'—a situation that can cause emotional, social, or intellectual damage—and without special arrangements for acceleration. Curricular content can be matched to individual abilities."[8] Ellen White indirectly touched upon this point when she wrote that "the system of confining children rigidly to grades is not wise," since it does not account for individual needs (CT, p. 177).

Another advantage in a school with three or fewer teachers is that it exposes the students to a wider range of experiences. John I. Goodlad, former dean of UCLA's School of Education, has noted that one of the difficulties of single-grade classrooms is that they cause "each group to lose some of its perspective on human experience by narrowing the social atmosphere within which the children live."[9] A classroom having children of several ages enables students to gain a perspective on what is happening in the lives and education of children both younger and older—it helps them gain a more accurate sense of the past and future in terms of the significance of their own development. Such a wider range of experiences and interests stimulates the entire learning environment.

A fourth advantage of multigrade classrooms is that children generally have more opportunity to help one another than in single-grade classrooms. With several age levels in the same room, it is only natural that the older children should at times assist the younger. At the same time, the teacher, who has several levels of students to instruct, will more likely foster such an arrangement. Such peer teaching aids the slower and younger children in ways often beyond the communicative ability of adults, since adults have generally forgotten the problems they had in learning a particular concept or skill in the remote past. By way of contrast, the older student has recently passed through the same learning process and can often explain a difficulty in a way that makes sense to a younger classmate. Not only does such an interchange aid the younger student, but there is evidence that the older children learn even more than their tutees. Alan Gartner and his colleagues found that the older students (tutors) were " 'turned on' " by becoming helping teachers. This stimulated their own interest in the learning process. As a result, they made "striking gains" in achievement. The conclusion was that *"children learn more from teaching other children,"* and, therefore, "every child should be given the opportunity to play the teaching role." In their review of studies on the topic, Gartner and his associates found that in situations where adult teachers assigned sixth-graders with reading difficulties to tutor fourth-graders with reading problems, both groups made more than average progress, with the sixth-graders being the chief beneficiaries.[10]

Peer tutoring is a natural tool for the multigrade classroom.

Furthermore, it is a part of the divine instructional plan. "Co-operation," wrote Ellen White, "should be the spirit of the schoolroom, the law of its life. The teacher who gains the co-operation of his pupils secures an invaluable aid in maintaining order. In service to the schoolroom many a boy whose restlessness leads to disorder and insubordination would find an outlet for his superfluous energy. Let the older assist the younger, the strong the weak, and, so far as possible, let each be called upon to do something in which he excels. This will encourage self-respect and a desire to be useful."—Ed, pp. 285, 286. She reinforced the benefits of the plan when she wrote that "one whose mind is apparently stolid will catch ideas more quickly from a fellow student than from a teacher."—7T, pp. 275, 276; cf. CT, pp. 552, 553. Both the tutor and the tutee learn from the experience. Given these facts, why not provide opportunities for older students with spare time to help drill younger or slower students with flash cards or in some other way? After all, if a sixth-grader doesn't know his multiplication tables, in what better way could he learn them than by helping a third-grader? The small multigrade classroom facilitates peer tutoring.

Closely related to peer tutoring are the opportunities small schools offer students for developing independent work habits, assuming responsibility for their own activities, and leading out in school activities. With fewer children, the opportunities multiply. Research has found that members of small schools (and small churches) report greater feelings of responsibility and involvement, and they commit more of themselves to their institutions.[11] Such situations certainly have the potential for developing character and Christian commitment.

Another advantage of small multigrade schools is that they provide a family atmosphere. Mrs. White has suggested that Adventist schools should be "family schools, where every student will receive special help from his teachers as the members of the family should receive help in the home" (6T, p. 152). Interestingly, the research literature often refers to multigrade classrooms as "family-grouped classrooms." Small multigrade classrooms facilitate the creation of a family environment, especially since nearly all of them have several sets of siblings in them.

The fact that children have the same teacher for more than one year also heightens the family effect, since the teacher gets to know the children quite well. Such closeness, ideally, leads to a climate of freedom and confidence. The children, meanwhile, gain the benefit of not having to go through the traumatic adjustment to a new teacher every year. Both teacher and children have opportunities for in-depth relationships on an ongoing basis afforded to few people in modern society. One of the most rewarding experiences in my varied professional life was teaching in a small multigrade school for two years. Nearly all of my students were with me for the entire time. It opened up opportunities for intensive personal ministry to individuals that I have not found in pastoral work, teaching in a larger school, serving as a school principal, or working in a university. Such personal relationships can be important stimuli in the academic, social, and spiritual development of both students and teacher.

Intimately related to the familylike advantages of the multi-grade classroom is the relationship the teacher can have with the children's parents. Generally he gets to know them better, since fewer families are represented in the classroom and both teachers and parents probably attend the same church, facilitating parent-teacher cooperation. Parent-teacher conferences generally don't need to be planned, since they "just happen" in the frequent contact that parents and teachers have with each other. Normally, therefore, we will find more opportunities for cooperation between home and school in a small school than in a larger one.

Another advantage of a small, closely related school is that community cooperation is often much better. Parents have more opportunities to become involved in school activities. Also, they frequently labor with both teachers and students on projects to improve the school and its grounds. People who work together generally come to understand each other better.

A final area in which the small school has an advantage over the larger is in the social realm. The social dynamics in my little two-teacher school thrilled me. All the students had to play together if they wanted to have a baseball game. It was of great interest to me to participate in school activities in which eighth-graders played ball with fourth-graders and enjoyed it. They were even—with a little encouragement at times—willing to help the younger students. What a contrast between that little school and some of the larger schools I have visited, in which the sixth-graders wouldn't think of playing with the "little kids" in the fifth grade. Goodlad reported that single-grade levels encourage "an unhealthy attitude within each age group toward other age groups, especially those who are younger and . . . have less status." [12] Several studies have found that multigrade classrooms improve personal and social development, improve attitudes toward school, and help students become more cooperative and less competitive.[13]

While it is comforting to realize that all of the advantages do not lie on the side of large schools, it is an ongoing challenge to develop the potential of small schools in a society dominated by large school mentality.

A Word About Teachers in Small Schools

We should realize that the many potential advantages of small schools with multigrade classrooms do not come about automatically. At the center of this complex classroom is the teacher, upon whom so much depends. The teacher stands in an even more crucial position in the small school than in a larger one, because he has influence over the same children for a series of years, makes decisions that he carries out without much input from colleagues, and has immediate contact with the parents and school board without the cushioning effect of administrators. Everything that makes the small multigrade school potentially advantageous is also fraught with difficulties. So very much depends upon the teacher.

One can claim, therefore, that it takes more talent and skill to teach in a one- or two-teacher school than in a larger institution. Ruth Ann Stringer hit on a major point when she recognized that "it is a mistake to send beginning teachers out to the one-teacher schools and then when they have learned how to teach to 'promote' them to larger schools. Of course they do well to have had that experience[,] but, actually, better qualifications are needed to become a successful teacher in a one room school." [14] It would make more sense to reverse our present practices and provide internships for beginning teachers in larger schools, where they have supervision and fellowship, and then "promote" the most successful of them to small schools. Here we have a special case of the problem of up and down that we discussed earlier. As a church, we could do many things to enhance the position of the teacher in a small school if we treated work there as a reward rather than a punishment. But it appears that we have our system of social incentives backwards.

It is interesting to note Chace's finding that teachers and administrators with experience in both multigrade and single-grade classrooms were consistently more favorable to multigrade groupings than were those who had taught only in multigrade classrooms.[15] Presumably they saw the freedom, flexibility, and other advantages of the multigrade classroom and could make a comparison, whereas teachers who had served exclusively in a multigrade school could not see the advantages and disadvantages of both sides. His conclusion agrees with my personal experience. I felt quite poorly about my isolated and "lowly" position in a small school until I had become locked into the structure of a larger school with its different type of problems.

Teachers in small schools have more challenges and opportunities for personal growth because they have to face difficulties on their own. The task of organizing the day's instructional work is much more complex for multigrade teachers than for those of a single grade. The constituency of a small school also has a ringside view of its teacher's virtues and faults. In addition, teachers of multigrade schools have administrative, organizational, and public relations tasks that those in charge of a single-grade classroom rarely face.

As a denomination and as local congregations, we would do well to do our best to support and help those who fill these demanding educational positions. We could certainly be more creative in rewarding and encouraging such teachers. All will benefit from quality teaching in small schools—especially parents and their children. If the small school is like a family—and it is—then we need to show the kinds of understanding and caring that make for success in family living to the teachers in such schools. I am quite convinced that if churches took the effort to respect their crucial role in their community, many more teachers would be willing to make a career of teaching in these all-important educational outposts.

A Word About the Small High School

In 1959 James Conant's influential first report on the American high school appeared—a report that bluntly stated that bigger is better. Conant claimed that any high school with a graduating class of less than one hundred students (this probably includes all Adventist schools) could not adequately perform its task, and should therefore be eliminated.[16]

Policymakers and educational leaders are currently reevaluating the "bigger is better" proposition. We have discovered that large high schools contribute to student alienation, provide young people less contact with their friends, make it difficult for them to hold positions of responsibility, and create distance between students and teachers and administrators. In large high schools, furthermore, students participate in fewer activities, become more competitive, and develop a narrower conception of their own worth. In addition, a correlation exists between large schools and the frequency of cheating. Even cost efficiency does not support the concept of the large high school. A study in Minnesota has suggested that secondary schools that graduate between 38 and 175 students per year are the least bureaucratic in atmosphere and the most economical.[17]

By way of contrast to large schools, in a small high school every student knows everyone else, teachers do not become overspecialized, and teachers tend to view young people in a wider context than the classroom. Each student becomes an individual rather than just one of the 150 faces the adult sees every day. Research has revealed that in small high schools teachers and students participate more in each other's lives, and that each individual can more adequately share decision-making and the management of discipline.[18]

James S. Coleman and others on the Panel on Youth of the President's Science Advisory Committee in the early 1970s proposed that the nation should reverse the long-term trend toward large, comprehensive high schools. They recommended much smaller schools in which students could play a more active part in school life and interact with teachers and administrators in more informal ways. As they saw it: "Youth in large schools are more often passive spectators of action, less often participants, more often followers, less often in leadership roles than youth in small schools." The crux of the solution, they indicated, lies in better relationships rather than in more expertise on the part of the faculty. It is true, they admitted, that many of the benefits of small schools are "intangibles" difficult to measure (such as quality relationships, better motivation, and involvement in common goals), but they are crucial elements in educational success.[19] Certainly the benefits attributed to small high schools are in line with the aims of Adventist education.

Some Concluding Remarks

In this chapter I have not claimed that small schools have all the advantages. They have some real disadvantages that we must take into consideration, but so do large schools. As the North Central Association study commission noted, it is not school size that matters as much as what each school is doing to maximize its strengths and minimize its weaknesses.

It is patently false that bigger is better, but it is not necessarily true that small is good. Size is one issue, quality another. The problem with many small schools is that they have tried to copy the ways of large schools. As a result, they have come out inferior. Small schools need different organizational, instructional, and curricular patterns than large ones. They must seek to be good small schools rather than mediocre large institutions. Because of their size, they need to develop patterns of operating that realize their potential. It means a different mind-set for teachers, who must learn how to teach several levels of students at the same time rather than acting as if they could teach four or five different grades independently, as they would if they were teaching each as a single grade in a single-grade classroom. Also, it calls for them to consciously provide opportunities for peer tutoring, independent study projects, and so forth. Chace concluded that "as long as single-grade standards and patterns of operation are duplicated in the multiple-grade class, personnel will be reluctant to work in the multiple-grade situation, and the results of multiple-grade grouping will be little different from those already achieved in single-grade grouping." [20]

It is encouraging to realize that the General Conference Department of Education and the denomination's colleges have taken distinct efforts to train teachers for the unique challenges of small elementary schools. Our next step, perhaps, should be to work on consciously restructuring Adventist secondary schools on an alternative model from Conant's concept of the comprehensive high school, so that Adventist academies can better capitalize on the instructional, organizational, and economic possibilities inherent in the small high school. [21]

An additional item on the agenda of improving the quality of Adventist education is to realize the need for all of us—professional educators and laity—to grasp intellectually the potential of the small schools so that we can actualize that potential more effectively. The North Central Association study commission on small schools pointed out that "the attitude too often permeates the total school—administration, teachers, pupils and patrons—that because the school is small that it cannot be good. Unless this defeatist attitude is changed, the school will probably continue to offer inferior educational experiences." [22]

As Christian Adventists, we can be thankful that big is not better. We have the blessing of having small schools—and it is a blessing because the aims of Christian education can be best achieved in a small school, where caring relationships are easier to form than in large impersonal "institutions." E. F. Schumacher wrote a delightful book entitled *Small Is Beautiful: Economics as if People Mattered*. I have often thought of writing a book called *Small Is Beautiful: Education as if People Mattered*. Quality smallness can be a blessing in disguise.

18 Recreational Myths

*T*he well-known Christian writer C. S. Lewis tells the story of the schoolboy who was asked what he thought God was like. He replied that, as far as he could make out, "God was 'the sort of person who is always snooping round to see if anyone is enjoying himself and then trying to stop it.' "[1] Unfortunately, many young people (and adults) have similar concepts of God's attitude toward recreation. To the contrary, however, Ellen White tells us that God "would have us enjoy everything that will ennoble, expand, and elevate our characters" (FE, p. 234). He is concerned with our growth and happiness rather than with arbitrary restrictions that separate us from the good things in life.

Recreation is an important aspect of life in a world in which people have more and more leisure time but must also learn to cope with greater and greater stress in a social order characterized by ever-increasing complexity. More than a hundred years ago Ellen White wrote that "recreation is needful to those who are engaged in physical labor and is still more essential for those whose labor is principally mental. It is not essential to our salvation, nor for the glory of God, to keep the mind laboring constantly and excessively, even upon religious themes."—1T, p. 514.

Seventh-day Adventists have long been aware of the delicate balance between the mental, physical, and spiritual components of human nature. In both our churches and our schools we have taught that "the health should be as faithfully guarded as the character" (Ed, p. 195), because what affects one part of a person affects the whole. Recreation is one of the gifts of God to help us maintain balance and guard both our health and character. It is therefore important to understand the nature of true recreation in terms of God's overall plan for the restoration of His image in mankind.

As we move into this topic each reader should recognize that most of us have strong feelings concerning recreation. They may be a result of the widespread belief that recreational activities are our personal business—that periods of recreation are times when we can escape from the issues of life. But this is a false conception. Recreation is not "time out" from the rigors of responsible Christian living—rather, it is a crucial aspect of stewardship to our Creator. It is important, therefore, for every Christian to think through recreational issues and develop a well-considered recreational philosophy within the context of God's plan for Christian living. At times it may be necessary to challenge our accepted recreational views and some of our favorite pastimes. This chapter will challenge some of these, but it also seeks to lay the foundation for a philosophy of recreation within a Christian framework. The important thing is not that every reader agrees with every idea set forth here, but that he or she has thought through the issues and makes decisions within the framework of Christian principles.

Myths About Recreation

One recreational myth centers upon the thought that recreation is an escape from reality and useful activity. A conceptual confusion between recreation and amusement has led to the myth. On this topic we read in *Education* that "there is a distinction between recreation and amusement. Recreation, when true to its name, *re-creation, tends to strengthen and build up.* Calling us aside from our ordinary cares and occupations, *it affords refreshment for mind and body,* and thus enables us to return with new vigor to the earnest work of life. *Amusement,* on the other hand, *is sought for the sake of pleasure and is often carried to excess; it absorbs the energies* that are required for useful work and thus proves a hindrance to life's true success."—Page 207. (Italics supplied.)

Mrs. White's use of the words *recreation* and *amusement* is in accordance with Webster's dictionary, which suggests that to recreate is "to restore, refresh, create anew; . . . to put fresh life into; refresh or restore in body or mind." *Amuse,* on the other hand, is more or less equated with entertainment by the lexicographical fraternity.

"Recreation," claimed Arthur Spalding, "is to be distinguished from mere amusement, though amusement may enter into recreation." When supposedly recreational activities have amusement as their only aim, the activities tend to degenerate into triviality and sometimes into immorality. In such cases, wrote Spalding, amusement becomes opposed to recreation, and re-creation is transformed into "wreck-creation."[2]

True re-creation focuses on the restoration of the mental and physical energies, rather than on just providing a meaningless escape from the business of daily living. Psychoanalyst Erich Fromm, in discussing self-discipline outside the sphere of work, indicated that modern people have a "wish for laziness" because of alienation from their work. Meaningless work leads to "infantile self-indulgence," which, in turn, creates a desire for meaningless amusement. "Man overcomes his unconscious despair by the routine of amusement, the passive consumption of sounds and sights offered by the amusement industry; . . . by the satisfaction of buying ever new things, and soon exchanging them for others." [3]

Philosopher John Dewey hit this same theme when he talked about the externally imposed demands of most modern workplaces. The essentially boring nature of much present-day work "fails to give adequate stimulus to emotion and imagination. So in leisure time, there is an imperious demand for their stimulation by any kind of means; gambling, drink, etc., may be resorted to. Or, in less extreme cases, there is recourse to idle amusement; to anything which passes time with immediate agreeableness." On the other hand, he noted that "recreation" is the "recuperation of energy. No demand of human nature is more urgent or less to be escaped." One of the most important tasks of education, therefore, is to develop the "capacity for seeking and finding" truly recreative activities as opposed to aimless amusement. [4]

Perhaps at this point it is important to note that work and play are not opposed to each other. [5] Work has elements of play in it and vice versa. For example, my son likes to play basketball, but if I require him to play basketball eight hours a day for five days a week, the task transforms from play into work. In a similar vein, we usually define digging in a garden as work, but when I come home after a hard day at the office, I can see it in terms of recreation and play. Both play and work are serious activities for their participants. As long as we have some control over our activities, there are no hard-and-fast lines between the two terms, except in our minds. The problem is that most people in industrial societies have lost control over their work activities.

One unfortunate outgrowth of the false dichotomy between work and play has been the fostering of a "distaste for useful labor, a disposition to shun practical duties and responsibilities," and the destruction of a "relish for life's sober realities and its tranquil enjoyments" (Ed, pp. 210, 211). In general, modern people have developed an extremely powerful drive to escape from the useful and responsible during their leisure hours. During the industrial age it has led to a progressive movement from re-creational activities to aimless spare-time amusement. This trend has been the stimulus and support behind such industries as popular professional entertainment and commercial sports. Not only are they largely escapist but they also set forth a value system often in direct contradiction to Christian principles.

Modern men, women, and children live in a fast-paced world of machines, schedules, turmoil, and tension. They spend much of their day in institutions that all too often have removed the possibility of play from their work, and they have a crucial need for re-creation. Never before have people required such great need of release from nervous tension if they are to live responsible and successful Christian lives. *Christian recreation is not an escape from reality, but an avenue to it.* Our task is to learn to think Christianly about leisure-time activities and the purposes of God for our lives.

A second recreational myth deals with the issue of games and playing ball. Some readers of the Bible and of Ellen White apparently have come to the conclusion that work without play is God's recreational ideal. Some "saints" are turned off by even the joyful shouts of laughing children in their sports. We can be thankful that God does not agree. In Zechariah 8:5 we read of part of God's ideal for Jerusalem: "And the streets of the city shall be full of boys and girls playing." This beautiful picture gives some insight into the Lord's thinking on the topic. In a similar vein, Ellen White has suggested that parents and teachers should take an interest in the sports of their children—even going so far as to unbend their dignity and participate with them in their games (FE, p. 18).

It is not games and sports that Ellen White frowned upon, but their abuse. She wrote, "I do not condemn the simple exercise of playing ball; but this, even in its simplicity, may be overdone."— AH, p. 499. The problem lies not in the doing, but in the overdoing and misdoing of ball playing in terms of both time and the complexity of arrangements that leads to difficulties in personal and interpersonal relationships. She went on to note that all too often the results of ball games lead to inordinate expenditures of money, self-glorification, a love and enthusiasm for games more than Christ, and a "burning passion" for supremacy. In addition, the way games are often played does not strengthen the intellect or character, distracts minds from studies, and tends to make their participants lovers of pleasure more than of God (*ibid.*, pp. 499, 500).

Arthur White, retired secretary of the White Estate, in

commenting on Mrs. White's several statements on ball playing, has stated: "I see very clearly a distinct difference between a day of recreation at which certain games may be played, and the development of well-trained teams in our academies and colleges to engage in a sports program. When a group of Christian young people, or the members of a church or an institutional family, gather for a day of recreation, they may play certain games. There is no long training period and no large outlay of means. A few hours are spent together, the games are over, and the day has been one of recreation. How different this is from a program where the young people may be called upon to spend hours in training day after day, where there are certain players who are glorified, and in the development of teams excitement runs high, competition is keen, and a few young people get the exercise while the others stand by and shout. This is not true recreation. The difference is obvious." [6]

A tragedy, however, is that many games have recreational potential that is often not developed. Part of the difficulty stems from the fact that too often we engage in games in order to win rather than to exercise and have a pleasant social experience. The desire to win, as we shall see in our discussion of competition, has a great number of built-in problems.

The compulsion to win and the problems generated by it often override the positive potential inherent in games. On the other hand, few want to play once we remove the drive to win. The negative aspects of competition are deeply rooted in the sinful human heart. Commercial sports have extended them to their logical extremes and serve as a constant illustration of the rationale behind organized sports. For instance, it is hard to imagine a professional, college, or even a high school coach advocating that his players do anything but play hard to win.

Ball games have some positive recreational potential. But it is also true that they are not, in most cases, the best possible form of recreation in terms of Christian development. Implicit in Ellen White's writings is a hierarchy of recreational activities for those with sedentary jobs. (The last section of this chapter will discuss recreation for those whose jobs involve strenuous physical activity.) At the top stands useful work in the open air (Ed, pp. 215, 219; CT, p. 308). Useful work not only gets our blood circulating after mental pursuits but develops character traits such as industry and perseverance, provides us the mental satisfaction of having achieved something worthwhile, and often gives us the spiritual blessing of having made someone else's life a little easier. In addition, work in the outdoors puts us in contact with fresh air and sunlight—two of God's natural remedies (MH, p. 127). As an added blessing, outdoor work can offer the peacefulness of nature, which is restorative in itself (CT, p. 186; FE, pp. 319, 320).

One problem in modern society, however, is that it is often difficult to find worthwhile activities in the open air that get our hearts pumping hard enough to be defined as exercise. Machines do most of our strenuous tasks.

On the other hand, there are some definite possibilities for useful work outdoors. Gardening, for example, can be both strenuous and peaceful. All too often, however, we frustrate its re-creational benefits with our handy Rototillers, which pollute the air with sound and smoke but allow us to rush through the task in time to plop in front of the "tube" for the Sunday football game. Perhaps the solution is to revert back to shovel and hoe. Walking to work is another example of a useful activity in the open air. Why not go on foot the three miles to work instead of taking the car or bus? You might find that the forty-five-minute excursion has not only invigorated you physically but has stimulated your powers of observation and thought. Besides, it's more peaceful, even in the city. With a little imagination, most of us can find useful outdoor activity that is recreational. At least we should try.

Second in the recreational hierarchy is contrived exercise in the outdoors, with indoor exercise coming in third (Ed, p. 210).[7] It is interesting to observe how many people drive their cars to the gym so they can get some exercise. They could, of course, jog, walk, or bike to the gym or health club, but on second thought, after all that exertion they might not need the indoor exercise.

At the bottom of the recreational hierarchy stand spectator sports. Spectator sports, in fact, are not recreational for either participants or onlookers. For the latter they are antirecreational, since they absorb the time and energy that might be given to physical and/or mental exercise, while supplying little of value in return. It is hard to imagine few things more absurd than the spectacle of thousands of men and women who desperately need exercise sitting in bleachers or in front of television sets to watch twenty-two men, who do not need physical exercise, exercise violently. It may pass the time of day, it may entertain in the sense of amusement, but we certainly cannot call it recreation for the spectators. Rather it is an escape from personal recreation and an intermission from reality. For the participants, on the other hand, success too often breeds self-centeredness. It is no accident that Muhammad Ali could write a book entitled *The Greatest: My Own Story*. Stardom and self-centeredness are built into the structure of highly competitive sports, and all too often the spectators merely aggravate the temptations of the participants.

Spectatorism is one of the most serious diseases of modern society. Massive doses of television and spectator sports introduce us to it, and we carry it into our political lives and our relationship to the church. Most of us would rather watch the "other guy do it" than become involved ourselves. Spectatorism is the antithesis of Christian concern and action. In addition, it certainly says something about the values of a human community that will collectively pay millions of dollars to an athlete to amuse them while untold millions of their fellow humans suffer physically, mentally, emotionally, and spiritually because they cannot meet their basic needs.

As Christians, we should never forget that Satan's main aim is to divert us away from the issues of life and from responsible action. In 1899 Ellen White wrote the following passage: "Once in Sydney I saw a great multitude on one of the streets. Hundreds and hundreds, and I might say thousands, were gathered together. 'What is the matter?' I asked. 'It is because of the cricket match' was the answer. And *while men were playing the game of cricket, and others were watching the game, Satan was playing the game of life for their souls.*"[8] In commenting on her statement, Ron Graybill has pointed out that the issues at hand in Christian recreation are more important than the pros and cons of basketball or baseball. "We're talking about a far more important game: the game of life. Our opponent is Satan, and only here may it truly be said, 'Winning isn't everything—it's the only thing.' "[9]

Recreation is not an area of life outside the scope of Christian living. Responsible thought and action regarding it are just as important as they are in any other area of our life. The words of Paul to the Romans are appropriate in our thinking about recreation: "Do not be conformed to this world but be transformed by the renewal of your mind, that you may prove what is the will of God, what is good and acceptable" (Rom. 12:2).

Myths About Competition

Several myths concerning competition touch Christian education and Christian life in general. The first is that we live in a society that is essentially competitive. Consequently, claim the proponents of the myth, young people need competitive experiences in school if they are to be prepared to live in adult society. This is false. We live in the most cooperative and interdependent society the world has ever known. We depend, for example, on countless hundreds of unknown people to produce, market, and deliver our food, clothing, shelter, and other needs. In turn, thousands of people are dependent on us. Modern society is essentially cooperative. Even modern industry—the supposed example of a competitive way of life—turns out on close examination to be an outstanding example of cooperation. Large industry thoroughly relies upon the cooperative activity of thousands and thousands of separate workers at all levels. The very concept of the assembly line is an example of cooperation.

While it is true that modern life does have competitive elements, we should realize that it is the exception rather than the rule. Most of us live for days without vying with another person, but we cooperate with others from morning to night. To prepare a young person for life, even in "secular" society, we would do better to teach the elements and rewards of cooperation rather than competition.

Even, however, if we lived in a fundamentally competitive society, we could never justify highly competitive activities within the framework of Christian truth. At its base, competition rests on strife for the supremacy—to be the first, the best, the most, and so on. Here, we should note, is the very disease that stands at the heart of sin. An emphasis on putting self first and most important brought Satan's downfall (Isa. 14:12-14) and Eve's failure (Gen. 3:1-7), while it provided grist for the disciples' favorite argument—who is the greatest? (Mark 9:34; Luke 9:46; 22:24; Matt. 20:20-28). Paul wrote that the works of the flesh include emulation, strife, and selfishness (Gal. 5:19-21).

The challenge for Christian education is not to promote emulation and competition, but to curb and moderate such attributes. Ellen White stated that "in God's plan there is no place for selfish rivalry. . . . But how widely different is much of the education now given! From the child's earliest years it is an appeal to emulation and rivalry; it fosters selfishness, the root of all evil."—Ed, p. 226. Those, claimed Paul, who measure themselves by themselves, and compare themselves among themselves, are not wise (2 Cor. 10:12). God's ideal is cooperation, not competition. In First Corinthians Paul stresses the point with his delightful and meaningful illustration of the gifts of the Spirit, which are to work in harmony like the parts of the body, rather than competing with each other as to which gift is the most important (1 Cor. 12:12-31). The better Christian way is that love that puts others before self (chaps. 12:31-13:13). The Christian ideal is not to exalt one's self through competition, but to follow Christ, who "emptied himself, taking the form of a servant" (Phil. 2:7).

Erich Fromm, in discussing the needs of modern society, pointed out that the principle underlying a competitive, capitalistic society and the principle of love are "incompatible." [10] George B. Leonard, in a similar vein, has written that "a society that encourages competition and acquisition is almost sure to encourage aggression as well." [11] Both authors, while not speaking from a Christian perspective, have certainly spoken to the Christian community. The goal of the Christian school and the Christian church must be to play down the competitive aspects of life and to uplift the cooperative.

A second myth related to competition is that the only problem area of competition in Adventism is in sports. Again, this is false. Competition in athletics is certainly an important issue, but it is also important to view competition in the light of scholastic and church events. What, for example, is the impact on a young person when he hears warnings against highly competitive sports and then finds banners broadcasting the relative accomplishments of the various Ingathering teams covering one wall of the sanctuary or being displayed in the church foyer? What is the message and impact of highly competitive academic grading? And what is the message and effect of conference-sponsored comparative lists of pastors or colporteurs, indicating their baptismal or sales records for the year? Graybill has even questioned the result of the gold stars on the memory verse chart in the kindergarten Sabbath school. "Does the child," queried Graybill, "learn to love the Scriptures or to love the sight of his name followed by the longest and brightest line of stars?" [12] In short, the area of sports and recreation comprises only one aspect of competition that we need to examine within the framework of Biblical Christianity. It is destructive to the confidence of youth when we focus on the one part of the problem they enjoy the most while overlooking other manifestations of the same issue.

A third myth is that competition is a generally effective motivator. Arthur Combs has pointed out that this myth, like so many others, contains an element of truth. Competition does motivate some people some of the time. But, he noted, "psychologists know three things about competition as motive: (1) *Competition is valuable as a motivator only for those people who believe that they can win;* (2) *People who do not feel that they have a chance of winning are not motivated by competition, they are* discouraged and disillusioned; *and* (3) *When competition becomes too important, morality breaks down and any means becomes* acceptable to achieve desired ends." [13]

George Lehner and Ella Kube, in studying the dynamics of personal adjustment, arrived at similar conclusions. They found that excessive competition among secondary students led slow learners to grow discouraged and fall behind their mates, put average students under constant strain and stress to keep up in their work, caused the brightest pupils to develop exaggerated feelings of superiority, and caused different students in the various achievement subgroups to develop an attitude of "aggressive non-cooperation" toward others in their group in an effort to maintain their relative positions.

On the other hand, Lehner and Kube observed a different set of characteristics in the behavior of students placed in situations that called for cooperation. They learned to work together in goal setting and developing plans for goal achievement, cooperated in working toward the goal, shared alike in success and failure, and became more goal-centered rather than self-centered in the pursuit of their common task.[14]

Moderating the Effects of Competition

While it is true that the results of excessive competition are inconsistent with the aims and purposes of Christian education, it is also true, given the nature of the world in which we live, that competition in human living will not vanish until the second coming of Jesus. Psychologist David P. Ausubel has noted that competition does have some positive effects. It "stimulates individual effort and productivity, promotes higher standards and aspirations, and narrows the gap between capacity and performance." [15] Not surprisingly, socialistic experiments have consistently failed to usher in utopia in a world in which the majority continue to remain self-centered and selfish. Early Christian socialistic policies broke down in the apostolic church (Acts 6:1-6). Even God places before us the glories of His kingdom and suggests that we strive to enter the "strait gate" (John 14:1-3; Luke 13:24, K.J.V.). Note, however, that He has set up His kingdom in such a way that all may enter. His program does not require a large number of losers for some to be winners—all can win.

This point gives us some leads on the uses of competition in a Christian setting. Since humans in their current status are not naturally ambitious, we might employ moderate amounts of competition as a stimulus for movement toward Christian excellence. For example, we could more often utilize competition with one's self rather than with others. Christianity concerns itself with growth rather than maintenance of the status quo. It challenges young people to better their performance across time. All can be winners in competition with themselves, since all have the capability of growth.

Even competition with one's own self, however, must remain in perspective. Francis Schaeffer has rightly remarked that if "my whole life turns upon knocking one second off my time on a downhill race, I am destroyed." [16] The same applies to academic pursuits. Christian growth in the context of Christian living is one thing, while growth as an end in itself provides a false integration point and merely leads one further into the self-centeredness of sin.

Also we should recognize that in the school setting we probably cannot and perhaps should not avoid sports and games in which winning is a factor. The Christian teacher who emphasizes teamwork, sportsmanship, and the social elements of such games rather than "beating" the other team can, however, moderate their influence. Teachers and other recreational leaders can also help young people control their competitive impulses by personally selecting balanced teams whose membership often changes. Few things do more damage to a student's self-image than being consistently chosen last or next-to-last in a sporting event while one's future teammates groan over the misfortune of getting the "dog" on their team. Those in charge can avoid this problem with a little forethought and planning. In like manner, we can moderate the "star" effect on the playing field by teaching young people how to work together for a common goal, and then rewarding cooperative behavior.

Beyond even moderate competition, however, is the ideal of cooperation. Mrs. White has written that "co-operation should be the spirit of the schoolroom, the law of its life," since it helps in developing self-discipline, directs student energy into healthy channels, gives each student a chance to excel, and encourages self-respect (Ed, pp. 285, 286; italics supplied). God's ideal is for us to create environments in work, play, and study that enable every student to be a winner who is continuously stimulated toward further growth in every area of life.

Selected Principles Related to Recreation

The recreational program in Christian education, like every other aspect of Christian living, must be integrated with the Christian worldview. No aspect of Christian life falls outside the scope of the law of love or the reign of Christ in the life. The Christian never comes to the place where he can say, "I have fulfilled my quota of Christianity for the week—now I can relax and be my natural self." Consequently, Christian education integrates the principles of the Bible into every activity so that the result is uplifting, restorative, and re-creative.

General Recreational Principles

The preceding discussion of various recreational myths suggests certain principles that should govern the Christian's choice of such activities. One basic principle underlying Christian recreation is that whatever we do, it should be done to "the glory of God" (1 Cor. 10:31). Paul also wrote that whatever we do in word or deed, we should "do everything in the name of the Lord Jesus, giving thanks to God the Father through him" (Col. 3:17). These admonitions allow everything that is wholesome and rule out only those things that we cannot pursue to the glory of Christ and with thanksgiving to God. Ellen White has observed that helpful recreational activities are those that better fit us for the more successful discharge of our duties, ennoble our influence with our associates, and allow us to return to our homes improved in mind, refreshed in body, and prepared to engage in our work with new hope and courage (CT, p. 336). On the other hand, "any amusement which disqualifies you for secret prayer, for devotion . . . , or for taking part in the prayer meeting, is not safe, but dangerous."—Ibid., p. 337. "Christians," she wrote, "have many sources of happiness at their command, and they may tell with unerring accuracy what pleasures are lawful and right. They may enjoy such recreation as will not dissipate the mind or debase the soul, such as will not disappoint and leave a sad after influence to destroy self-respect or bar the way to usefulness."—Ibid., p. 342.

As with most things in life, room exists for individuality and responsible choice in the area of recreation. We must never forget, however, that each of us is in the midst of the struggle between good and evil, and activities may either be recreative and restorative in their impact upon us or diversionary and destructive. C. S. Lewis highlighted this point when he wrote that "our leisure, even our play, is a matter of serious concern. There is no neutral ground in the universe: every square inch, every split second, is claimed by God and counterclaimed by Satan. . . . It is a serious matter to choose wholesome recreations." [17]

The Christian question is not "Can I do this and still be a Christian?" This stems from an anti-Christian frame of mind that looks for the minimum rather than the maximum in life. Underlying such questions is a legalistic attitude more concerned with immediate pleasure than maximum effect in terms of God's glory and human betterment. The Christian inquiry might be "What is the effect of this activity on Christian character? Will it lead its participants to be more sharing, polite, helpful, and generous to others, or will it cause them to be more self-centered and contentious? Will it produce a better relationship with God, our fellow men, ourselves, and our environment, or result in a deterioration of relationships? Will it contribute to social, mental, physical, and spiritual balance in the re-creative process, or will it make its participants one-sided and overdeveloped in one area?" The Christian is interested in the maximum glorification of God through the human life.

A second principle relating to recreation is the concept of balance between the mental and the physical. The ideal is that we exercise both the mental and physical powers daily for the maximum health of the whole person (e.g., Ed, p. 209). The nature of recreation, therefore, varies with an individual's daily activities. If, for example, a person has a physically taxing job, reading would be recreational. On the other hand, for students and sedentary people, that which is recreative is vigorous physical activity. Unfortunately, few often achieve such a balance. In daily life, for instance, the carpenter likes to go home and work in his shop, while the English teacher prefers to read in the evening. Here is one reason why Ellen White recommended useful work for students— so that each day the whole person, rather than just part, would experience the re-creative process. She claimed that "study [among students] is not the principal cause of breakdown of the mental powers. The main cause is improper diet, irregular meals, a lack of physical exercise, and careless inattention in other respects to the laws of health."—CT, p. 299. Physical-mental balance is God's ideal, because the health of the mind has an intimate relationship to that of the body.

A principle closely related to mental-physical balance is the student's need of "vigorous exercise" (Ed, p. 210). Some interpreters of Ellen White have indicated that useful work should be the only, or at least the major, form of recreation in Adventist schools. This may have been true with nineteenth-century work, but little twentieth-century labor in the developed countries offers vigorous exercise. Most of it is either sedentary or minimally active. It does not generally get the blood circulating sufficiently. We can no longer view work in mechanized agriculture and modern industries as re-creative in the physical sense. Ellen White indicated that changes in circumstances alter "the relation of things" (3SM, p.

217). The role work plays in education in the last quarter of the twentieth century illustrates this point. While work is still educative in the vocational sense, it is no longer recreational in most cases. In fact, much of it is more closely related to mental activity than physical exercise. Therefore, a genuine need exists for physical education departments in Adventist schools. We must now consider the type of physical education that will best meet the needs of students during both their school days and their postschool life.

Criteria for Physical Education Programs

People have a crying need for both recreation and physical fitness for as long as life shall last. If "physical education" in school is to be true to its name, it must satisfy two criteria. First, it must help every student. Graybill has rightly remarked that "the purpose of the physical-education program in an Adventist school is to aid every student's physical development, not to groom a few for excellence. Varsity teams monopolize the time and equipment of a school to the detriment of other students who need physical training." [18] While Adventist schools have shied away from varsity sports, they have at times created their own road to stardom through an overemphasis on gymnastics. Perhaps it is time to reconsider the amount of time, energy, and money devoted to a portion of the student body in many schools, to the detriment of the nonparticipating students. In many cases, gymnastics has become the Adventist equivalent to football, even in its public relations effects. At times, the first question a potential employer asks a prospective PE teacher is whether he can organize a gymnastics team. Sometimes it is the only question, since some employers feel that a good team is a must for public relations and recruitment. Such administrative concerns are necessary, but they have only a tangential relationship to the physical education of every student and may actually hinder the hiring of teachers who have a burden for those who most need physical education—those young people who don't like sports. Despite many of the positive opportunities for Christian witnessing provided by gymnastic tours, it might be proper to question whether a little creative thought might not provide more effective means for witnessing along with more abundant opportunities for the "physical education" of every student—especially those who need the most help. Current programs in both public and Adventist education tend to focus the most energy and means on those who least need physical education.

A second criterion for physical education activities, when we see education as a lifelong process, is an activity's *carryover value.* Carryover deals with that element of physical education that the student can use to enrich his recreational life after graduation. Many team sports that provide physical exercise to students while they are in school have limited value after graduation, since it becomes increasingly more difficult to bring enough friends together for a game on a regular basis. Other activities become impractical after graduation because they demand expensive equipment if one is to do them properly. Many physical education teachers have begun to realize that the subjects they have most often taught in the past have generally had the least carryover value. Even students who enjoy flagball, volleyball, soccer, softball, and gymnastics in school will find it difficult to continue *regular* participation in such activities after graduation. From the perspective of the physical education of the whole person for his entire life, it is gratifying to see many schools moving to programs that emphasize personal activities such as jogging, cycling, swimming, cross-country skiing, tennis, backpacking, and so on. Physical education stressing activities with carryover potential emphasizes physical fitness both during and after school days.

In conclusion, the Christian educator can never forget the fact that recreation is re-creation in the broadest sense of the word. It should aid in developing the character and the mind as well as the body. It seeks to refresh and restore our minds and bodies so that we might be better able to serve our fellow beings and glorify God. Recreation is an integral and important part of Christian living.

19 Manual Labor Myths and Concept of Balance

*P*erhaps the most widely discussed and energetically argued aspect of education among Adventists has been the role of manual labor in the school program. The "practical educators" have seemed at times to suggest that manual labor experience is the most important item in the curriculum, while Adventist "academicians" have often tended to treat it, in practice if not in words, as a necessary evil. As in most arguments, both extremes are in error.

Myths in Favor of Manual Labor

Among the ideas sometimes voiced in Adventist circles is the myth that manual labor combined with study was one of the unique contributions of Adventism to education. Nothing could be further from the truth. Throughout the nineteenth century many reformers put a stress on improving physical health as a basis for mental achievement and on combining work and study in the curriculum. The 1830s witnessed the rise of scores of reform institutions based on "Adventist" principles forty years before any Adventist schools ever existed. An entire society promoted manual labor in literary institutions.[1] This practical emphasis later became reflected in Federal legislation with the passage of the Morrill Act in 1862, which made financial provision for the teaching of the mechanical trades and agriculture in State colleges. Furthermore, in the 1880s the issues of vocational education and manual labor in education became central topics for discussion and reform in American secondary education.[2]

It is important that we forever put to rest the myth that Adventist educational ideals were unique or ahead of the reform ideas of the times. Adventists did not pioneer the expulsion of the Latin and Greek classics from the curriculum—it was a major area of curricular struggle in non-Adventist secondary and higher education throughout the last half of the nineteenth century. Neither were Adventists ahead of evangelical reformers in placing the Bible at the center of the curriculum—evangelical Christians, setting forth the same ideals as Adventists, spearheaded the Bible institute and Bible college movement during the 1880s and 1890s. Likewise, Adventists were not out of step with other reformers in the area of combining work with study. While it is true that they were ahead of the mainline educators of their time, they were not in advance of other reformers. Rather, they were in step with contemporary reformers in battling common educational problems.[3] As such, the Adventist contribution was important, but not unique.

A second myth heard from time to time in Adventist circles is that work-study programs are the educational panacea—especially, note some of its advocates, when every teacher works with students every day. They have extrapolated their position from *Counsels to Parents and Teachers,* which plainly states that "our teachers should not think that their work ends with giving instruction from books. Several hours each day should be devoted to working with the students in some line of manual training. In no case should this be neglected."—Page 211. The interpretive emphasis generally falls on the last sentence. Unfortunately for the myth's proponents, Ellen White emphasized this point only once in her entire corpus of writings, and she made that one mention to the faculty of the Fernando school in California, who had totally missed the reason for their school's existence. The faculty and administration at the Fernando school had been boasting of its curriculum, emphasizing its many languages, its "college" status, and its advanced intellectual program, while neglecting the reason for its existence—sending practical missionaries directly into the field prior to a collegiate education.

A study of the manuscripts concerning the problem of the Fernando school makes it clear that Ellen White had been speaking with both the teachers and the administration concerning their educational role. She specifically noted that Fernando was not a college, that colleges had a different function from intermediate schools, that the institution should delete "flowery notices" of what it intended to do from its bulletin, and that it was to uplift labor and basic educational skills rather than advanced studies.[4]

It is in this concrete context that Mrs. White made her strong statement in *Counsels to Parents and Teachers.* To develop it into a universal mandate and a divine command for every teacher in every school is to go beyond the evidence, to obscure the moderation of other Ellen White statements,[5] and to divorce her writings from the historical context that gives them meaning.

Building educational theory on isolated statements removed from their historical context is the problem involved in the "blueprint myth" discussed in the first chapter of this book. There I pointed out that Mrs. White had to combat such misuse of her writings even during her own lifetime. Interestingly enough, she wrote to the educators at Fernando that "it would be a sad mistake for us to fail to consider thoroughly the *purpose* for which each of our schools is established." [6] This is exactly what the faculty of the Fernando school had not done when they sought to act as if they were running a college.

A work-study program with every teacher laboring daily with students may not be a panacea or the "perfect answer for the community of Christ," [7] yet it is an excellent way to build relationships wherever we can practically carry it out. While Mrs. White's remark that "in no case should this be neglected" was aimed at a specific school with a specific mission, she repeatedly emphasized that it is a rewarding experience for teachers and students to work together (FE, p. 325; CT, pp. 203, 208; 6T, p. 179; Ed, pp. 212, 219). This concept is one of many helpful ideas that she put forth to facilitate Christian education. A one-to-one teacher-student relationship in outdoor work is certainly a desirable state of affairs, but we should not view it as the ultimate educational accomplishment. Rather, it is one of many avenues available to maximize our educational effectiveness.

A third myth related to manual labor is that work combined with study is the *most* important element in Ellen White's educational philosophy. (No one, of course, really believes this, but some Adventist reformers have talked and acted as though they did.) Undoubtedly the myth finds its roots in Mrs. White's first major statement on education, "Proper Education" (FE, pp. 15-46), and in the emphasis that she put on work during the nineties in the counsel given during the establishment of the Avondale school.

A casual reading of Ellen White's educational writings separated from their historical context might create the impression that a work-study combination was indeed the most important thrust in her educational message. "Proper Education" (1872), for example, can be broken down into three parts. The first, roughly four and one-half pages long, concerns the importance of education, training, and discipline as self-control. The second section is the big one; it deals with physical health and manual labor and gets the mammoth share of the treatment—twenty-four of the thirty pages. Meanwhile, the third segment, only one and one-half pages long, discusses the teaching of the Bible and the "common branches" for those preparing for the ministry. Missing totally are any statements concerning the study of the Bible as the great agent for developing mental power and any condemnation of the pagan classics or infidel authors. These missing points would become major emphases in her later educational writings.

The question that naturally arises is Why the unbalanced emphasis on the physical and practical work in education in this important document that she wrote to give guidance in the founding of the first Adventist school? I would like to set forth two hypotheses that I have previously discussed more fully within their historical context.[8] First, the need for manual labor in a literary institution was a point of almost total blindness among the men who established Battle Creek College. Mrs. White, who was advocating a balanced education of the physical, mental, moral, and religious powers of each student (FE, p. 15), needed to emphasize it. Second, there seemed to be no problem with the founders' understanding of a school that had a Biblically based curriculum. The church leaders had regularly written in the *Review and Herald* of their desire to establish a college that would teach the Bible.[9] Ellen White, therefore, quite naturally addressed the needs of the founders. It was apparently incomprehensible, after all that the leadership had said about the Bible in education, that the denomination's first school would neglect the Bible while giving the pagan classics the place of honor.

In terms of historical fact, neither the Bible nor manual labor found its rightful place in Adventist education during the 1870s. Problems at Battle Creek led Mrs. White in 1881 to pen a crucial statement, "Our College" (5T, pp. 21-36), which spoke to Battle Creek's curricular problems. In her article, which was read before church leaders there, she went so far as to suggest the selling of the school and the building of another upon the plan specified by God if they could not bring the college in Battle Creek in line with its philosophy. It is of interest to note that in this important message she repeatedly stressed the central place of the Bible in education, while devoting only one paragraph to manual labor. The amount of space given to the Bible and the manual labor aspects of education in "Our College" had just the opposite proportion to that found in "Proper Education." Once again, we might ask Why? The answer seems to be that what was incomprehensible in 1872 had actually come to pass—Adventist education had largely ignored the primacy of the Bible. It is true that the practical, physical, work-study program had also suffered neglect, but that problem paled into relative insignificance in her eyes in 1881 next to the neglect of the Bible.

Her major emphasis from 1881 up through the early nineties was the placing of the Bible at the center of the curriculum. During 1891 she would also begin to emphasize dropping the Greek and Latin classics. By 1894 both objectives were on their way to being accomplished. Subsequently, she once again placed greater emphasis on the last of the education reforms to be achieved in Adventist circles—the introduction of manual labor into the educational program, an emphasis at the forefront of her writing during the founding of Avondale, the pattern school.

It is enlightening to read Mrs. White's educational writings chronologically in the light of their historical background. She always advocated a balanced approach to the mental, physical, and spiritual in education, but her emphasis changed over time, depending upon the needs and condition of Adventist education. If any one part of education was more important than others, it would, from her point of view, appear to be the spiritual. On the other hand, it is easy to gain the impression that the physical, practical, and manual labor aspects were her major emphases, since it was on those topics that she had to "shout the loudest and longest" to make herself heard by educators with a bookish orientation.

However, manual labor is only one part of her reform package. Some of her sincere followers lost her balanced perspective. For example, Edward Sutherland, during his early years at Emmanuel Missionary College, turned the school largely into a work program with minimal emphasis on mental development. It is unfortunate that in our attempts to counteract one extreme, we move, at times, to its polar opposite. The ideal is balance.

A final myth related to work combined with study is that we can define practical training in the last quarter of the twentieth century in the same terms as that of the nineteenth century. What was practical one hundred years ago is often extremely impractical today. While principles remain unchanged, application varies across time and cultures. Agriculture is a case in point. One could certainly question the propriety of making traditional land-intensive agriculture (and other trades that were "practical" in the late 1800s) the focal point of practical education for the world of work in the latter part of the twentieth century. Mrs. White emphasized again and again that each young person should learn a practical trade in school so that, "if need be, he may obtain a livelihood" in times of adversity (CT, p. 307). The big question is "What is practical in the 1980s?" In the nineteenth century, agriculture was quite relevant and useful for almost everyone. Land in many places was nearly free, and all one needed to set up business was a horse and plow. Good farmers were needed, and farming was easy to break into. This has all changed. Today, in the industrialized countries, traditional agriculture (outside of gardening to supply family needs) is an expensive business requiring a major financial investment for both land and equipment. Unless a person has inherited land or has a large savings account, farming is hardly the practical trade to fall back on in difficult times.

In the late nineteenth century the United States had a great need for many small-time farmers. The same was true of Australia. Ellen White could therefore comment, "This country [Australia] needs educated farmers."—FE, p. 319. That was a true statement in Australia in 1894, and Mrs. White accordingly emphasized agricultural training at Avondale. The principle underlying it was that education should be practical—it should prepare students to meet society's needs. Agricultural training was the application of the principle within the context of that time and place.

Adventist Christians in the 1980s, however, live in a different context. We need to ask how we can apply the unchanging principle that education should be practical in our time and place. What does our country need today? What is "practical" in the 1980s? What can we teach to young people that they can fall back on during hard times in the postindustrial era? It is evident that both needs and practical opportunities have largely shifted from production to service. What does the United States require today in terms of practical workers? It still needs carpenters, plumbers, and farmers, but it also calls for computer programmers, nurses, and social workers in ever-increasing numbers. Training to meet today's practical demands should find a place in Adventist curricula.

Because of changing technology, economic conditions, and business realities, marketable skills have changed. Ellen White never sought to give hidebound counsel that would make her readers anachronistic. As we have already noted, she specifically remarked that "circumstances change the relation of things," and God "wants us to reason from common sense" (3SM, p. 217). He wants us to prepare young people for the "practical" side of life in the twentieth century. We must not teach the upcoming generation to live in contemporary society by *unthinking* and *inflexible* application of counsel given to meet the needs of the first, tenth, or nineteenth centuries. Although we Adventists have no problem in seeing that the Amish have committed this fallacy, we get all befuddled when we face the same issue in our attempts to be faithful to Ellen White. Inherent in her very counsel, however, is the duty of abstracting the eternal principles, thinking them through in the context of present realities, and applying their intent to current situations. Such a procedure does not "explain away" the counsel. Rather, it provides the only avenue to real faithfulness to its goals.

Some may object to the above line of reasoning. They may rightly accuse me of not accounting for the physical regeneration of the students when I suggest that practical work-study might focus on gaining experience with computers. They are correct. But, as I noted in my chapter on recreation, most modern work (including machine-oriented agriculture) does not sufficiently exercise the body. It is hard to escape the conclusion that students need re-creational activities for physical exercise beyond the realm of work in a modern industrialized society. This, of course, does not always hold true in those developing Third World nations where machines have not replaced human muscle in the competitive production of goods.

Others might fault me for seemingly implying that agricultural study is no longer the "A, B, and C of the education" we should provide in our schools (6T, p. 179). That is not what I intended. While I did say that traditional land-intensive forms of single-crop agriculture are not practical for the majority of students, I will demonstrate later that some labor-intensive forms of agriculture could easily be quite practical and profitable for both schools and students in postindustrial societies in the last quarter of the twentieth century. It is also true that we can effectively teach many spiritual lessons to young people through school gardens and even by growing seeds and plants in window boxes in the classroom in areas of the world that have severe winters. Ellen White's chapters entitled "God in Nature," "Lessons of Life," and "Other Object Lessons" in *Education* (pages 99-120) set forth appropriate means to teach the A, B, and C of life through nature and agriculture. We need to carry out her suggestions much more frequently than we have carried them out in the past. Even though agriculture as a business has radically altered, it is still true that the study of the processes of germination and growth in connection with Christ's parables is one of the best ways to help young people come to grips with the mysteries of life and the power of God. Agricultural lessons should be at the foundation of every young person's education, both at home and in the school.

The Important Place of Work in the School Program

If those who overplay the role of work in education are not correct, neither are those who underplay its importance. Mrs. White was emphatic in her advocacy of practical work in the curriculum. She wrote that "if the youth can have but a one-sided education, which is of the greater consequence, a knowledge of the sciences, with all the disadvantages to health and life, or a knowledge of labor for practical life? We unhesitatingly answer, the latter. *If one must be neglected, let it be the study of books.*—CT, p. 289. (Italics supplied.) The ideal, of course, is that every student gain both cognitive knowledge and practical skills. Again, she wrote that many branches of study that take up the student's time "are not essential to usefulness or happiness; but it is essential for every youth to have a thorough acquaintance with everyday duties. If need be, a young woman can dispense with a knowledge of French and algebra, or even of the piano; but it is indispensable that she learn to make good bread, to fashion neatly-fitting garments, and to perform efficiently the many duties that pertain to homemaking," since the health and happiness of her family depend on such skills (Ed, p. 216). She also wrote that "while every person needs some knowledge of different handicrafts, it is indispensable that he become proficient in at least one. *Every youth, on leaving school, should have acquired a knowledge of some trade or occupation by which, if need be, he may earn a livelihood.*"—*Ibid.*, p. 218. (Italics supplied.)

Ellen White left us with no doubt as to her evaluation of the role of practical work in education. Part of the function of Christian education is to provide every student with a marketable skill. Apparently, her recommendation does not mean that every student should be at the journeyman level in a trade, but it does imply that each should have enough experience to recommend him or her for successful work of the same type in the larger world outside the school (i.e., job-entry-level skills). Thus, a young lady studying to be an engineer might pick up secretarial skills while working her way through school. Or a premed or ministerial student might have achieved enough experience as a maintenance painter to recommend him for a job if and when he needed it. For many students such school-developed skills might be important avocationally as well as vocationally, an especially important consideration in an age of shortened workweeks and increased leisure time.

According to Ellen White, such training in work skills should begin in the home and then be extended by the school. "For every child the first industrial school should be the home. And, so far as possible, facilities for manual training should be connected with every school."—*Ibid.*, p. 217. Young people can and should learn many things in their homes from their earliest days. These include housecleaning, gardening, maintenance, baking, cooking, and so on. Useful tasks are a blessing. They not only strengthen the body but also help our children apply their minds to real-life situations. In addition, they provide opportunities to develop character as children learn to persevere at tasks and be helpful to other people (*ibid.*, p. 215). The work at the elementary school should ideally be a continuation of this development.

Needed: Serious Thought and Action
Concerning Work Programs in Schools

Seventh-day Adventist educators have done a great deal to develop work-study programs in their schools, but they have much yet to accomplish. The area of the curriculum dealing with practical work has always been harder for academicians to visualize and actualize than those aspects involving mental education. Yet developing better work programs is of utmost importance if students and their families are going to be able to meet the rising costs of private schooling. It seems to me that the continued health, and even existence, of Adventist education depends upon at least two factors: (1) that the education is distinctively Christian, and (2) that its customers can pay for it.

We must face both factors at all levels of education. The first issue deals with whether Seventh-day Adventist education is worth the cost. Is it really different from public education in a significant way, or is it merely the same approach to the same topics with religion and chapel pasted on? It is no small matter to parents who must pay the bill. For example, at the beginning of this school year I had two children wanting to attend boarding academy. The cost was roughly 50 percent of my gross income. Adventist families have been, and continue to be, willing to pay the price for an education that is truly Christian, but I doubt if large numbers would continue to sacrifice if Adventist schools did not deliver what they had promised in such areas as developing the Christian mind (see chapters 10-14) and providing caring personal relationships between faculty and students (see chapter 15).

The second factor is no less serious. Even if Seventh-day Adventist education is worth the cost, we still struggle with the problem of financing it. At the present time this is especially a problem at the secondary level, where tuition and living costs are high, while grants and loans are not as plentiful as they are for college. However, it is not merely a problem for our secondary schools, since what affects the vitality of one part of the Adventist educational system will eventually make an impact upon the whole. Paying for this expensive education makes work programs loom large for many parents and students.

It seems that the development of work opportunities that are both profitable and educative should be a major priority in Adventist educational discussion and planning if we hope to survive in an increasingly competitive educational marketplace. If Adventist schools do not provide the means for purchasing their educational commodities, they will eventually dwindle and die or become exclusive private schools for the church's upper-middle class.[10] Here is an issue among issues on our educational agenda.

What follows in this chapter is not a full-blown program for the revitalization of the work-study idea, but rather a few suggestions in the direction of a solution. Some may be impractical, but even if only a spark of light exists in them, it will be worth the effort needed to set them forth.

First, it is imperative that the development of work programs that are both educative and profitable receive our best thought and energy. At times it seems that our imaginations suffer from stagnation in regard to industrial development. Many Adventist schools have fixated on certain types of work for students such as binderies, furniture factories, dairies, and bakeries. Such industries are now rooted in tradition, and we may be tempted to think like our fathers, who were often in touch with the needs of their era but whose ideas may or may not meet the demands and opportunities of the 1980s. Perhaps what we need is fresh thought—not more thought from educators and school business managers, but fresh thought from some self-made Christian "millionaires" (not necessarily Adventists), men and women who see opportunities that the rest of us miss, who have had above-average successful experience. After we have decided exactly what our needs and goals are in terms of work-study, why not bring a dozen or so of these people together with a dozen of our most innovative educators and their business managers for a two- or three-day brainstorming convention focused on developing new work programs? There are innovative ideas. Why not seek them out? Educators and other church leaders can benefit by aggressively seeking the expertise of those whom the Lord has blessed with special talents in conducting creative and innovative businesses.

A second suggestion focuses on more flexible attitudes toward student workplaces. Too often in the past we have developed work facilities that employ a large number of students and demand heavy capital investments. Under such circumstances, establishing new industries is a risky business, since their failure would jeopardize the economic structure of the school. I am encouraged to see many of our schools developing cooperative programs wherein local private industries arrange to hire a certain number of students each quarter. This plan provides the industries with a needed supply of dependable labor, the students with tuition money, and the school with tuition income without the expense of extending its industrial capabilities. Other Adventist schools have offered school-owned buildings at low cost to businesses that will occupy them and utilize student labor.

Closely related to flexible attitudes toward student workplaces is the need to recognize the changed nature of much modern work, business, and industry. Agriculture is a case in point. In the nineteenth century, farmers had access to inexpensive land that they could competitively work with a minimal capital investment in equipment. Success came through putting as much land under cultivation as possible. Today, both land and equipment are extremely expensive, making traditional agriculture a capital-intensive enterprise. Complicating the picture for schools is the fact that advances in technology make it possible for a half-dozen workers to farm the same amount of land as a couple hundred using traditional equipment. In effect, it means that it would take immense amounts of land and a large outlay for equipment (capital investments) to employ the young people in a small college.

Schools in industrialized nations can no longer view agriculture from the perspective of the nineteenth-century model. They need to move from machine- and land-intensive (i.e., capital-intensive) models to labor-intensive models. Therefore, with their large labor supply and shortage of liquid capital, schools might be wiser to move away from visions of single-crop agriculture utilizing vast acreage to such activities as truck farming, hydroponic tomato production, or growing green plants and shrubs for florists and nurseries. Such activities not only have the potential of more profit with less investment but they also provide more carryover options for those students who want to establish their own businesses after graduation. Agricultural opportunities for schools in postindustrial societies are not dead, but they have been transformed.

We might say the same about other school industries. Adventist schools need to move beyond industrial formats that are capital-intensive to those that can use the maximum labor with minimal investment. Perhaps we have something to learn from E. F.

Schumacher, who in *Small Is Beautiful* and *Good Work*[11] has demonstrated innovative ideas for putting people to work by scaling down the modern economic means of production. Not being big offers many economic advantages—not the least of which is a flexibility that can respond to changing market conditions.

Paul Damazo, a highly successful Adventist businessman who is chairman of the board of Versitron Industries, has been a leader among Adventists in providing ideas and developing programs for low-investment "cottage industries" in which students can produce salable items, such as Christmas tree ornaments, bean sprouts, or recipe boxes, for either local or international markets. Adventist schools have a ready-made international marketplace if they will competitively produce goods that people need to buy anyway. We have not, however, taken full advantage of this vast market for the financial health of Adventist schools. Damazo has recommended that we "encourage SDA businessmen to start many import-export businesses worldwide to facilitate the sales and distribution of products produced at our . . . schools worldwide."[12]

A school does not need expensive equipment or a fancy building to develop industries. The assembling and packaging of many products, for example, can be done in quite humble environments. Industries without expensive equipment have advantages since they allow for flexibility when one market dries up. It is also important to realize that a successful industry does not need to employ a large number of students. In many ways a school with twenty-five profitable enterprises, each employing four students, is in a better situation than an institution that has one industry employing one hundred students. When something curtails the larger industry's market, it threatens the school, but when a small enterprise's market gets wiped out, the school can redeploy the students into more promising endeavors with minimal effect. Diversity and flexibility are safety features.

Being safe and being efficient, however, may be two different things. A large number of small industries could degenerate into a real mess without adequate professional guidance. Damazo has suggested that colleges should "employ a *successful* business executive to assist the college business manager. His sole responsibility should be to coordinate all industries on campus and to make them more efficient and profitable for the student and college."[13] The secondary schools of a union conference might jointly employ a similar specialist. A large part of his function would be to investigate possible ideas, do market analyses, and develop plans for their implementation. It would not take too much success to pay his salary, and there is almost unlimited potential for the results of his work.

Another suggestion for the revitalization of Adventist work programs is that we study the types of industries and the marketing procedures developed by other educational institutions. For example, the School of the Ozarks, an independent college in Point Lookout, Missouri, has developed a weaving industry that includes hand spinning and traditional loom weaving. The finished articles are quality collector items and make excellent gifts in an affluent society in which people have learned to value their heritage and its crafts. In addition, the school produces quality fruitcakes and jellies. The college packages them in fancy gift boxes and markets them around the world, along with other of the school's products, through the *Ozark Visitor*, which goes to 170,000 homes bimonthly. The *Visitor* advertises the school at the same time that it taps a vast mail-order market for both its own products and other items that it retails. Besides the School of the Ozarks, we could learn lessons from other educational institutions.

Still another suggestion is that we move away from the concept that a profitable school industry is one that makes a profit in the same way that a private business does. Ellen White suggested that we must consider more than merely the account books. Side benefits such as character development and other unseen advantages "cannot be measured or estimated" (CT, p. 317). Because of this, the large outlay for industrial training is worth the cost (Ed, p. 218). Frederick Griggs, a leading Adventist administrator earlier in the century, faced the shortsightedness of looking at industries only in terms of financial profit. In 1908 he wrote to W. C. White that he was "aware that many industrial features cannot be made remunerative to our schools, which, whether they can be or not, ought to come in. We do not get anything back in a money way from arithmetic and grammar save in tuition. We should recognize that manual education is highly valuable from an intellectual point of view and as a character builder."[14] Following Griggs's suggestion, we must learn to see the school's work program in the context of the entire instructional program. Unlike other parts of the instructional package, however, the work program does pump money into the school through tuition, even though its industries may not be totally in the black. Under the circumstances, a school still may gain $10,000 in tuition even though it has to subsidize a particular industry $2,000 per year. A work program involving instructional benefits and the generation of tuition by students who would not otherwise be able to attend the school involves a different calculus in relation to profit than does a private business enterprise.

Two final suggestions move away from the financial aspect of work-study programs to the educative aspect. If we as Seventh-day Adventists really want to make work a quality part of our educational system, then we can improve in at least two areas. First, work must take place under quality supervision. All too often our work programs teach young people how not to work. At times we place an overworked academy teacher in charge of a large number of students whom he cannot properly supervise because of other responsibilities. The result is that they learn to get paid for standing around and avoiding productive activity. If that happens, then we are doing more damage than if we had no work program at all. For students to be responsible in work, they must have well-planned and carefully supervised programs. Moreover, Ellen White has suggested that the best work education takes place under "experienced workmen" (6T, p. 176). It is foolish to place students under the supervision of a teacher who himself doesn't understand the work. Likewise, it is a false economy to hire craftsmen as work leaders and then reward them at a lower level than the academic faculty. They have a responsibility commensurate with that of those who instruct in the classroom, and the school should reward them accordingly. It will be impossible to keep first-class craftsmen if the administration treats them as second-class citizens.

Another way we can improve the quality of work in Adventist schools is to provide incentives that will motivate student workers to do their best. One of my students pointed out to me that we too often have hired students on a pass-fail system, and have then wondered why they are not returning A and B quality output. Schools that have graded academic progress on a pass-fail basis have generally found that students soon gravitate to the minimum required. Whether we like it or not, grades do help people living in a sinful environment to put forth more effort. Too often students take a job at an Adventist school for granted. One must be an extremely poor worker to get fired and, on the other hand, one finds little incentive to put forth quality output in campus industries. This state of affairs frustrates some of the major purposes for even having work-study programs.

Once again we might learn from such institutions as the School of the Ozarks. This fully accredited, 1,200-student college has a work coordinator who keeps performance records showing the effectiveness of each student on the job. Students receive letter grades (but not academic credit) for their labor at the end of each semester. The coordinator bases their grade on the categories of cooperation, interest and enthusiasm, initiative and responsibility, quality of work, attendance and punctuality, and care of school equipment. The work grade becomes a part of the student's permanent record and indicates that the college "expects not only adequate academic performance but also places a high value on performance in the work program." The school places the students on work probation if their grade falls below a C, and they receive one semester to improve or be terminated. A grade of F usually results in immediate dismissal without a probationary period. The records are available to employers after graduation and, notes the school, often help students obtain future employment.[15] Although the School of the Ozarks does not practice it, there is no reason why we might not add "small" financial incentives for above-average and, especially, superior work grades. At times we lose much in both production and attitude by seeking to hold students to the inflexible minimum, when we could gain a lot by offering even small tokens of appreciation for work well done.

A Note on Work-Study Programs
in the Elementary School

In our discussion thus far, we have mostly addressed topics and ideas applicable for secondary schools and colleges. Even though space is short, it is important to note the many excellent opportunities to develop work skills and attitudes at the local elementary school also. In many ways the task is easier because of the relative smallness of such schools. I have been impressed by the program developed by one of the teachers in the Berrien Springs Adventist School. Harry Rogers has made arrangements with local businesses for seventh- and eighth-grade students to gain experience in their establishments. On Wednesday afternoon those young people who so choose can work in grocery stores, offices, garages, and several other places. Students stay on the same job for at least one quarter. After that time they can elect another type of work experience. The program has turned out to be an excellent introduction to the world of work. Even though the young people do not receive any pay, it has provided them with skills that have in some cases led to employment.

Local elementary schools also have opportunities to develop work experience in their curriculum through school improvement projects, grounds beautification, school gardens, and "cottage industries," and through arranging with parents to provide part of the work curriculum through jobs around the house. One major reservoir of talent often overlooked is retirees. Many of them have both the ability and desire to share their knowledge with young people. Educators, however, need to take the initiative to develop plans if they are to tap this reservoir of talent. I can easily imagine the fifteen students in grades 5 through 8 in a two-teacher school dividing up into three or four groups on Wednesday afternoon to participate in work education in the community. Four work with a retired carpenter on some new cabinets and shelving for the school, three with a retired mechanic in his home shop as they learn to rebuild a lawn-mower engine, three with a seamstress in her home, and the remaining four with a first-class cook. In small schools, educative work programs often suffer only because of our lack of imagination.

Some Concluding Remarks

This book closes with the quotation that most authors on Adventist education might choose for their introduction. In the opening paragraph of *Education*, Mrs. White wrote: "Our ideas of education take too narrow and too low a range. There is need of a broader scope, a higher aim. *True education* means more than the pursual of a certain course of study. It means more than a preparation for the life that now is. It *has to do with the whole being*, and with the whole period of existence possible to man. *It is the harmonious development of the physical, the mental, and the spiritual powers.* It prepares the student for the joy of service in this world and for the higher joy of wider service in the world to come."—Page 13. (Italics supplied.)

This quotation uplifts the ideal of balance in Christian education. The Fall fractured the image of God in man in its physical, spiritual, and mental aspects. Christian education, therefore, must seek the restoration of that balanced image in each person's life. Redemptive education works to restore the whole man to God's original ideal. It must not overly emphasize the mental or the physical or the spiritual or the social or the vocational or the emotional. Rather, it must develop the total person in integrated wholeness. Both the formal and the informal curricula of the school must aim at fostering this balanced harmony in the Lord's children. Producing educational programs that facilitate it in a constantly changing world is an ongoing challenge that will continue to take the best thinking and most earnest efforts of Adventist educators in the home, the school, and the church.

Jesus "increased in wisdom [mentally] and in stature [physically], and in favor with God [spiritually] and man [socially]" (Luke 2:52). Here is God's ideal for all of His children.

Epilogue

I selected the myths discussed in this book because Seventh-day Adventists widely hold them. I might have chosen other examples (e.g., the myth of the truly "self-supporting" school, the myth that conformity is good, myths in music, and so on), but hopefully the chapters in this book have provided a method for thinking about other misconceptions and arriving at sounder views on any topic.

Christians should be in the habit of evaluating the truthfulness of everything they hear. A great deal of damage occurs through the uncritical acceptance of widely held myths. Historical tradition has sanctified many of them, but this does not make them valid. Ellen White spoke to the point when she wrote that "errors may be hoary with age; but age does not make error truth, nor truth error."—6T, p. 142.

A thoughtful examination of their underlying assumptions and their historical roots could clarify many misconceptions. This, however, does not go far enough. The problem with much "intellectual" Christianity is that it remains satisfied with debunking myths and exposing error, while failing to move to the constructive side of its task. Being able to analyze error is important, but the most important function of Christian thinking is building a positive approach to Christian living and Christian education from the basic documents of our faith.

On the other hand, even constructive thought falls short of the Christian ideal. Christianity is an active, living faith. Whereas the first step in the continuous revitalization of the church and its educational system is clear thought about goals and the means to achieve them, the second step is positive action toward fulfilling those goals by individuals and the corporate membership of the church. Action informed by thought based on revealed principles is the Christian ideal that stimulated the writing of *Myths in Adventism*.

References

Chapter 1

[1] "Counsel Regarding Age of School Entrance," MS 7, 1904. This was published in full for the first time in the *Review* of April 24, 1975. Much of it has been republished in *Selected Messages*, book 3, pp. 214-226.

[2] Odell Shepard, ed., *The Heart of Thoreau's Journals* (Boston: Houghton Mifflin, 1927), p. 176.

[3] I have provided a fuller discussion of the relationship between revelation and reason in *Philosophy and Education: An Introduction in Christian Perspective* (Berrien Springs, Mich.: Andrews University Press, 1980), pp. 157-162.

[4] David Elton Trueblood, *Philosophy of Religion* (Grand Rapids, Mich.: Baker Book House, 1973), p. 112.

Chapter 2

[1] Otto L. Bettmann, *The Good Old Days—They Were Terrible!* (New York: Random House, 1974), p. xi.

[2] C. P. Snow, *The Two Cultures and a Second Look: An Expanded Version of the Two Cultures and the Scientific Revolution* (New York: Cambridge University Press, 1969), p. 82.

[3] Quoted in Bettmann, *op. cit.*, p. 157. From Edward Eggleston, *The Hoosier School-Master* (New York: Grossett and Dunlap, 1913), p. 53.

[4] Colin Greer, *The Great School Legend: A Revisionist Interpretation of American Public Education* (New York: The Viking Press, 1972), p. 4.

[5] School Committee, "The Proposed School," RH, May 7, 1872, p. 168. Cf. George I. Butler, "What Use Shall We Make of Our School?" RH, July 21, 1874, pp. 44, 45.

[6] W. C. White, "Pioneer Pilots in Christian Education," In *Founders' Golden Anniversary Bulletin of Battle Creek College and Emmanuel Missionary College: 1874-1924*, p. 29.

[7] For the fullest account of this struggle see George R. Knight, "Battle Creek College: Academic Development and Curriculum Struggles, 1874-1901," a paper presented at Andrews University Founders' Weekend, March 10, 1979, AUHR; see also George R. Knight, "Ellen G. White: Prophet," in George R. Knight, ed., *Early Adventist Educators* (Berrien Springs, Mich.: Andrews University Press, 1983), pp. 26-49.

[8] Sidney Brownsberger, "Personal Experiences, Conditions, and Impressions in Connection With the Educational Work Among Seventh-day Adventists," AUHR.

[9] James White, ed., *Health: or How to Live* (Battle Creek, Mich.: Seventh-day Adventist Pub. Assn., 1865), No. 5, pp. 19-26; No. 6, pp. 25-47. E. G. White to J. E. and E. L. White, June 5, 1899, EGWRC-AU.

[10] Robert Samuel Fletcher, *A History of Oberlin College From Its Founding Through the Civil War* (Oberlin, Ohio: Oberlin College Press, 1943); cf. George R. Knight, "Oberlin College and Adventist Educational Reforms," *Adventist Heritage*, Spring, 1983, pp. 3-9, documented copy in AUHR.

Chapter 3

[1] E. A. Sutherland, "Why the Battle Creek College Can Not Confer Degrees," RH, Oct. 10, 1899, p. 655; Nov. 14, 1899, p. 740.

[2] E. A. Sutherland, *Studies in Christian Education*, reprint ed. (Payson, Ariz.: Leaves-of-Autumn Books, 1977), pp. 137, 138.

[3] W. W. Prescott to E. A. Sutherland, April 29, 1896, EGWRC-DC.

[4] Sutherland, *op. cit.*, pp. 38-40.

[5] Ernest R. Sandeen, *The Roots of Fundamentalism: British and American Millenarianism 1800-1930* (Grand Rapids, Mich.: Baker Book House, 1978), pp. 181, 182.

[6] Everett Dick, *Union: College of the Golden Cords* (Lincoln, Nebr.: Union College Press, 1967), p. 159.

[7] Dores Eugene Robinson, *The Story of Our Health Message*, 2d ed. (Nashville, Tenn.: Southern Pub. Assn., 1955), pp. 371-389.

[8] Ellen G. White, letter reproduced in "A Medical School at Loma Linda," RH, May 19, 1910, p. 18 (italics supplied); cf. CT, p. 480.

[9] Warren E. Howell, "Letter From Prof. W. E. Howell," RH, Oct. 16, 1930, pp. 6-9.

[10] [E.A. Sutherland], "Why Should Madison Become a Senior College," *The Madison Survey*, Jan. 7, 1931.

[11] Clifford G. Howell to E. A. Sutherland, March 18, 1932, LLUHR.

[12] O. J. Graf to E. A. Sutherland, Jan. 16, 1931, LLUHR.

[13] E. A. Sutherland to O. J. Graf, May 18, 1931, LLUHR.

[14] O. J. Graf to E. A. Sutherland, June 8, 1931; C. G. Howell to E. A. Sutherland, May 11, 1932; LLUHR.

[15] William G. White, Jr., "Another Look at Those Pioneers of Adventist Accreditation," *Focus*, Winter, 1978, p. 11.

[16] W. H. Branson, "On Presentation of the Report of the Survey Commission on Education Regarding Accreditation," speech delivered at the Fall Council, Oct. 30, 1935, EGWRC-AU.

[17] W. W. Prescott to E. A. Sutherland, April 29, 1896, EGWRC-DC.

Chapter 4

[1] Trueblood, *Philosophy of Religion*, p. xiv.

[2] The image of God aspect of man, its change at the Fall, and man's potential will be more fully treated in chapter 8, "Myths About Human Nature."

[3] Edwin H. Rian, "The Need: A World View," in John Paul von Grueningen, ed., *Toward a Christian Philosophy of Higher Education* (Philadelphia: Westminster Press, 1957), pp. 30, 31; Herbert Welch, "The Ideals and Aims of the Christian College," *The Christian College* (New York: Methodist Book Concern, 1916), p. 21.

[4] Carlyle B. Haynes, *Righteousness in Christ: A Preacher's Personal Experience* (Takoma Park, Md.: General Conference Ministerial Association, n.d.), pp. 9, 10, cf. Gal. 2:20.

[5] C. B. Eavey, "Aims and Objectives of Christian Education," in J. Edward Hakes, ed., *An Introduction to Evangelical Christian Education* (Chicago: Moody Press, 1964), p. 62.

[6] See Harry Blamires, *The Secularist Heresy: The Erosion of the Gospel in the Twentieth Century* (Ann Arbor, Mich.: Servant Books, 1980), p. 56.

[7] Hans K. LaRondelle, *Christ Our Salvation: What God Does for Us and in Us* (Mountain View, Calif.: Pacific Press Pub. Assn., 1980), pp. 81, 82.

[8] For a helpful discussion of this topic see Edward M. Norton, "Character Development—A Process in Harmony With Righteousness by Faith," term paper, 1979, AUHR.

[9] Gene Garrick, "Developing Educational Objectives for the Christian School," in Paul A. Kienel, ed., *The Philosophy of Christian School Education*, 2d ed. (Whittier, Calif.: Association of Christian Schools International, 1978), p. 73.

[10] Welch, *op. cit.*, pp. 23, 22.

¹¹ J. Crosby Chapman and George S. Counts, *Principles of Education* (Boston: Houghton Mifflin Co., 1924), p. 498. (Italics supplied.)
¹² See Knight, *Philosophy and Education,* pp. 220-225.

Chapter 5

¹ Horace Mann, "Twelfth Annual Report of the Board of Education Together with the Report of the Secretary of the Board" [1848] in Mary Mann, ed., *Life and Works of Horace Mann,* 5 vols. (Boston: Lee and Shepard Publishers, 1891), vol. 4, pp. 251, 252.
² Marvin Grandstaff, "The Family as an Educational Institution: The Lost Perspective," in Cole S. Brembeck and Marvin Grandstaff, eds., *Social Foundations of Education: A Book of Readings* (New York: John Wiley and Sons, 1969), pp. 127, 129.
³ Jacques Maritain, *Education at the Crossroads* (New Haven, Conn.: Yale University Press, 1943), p. 24.
⁴ James S. Coleman et al., *Equality of Educational Opportunity* (Washington, D.C.: U.S. Department of Health, Education, and Welfare, 1966).
⁵ Christopher Jencks et al., *Inequality: A Reassessment of the Effect of Family and Schooling in America* (New York: Harper and Row, 1972).
⁶ Frank E. Gaebelein, "The Greatest Educational Force," *Christianity Today,* Aug. 28, 1964, pp. 28, 29.
⁷ Benjamin S. Bloom, *Stability and Change in Human Characteristics* (New York: John Wiley and Sons, 1964), pp. 72, 88, 110.
⁸ John Bowlby, *Maternal Care and Mental Health* (Geneva: World Health Organization, 1952), p. 68.
⁹ Quoted in Sarane Spence Boocock, *Sociology of Education: An Introduction,* 2d ed. (Boston: Houghton Mifflin Co., 1980), p. 65. (Italics supplied.)
¹⁰ Lawrence A. Cremin, *Public Education* (New York: Basic Books, 1976), p. 68.
¹¹ See Paul A. Kienel, *The Christian School: Why It Is Right for Your Child* (Wheaton, Ill: Victor Books, 1974), p. 63.
¹² Garrick, "Developing Educational Objectives for the Christian School," in Kienel, ed., *The Philosophy of Christian School Education,* p. 91.
¹³ Quoted in Kienel, *op. cit.,* p. 44.
¹⁴ Kenneth Keniston et al., *All Our Children: The American Family Under Pressure* (New York: Harcourt Brace Jovanovich, 1977), p. 7.

Chapter 6

¹ Carle C. Zimmerman, *Family and Civilization* (New York: Harper and Brothers, 1947).
² James Dobson, *What Wives Wish Their Husbands Knew About Women* (Wheaton, Ill.: Tyndale House Publishers, 1975), p. 55.
³ Urie Bronfenbrenner, "Nobody Home: The Erosion of the American Family," *Psychology Today,* May, 1977, p. 41.
⁴ Note, for example, that many of the Ellen White quotations in the "Toward a Solution" section of this chapter emphasize the parenting role of both mother *and* father, while others stress the primary role of the mother.
⁵ Bronfenbrenner, *op. cit.,* p. 42.
⁶ Alvin Toffler, *The Third Wave* (New York: Bantam Books, 1981), pp. 194, 221. Toffler also predicts the "possible resurrection of the expanded family" (page 222).
⁷ John Naisbitt, *Megatrends: Ten New Directions Transforming Our Lives* (New York: Warner Books, 1982), pp. 36, 45, 46.
⁸ Paul Goodman, *Growing Up Absurd: Problems of Youth in the Organized Society* (New York: Vintage Books, 1960), p. x.
⁹ See Toffler, *op. cit.,* pp. 42-45.
¹⁰ Mike McGrady, *The Kitchen Sink Papers: My Life as a Househusband* (Garden City, N.Y.: Doubleday & Co., 1975); Mike McGrady, "Let 'em Eat Leftovers," *Newsweek,* Feb. 2, 1976, p. 13.

[11] One obvious candidate is the need for more social relationships. The isolation of the housewife-mother is an obvious fact in many cases, but in and of itself it may not be a major determinant in the choice to work outside the home, since a woman can find many ways of enriching her social life without "binding" herself to a full-time job. It is probably more of a contributary cause.

[12] Grace Hechinger, "Happy Mother's Day," *Newsweek*, May 11, 1981, p. 19.

[13] Burton L. White et al., *Experience and Environment: Major Influences on the Development of the Young Child* (Englewood Cliffs, N.J.: Prentice-Hall, 1973), p. 242.

[14] Dobson, *op. cit.*, pp. 22, 25.

[15] *Ibid.*, p. 55.

[16] Cole S. Brembeck, *Social Foundations of Education: Environmental Influences in Teaching and Learning*, 2d ed. (New York: John Wiley and Sons, 1971), pp. 111-113.

[17] John Bowlby, *Attachment, Attachment and Loss* (New York: Basic Books, 1969), vol. 1, pp. 177-209.

[18] ———, *Maternal Care and Mental Health*, pp. 11, 12.

[19] W. Peter Blitchington, *Sex Roles and the Christian Family* (Wheaton, Ill.: Tyndale House Publishers, 1980), p. 81.

[20] Dobson, *op. cit.*, pp. 57, 58.

[21] *Ibid.*, p. 55.

[22] Hechinger, *op. cit.*, p. 19.

[23] Dobson, *op. cit.*, p. 58.

[24] Bronfenbrenner, *op. cit.*, p. 41.

Chapter 7

[1] This is true even though unequal reward distribution makes it appear as if the more highly rewarded roles are more important. Unequal rewards do, however, provide power for those in prestige positions while supplying a sense of awe for those lower in the hierarchy. Such results contribute to social stability. Like many myths, the myth of up and down has some utility value.

[2] A fuller discussion of the primacy of teaching can be found in George R. Knight, "Reschooling Society: A New Road to Utopia," *Phi Delta Kappan*, December, 1978, pp. 289-291.

[3] ———, *Philosophy and Education*, p. 191

[4] Blitchington, *Sex Roles and the Christian Family*, p. 90.

[5] Arthur W. Combs, *Myths in Education: Beliefs That Hinder Progress and Their Alternatives* (Boston: Allyn and Bacon, 1979), p. 34.

[6] *Ibid.*, p. 35.

[7] Laurence J. Peter and Raymond Hull, *The Peter Principle* (New York: William Morrow and Co., 1969), p. 25.

[8] Paulo Freire, *Pedagogy of the Oppressed*, trans. Myra Bergman Ramos (New York: Seabury Press, 1970), passim.

[9] David Elton Trueblood, "The Marks of a Christian College," in Von Grueningen, ed., *Toward a Christian Philosophy of Higher Education*, p. 170.

[10] Laurence J. Peter, *The Peter Prescription* (New York: Bantam Books, 1973), pp. 114, 115.

[11] C. Northcote Parkinson, *Parkinson's Law and Other Studies in Administration* (Boston: Houghton Mifflin Co., 1957), p. 4.

[12] At times Ellen White used words like *greatness* and *large* with their "worldly" meaning in order to communicate her point. Beyond her specific use of words, however, lies a conceptual distinction, since God's definition of greatness differs from human definitions.

Chapter 8

[1] G. C. Berkouwer, *Man: The Image of God* (Grand Rapids, Mich.: William B. Eerdmans Pub. Co., 1962), p. 9.

² Trueblood, *Philosophy of Religion,* p. xiv.

³ Blaise Pascal, *Pensées* (London: J. M. Dent and Sons), p. 99.

⁴ Quoted in Pascal, *op. cit.,* p. iii.

⁵ Abraham J. Heschel, *Who Is Man?* (Stanford, Calif.: Stanford University Press, 1965), p. 13.

⁶ *Ibid.,* p. 24.

⁷ C. S. Lewis, *The Abolition of Man* (New York: Macmillan Pub. Co., 1965), p. 77.

⁸ Francis A. Schaeffer, *Genesis in Space and Time: The Flow of Biblical History* (Downers Grove, Ill.: InterVarsity Press, 1972), p. 100.

⁹ ———, *Escape From Reason* (Downers Grove, Ill.: InterVarsity Press, 1968), p. 90.

¹⁰ C. S. Lewis, *The Screwtape Letters* and *Screwtape Proposes a Toast* (New York: Macmillan, 1972), p.11.

¹¹ Heschel, *op. cit.,* p. 40.

¹² *Ibid.,* p. 3.

¹³ E. F. Schumacher, *A Guide for the Perplexed* (New York: Harper and Row, 1977), pp. 18, 20. Cf. Reinhold Niebuhr, *The Nature and Destiny of Man: A Christian Interpretation* (New York: Charles Scribner's Sons, 1964), vol. 1, p. 14.

¹⁴ Niebuhr, *op. cit.,* p. 4.

¹⁵ C. S. Lewis, *Mere Christianity* (New York: Macmillan Pub. Co., 1960), p. 52.

¹⁶ B. F. Skinner, *About Behaviorism* (New York: Vintage Books, 1976), p. 24; B. F. Skinner, *Beyond Freedom and Dignity* (New York: Bantam Books, 1972), pp. 191, 192.

¹⁷ David G. Myers, *The Human Puzzle: Psychological Research and Christian Belief* (San Francisco: Harper and Row, 1978), p. 243.

¹⁸ In agreement with this point, Mark P. Cosgrove has written that *"a careful analysis of the data suggests that influence, not determinism, is a more convincing description of what Skinner has demonstrated.* Human freedom does not mean that a person is not *influenced* by the environment.... It simply means that the persons are agents, capable of making choices about what they do."—*B. F. Skinner's Behaviorism: An Analysis* (Grand Rapids, Mich.: Zondervan Pub. House, 1982), p. 71; cf. p. 115.

¹⁹ Donald M. MacKay, *Human Science and Human Dignity* (Downers Grove, Ill.: InterVarsity Press, 1979), pp. 45-48. See also Cosgrove, *op. cit.,* pp. 103, 104, 108; Malcolm A. Jeeves, *Psychology and Christianity: The View Both Ways* (Downers Grove, Ill.: InterVarsity Press, 1976), pp. 61, 62.

Chapter 9

¹ Richard Hofstadter, *Anti-intellectualism in American Life* (New York: Vintage Books, 1963), pp. 55-141.

² Quoted in Hofstadter, *op. cit.,* p. 122.

³ "Questions and Answers," RH, Dec. 23, 1862, p. 29.

⁴ Arthur F. Holmes, *All Truth Is God's Truth* (Grand Rapids, Mich.: William B. Eerdmans Pub. Co., 1977), pp. 28, 29.

⁵ *Ibid.,* p. 37.

⁶ H. Richard Niebuhr, *Christ and Culture* (New York: Harper and Brothers, 1956), p. 70.

⁷ M. L. Andreasen, "Autobiography," EGWRC-AU, quoted in Virginia Steinweg, *Without Fear or Favor: The Life of M. L. Andreasen* (Washington, D.C.: Review and Herald Pub. Assn., 1979), p. 31.

⁸ See George R. Knight, *Issues and Alternatives in Educational Philosophy* (Berrien Springs, Mich.: Andrews University Press, 1982), p. 25.

Chapter 10

¹ A. Victor Murray, *Education Into Religion* (New York: Harper and Brothers, n.d.), p. 1.

[2] Warren C. Young, "Supernatural, Supernaturalism," in Everett F. Harrison et al., eds., *Baker's Dictionary of Theology* (Grand Rapids, Mich.: Baker Book House, 1960), p. 507.

[3] Jack W. Provonsha, *God Is With Us* (Washington, D.C.: Review and Herald Pub. Assn., 1974), pp. 81, 82.

[4] Trueblood, *Philosophy of Religion*, p. 19.

[5] Carl F. H. Henry, *Aspects of Christian Social Ethics* (Grand Rapids, Mich.: Baker Book House, 1980), p. 12. (Italics supplied.)

[6] Richard H. Bube, *The Human Quest: A New Look at Science and the Christian Faith* (Waco, Texas: Word Books, 1976), pp. 52, 53.

[7] Knight, *Issues and Alternatives in Educational Philosophy*, p. 25.

[8] George Arthur Buttrick, *Biblical Thought and the Secular University* (Baton Rouge, La.: Louisiana State University Press, 1960), p. 65; cf. p. 26.

[9] J. E. Barnhart, *Religion and the Challenge of Philosophy* (Totowa, N.J.: Littlefield, Adams and Co., 1975), p. 30.

[10] Ira Eisenstein, "Is the U.S. Ready for a Civil Religion?" *Religious Education*, May-June, 1976, p. 227.

[11] John Henry Newman, *The Idea of a University* (Notre Dame, Ind.: University of Notre Dame Press, 1982), p. 19.

[12] Holmes, *All Truth Is God's Truth*, p. 28.

[13] Frank E. Gaebelein, *The Pattern of God's Truth: Problems of Integration in Christian Education* (Chicago: Moody Press, 1968), p. 20.

[14] Bube, *op. cit.*, pp. 119, 120.

[15] One problem is that people do not always have a correct view of the meaning of the Bible. In some cases science helps clarify Bible truth (see Ed, p. 128). This is especially true in regard to points of fact that are not central to understanding the plan of salvation, the central purpose for which God gave the Bible. Calvin, for example, resisted Copernicus' discovery that the earth went around the sun by quoting Psalm 93:1: "The world is established; it shall never be moved." But he was wrong on a point that is tangential to the Biblical message. In this case science corrected a misunderstanding in Biblical interpretation. On the other hand, to apply this line of reasoning to the concept of macroevolution is fallacious, since man's special creation in God's image, his fall from his exalted position, and his need of restoration is what the Biblical revelation is all about. It is at this very point—the illogical jump from a Copernican correction to a Darwinian correction of Scripture—that some Christian theorists have gotten off the track.

[16] Bernard Ramm, *The Pattern of Religious Authority* (Grand Rapids, Mich.: William B. Eerdmans Pub. Co., 1959), p. 44.

[17] Gaebelein, *op. cit.*, p. 21.

[18] Michael J. Christensen, *C. S. Lewis on Scripture* (Waco, Tex.: Word Books, 1979), p. 95.

[19] Harry Blamires, *The Christian Mind* (London: S.P.C.K., 1963), pp. 3, 4.

[20] *Ibid.*, p. 44.

[21] Holmes, *op. cit.*, p. 125.

[22] Niebuhr, *Christ and Culture*, pp. 1-11.

[23] Arthur F. Holmes, *The Idea of a Christian College* (Grand Rapids, Mich.: William B. Eerdmans Pub. Co., 1975), pp. 33, 45.

Chapter 11

[1] E. A. Sutherland, *Living Fountains or Broken Cisterns* (Battle Creek, Mich.: Review and Herald Pub. Co., 1900), p. 112; A. T. Jones, *The Place of the Bible in Education* (Oakland, Calif.: Pacific Press Pub. Co., n.d.), p. 149.

[2] E.g., Dave Schwantes, "Country Garden School: Back to the Basics," *Spectrum*, November, 1979, pp. 50-52.

[3] E. G. White to J. E. White, Aug. 14, 1898; E. G. White to S. N. Haskell, Aug. 1, 1899; cf. W. C. White to E. A. Sutherland, Sept. 25, 1899; EGWRC-DC.

[4] "General Conference Proceedings," *General Conference Bulletin*, Feb. 20, 1899, p. 35.

[5] A. T. Jones, "Christian Education," RH, Oct. 17, 1899, p. 663.

[6] E. A. Sutherland, "Textbooks for Church Schools," *Training School Advocate*, April, 1899, pp. 198, 199.

[7] Jones, *The Place of the Bible in Education*, pp. 63-76; E.A. Sutherland, "Why the Battle Creek College Cannot Confer Degrees," RH, Oct. 10, 1899, p. 655.

[8] Sutherland, *Living Fountains*, p. 112.

[9] E. J. Waggoner to W. W. Prescott, June 1, 1902, GCAr.

[10] Frederick Rudolph, *Curriculum: A History of the American Undergraduate Course of Study Since 1636* (San Francisco: Jossey-Bass Publishers, 1977), pp. 151-202.

[11] Alfred North Whitehead, *The Aims of Education and Other Essays* (New York: The Free Press, 1967), p. 7.

[12] Philip H. Phenix, *Realms of Meaning* (New York: McGraw-Hill Book Co., 1964), p. 3. (Italics supplied.)

[13] *General Education in a Free Society* (Cambridge, Mass.: Harvard University Press, 1945), p. 40.

[14] Herbert Spencer, *Education: Intellectual, Moral, and Physical* (New York: D. Appleton and Co., 1909), pp. 1-87.

[15] Gordon H. Clark, *A Christian Philosophy of Education* (Grand Rapids, Mich.: William B. Eerdmans Pub. Co., 1946), p. 210.

[16] Frank E. Gaebelein, "Toward a Philosophy of Christian Education," in Hakes, ed., *An Introduction to Evangelical Christian Education*, p. 41.

[17] Holmes, *The Idea of a Christian College*, p. 26. (Italics supplied.)

[18] Trueblood, "The Marks of a Christian College," in Von Grueningen, ed., *Toward a Christian Philosophy of Higher Education*, p. 163.

[19] Gaebelein, in Hakes, ed., *op. cit.*, p. 37.

[20] ————, *The Pattern of God's Truth*, p. 79.

[21] Hastings Rashdall, *The Universities of Europe in the Middle Ages* (London: Oxford University Press, 1936), vol. 3, p. 442.

[22] Henry P. Van Dusen, *God in Education* (New York: Charles Scribner's Sons, 1951), p. 82.

[23] Gaebelein, in Hakes, ed., *op. cit.*, pp. 47, 48; cf. Newman, *The Idea of a University*, p. 54.

[24] For Gaebelein's discussion of the integration of Christianity and mathematics see *The Pattern of God's Truth*, pp. 57-64.

[25] Garrick, "Developing Educational Objectives for the Christian School," in Kienel, ed., *The Philosophy of Christian School Education*, p. 79.

[26] Holmes, *op. cit.*, p. 48.

Chapter 12

[1] "Guide to the Teaching of Literature in Seventh-day Adventist Schools" (Washington, D.C.: Department of Education, General Conference of Seventh-day Adventists, 1971), p. 7. Cf. John O. Waller, "A Contextual Study of Ellen G. White's Counsel Concerning Fiction," paper presented to the Quadrennial Section Meeting of SDA College English Teachers, La Sierra College, August, 1965, AUHR.

[2] "Guide to the Teaching of Literature," pp. 6, 7; Minutes of the Committee on the Teaching of Literature, Columbia Union College, June 14-17, 1971, GCDEd.

[3] Paul T. Gibbs, "Literature in Adventist Schools," paper presented to SDA English teachers, Southern Missionary College, 1961, GCDEd; Max Phillips, "Fiction, E. G. White, and the Bible," *Insight*, June 15, 1971, pp. 6-11.

[4] W. C. White to F. M. Wilcox, June 2, 1921, EGWRC-DC.

[5] Alma McKibbin, "Fundamental Principles on Fiction," *Ministry*, August, 1941, pp. 37, 38.

[6] Francis A. Schaeffer, *Art and the Bible: Two Essays* (Downers Grove, Ill.: InterVarsity Press, 1973), p. 56.

[7] Kenneth H. Wood, "An Editor Looks at the Teaching of Literature in SDA Schools," paper presented to the Committee on the Teaching of Literature, June 14, 1971, GCDEd. On this point Harry Blamires made a meaningful observation when he wrote that it is not the content of a book that makes it moral or immoral, but "the extent to which it recommends moral as opposed to immoral behavior" *(The Christian Mind,* p. 98).

[8] T. S. Eliot, "Religion and Literature," in Leland Ryken, ed., *The Christian Imagination: Essays on Literature and the Arts* (Grand Rapids, Mich.: Baker Book House, 1981), pp. 148-150.

[9] Gibbs, *loc. cit.*

[10] Joyce Rochat, "Teaching Contemporary Literature in the Christian Classroom," paper presented at the North American Division Higher Education Convention, Andrews University, 1976, GCDEd.

[11] Virginia Lowell Graybill, "English Literature," in Robert W. Smith, ed., *Christ and the Modern Mind* (Downers Grove, Ill.: InterVarsity Press, 1972), p. 21.

[12] C. S. Lewis, quoted in Gaebelein, "What Is Truth in Art?" in Ryken, ed., *op. cit.,* p. 103.

Chapter 13

[1] For a discussion of this problem see George R. Knight, "Battle Creek College: Academic Development and Curriculum Struggles," a paper presented at Andrews University Founders' Weekend, March 10, 1979, AUHR; Knight, "Ellen G. White: Prophet," in Knight, ed., *Early Adventist Educators,* pp. 27-37. It should be noted that Ellen White used the term *infidel authors* in at least two senses: (1) to refer to the classics (FE, p. 467), and (2) to refer to a class of prominent late-nineteenth-century skeptics who put all their trust in science (CT, pp. 423, 424; COL, p. 41).

[2] John Wood, "The Trashy Novel Revisited: Popular Fiction in the Age of Ellen White," *Spectrum,* April, 1976, pp. 16-24; Don Russell, "Foreword," in William F. Cody, *The Life of Hon. William F. Cody: An Autobiography* (Lincoln: University of Nebraska Press, 1978), p. viii.

[3] Ellen G. White, "What Shall We Read?" *The Youth's Instructor,* Oct. 9, 1902, p. 1; Ellen G. White, comp., *Sabbath Readings for the Home Circle: Moral and Religious Lessons* (Oakland, Calif.: Pacific Press, 1877-1878), vol. 3, p. iii.

[4] *Signs of the Times,* July 9, 1902, pp. 1, 2. Mrs. White replied to this *Signs* article six days later. See "E. G. White to Those Connected With the Management of the *Signs of the Times,*" July 15, 1902 (CW, pp. 172-176); see also the remarks of Ellen White to the executive committee of the California Medical Missionary and Benevolent Association, July 14, 1902; EGWRC-AU.

[5] Dudley M. Canright, "A List of Good Books for Young Folks," RH, Sept. 7, 1886, p. 570. For Mrs. White's reply, see 5T, pp. 516-520.

[6] Gibbs, "Literature in Adventist Schools."

[7] *Ibid.*

[8] Andreasen, "Autobiography," quoted in Steinweg, *Without Fear or Favor: The Life of M. L. Andreasen,* p. 31.

[9] Perry LeFevre, *The Christian Teacher* (New York: Abingdon Press, 1958), p. 51.

[10] Gaebelein, *The Pattern of God's Truth,* pp. 64, 65.

[11] Donald Whittle, *Christianity and the Arts* (Philadelphia: Fortress Press, 1967), p. 68.

[12] Nathan A. Scott, Jr., "Faith and Art in a World Awry," in Nathan A. Scott, Jr., ed., *The Climate of Faith in Modern Literature* (New York: Seabury Press, 1964), pp. 14-18. See also ———, *Rehearsals of Decomposure* (New York: King's Crown Press, 1952); H. R. Rookmaaker, *Modern Art and the Death of a Culture,* 2d ed. (Downers Grove, Ill.: InterVarsity Press, 1973).

[13] See Stephen D. Ross, *Literature and Philosophy* (New York: Appleton-Century-Crofts, 1969), p. 3 and passim.

[14] Sallie McFague TeSelle, *Literature and the Christian Life* (New Haven, Conn.: Yale University Press, 1966), p. 106.

¹⁵ John O. Waller, "Keynote," in *Official Report: North American Division Quadrennial Council for Higher Education* (Washington, D.C.: General Conference Department of Education, 1968), p. 608.

¹⁶ James J. Londis, "God Loves Stories: A Theological Rationale for the Literary Art," *Spectrum,* April, 1976, p. 27.

¹⁷ Christensen, *C. S. Lewis on Scripture,* pp. 51, 54.

¹⁸ "Guide to the Teaching of Literature in Seventh-day Adventist Schools," pp. 5, 6.

¹⁹ Garrick, "Developing Educational Objectives for the Christian School," in Kienel, ed., *The Philosophy of Christian School Education,* p. 89. (Italics supplied.)

²⁰ H. M. Tippett, "The Literature Program for SDA Schools," in *Report of the Blue Ridge Educational Convention* (Washington, D.C.: Washington College Press, 1937), pp. 264, 265.

²¹ Reuben Hilde, *Showdown: Can SDA Education Pass the Test?* (Washington, D.C.: Review and Herald Pub. Assn., 1980), pp. 105-108.

Chapter 14

¹ LeFevre, *The Christian Teacher,* p. 35.

² William Temple, *Nature, Man and God* (London: The Macmillan Co., 1956), pp. 54, 30, 31.

³ Trueblood, *Philosophy of Religion,* p. 8.

⁴ Pascal, *Pensées,* p. 79.

⁵ Francis A. Schaeffer, *True Spirituality* (Wheaton, Ill.: Tyndale House, 1971), p. 144.

⁶ Hilde, *Showdown: Can SDA Education Pass the Test?* pp. 171, 173.

⁷ H. E. Carnack, quoted in C. B. Eavey, *Principles of Teaching for Christian Teachers* (Grand Rapids, Mich.: Zondervan Pub. House, 1968), p. 52.

⁸ Trueblood, *op. cit.,* pp. 9, 11.

⁹ Holmes, *All Truth Is God's Truth,* p. 71.

¹⁰ Robert Webber, "Educating Toward a Christian Lifestyle: A Look at Theological Education," in Marvin K. Mayers, Lawrence O. Richards, and Robert Webber, eds., *Reshaping Evangelical Higher Education* (Grand Rapids, Mich.: Zondervan Pub. House, 1972), p. 100.

¹¹ Lois E. LeBar, *Education That Is Christian* (Old Tappan, N.J.: Fleming H. Revell, 1981), p.125.

¹² Blamires, *The Christian Mind,* p. 60.

¹³ Schaeffer, *True Spirituality,* p. 144.

¹⁴ Webber, in Mayers, Richards, and Webber, eds., *op. cit.,* p. 106.

¹⁵ For a helpful discussion of the contents and format of this course, see Robert Webber, "Reshaping Theological Education in a Liberal Arts Setting," in Mayers, Richards, and Webber, eds., *op. cit.,* pp. 170-182.

¹⁶ Robert D. Baird, "Religion," in Smith, ed., *Christ and the Modern Mind,* p. 93.

¹⁷ Statement of the Committee on Biblical Studies of Fort Wayne Bible College, 1959. Quoted in H. W. Byrne, *A Christian Approach to Education: Educational Theory and Application,* 2d ed. (Milford, Mich.: Mott Media, 1977), pp. 236, 237.

¹⁸ George H. Akers and Robert D. Moon, "Integrating Learning, Faith, and Practice in Christian Education," *Journal of Adventist Education,* April-May, 1980, p. 23.

Chapter 15

¹ Combs, *Myths in Education,* pp. 191-197.

² Millicent C. McIntosh, *Education for What?* (Stamford, Conn.: Overbrook Press, 1948), p. 6.

[3] David Elton Trueblood, *The Idea of a College* (New York: Harper and Brothers, 1959), p. 33; Trueblood, "The Marks of a Christian College," in Von Grueningen, ed., *Toward a Christian Philosophy of Higher Education,* p. 168.

[4] Coleman, *Equality of Educational Opportunity.* See also George Mayeske et al., *A Study of the Achievement of Our Nation's Students* (Washington, D.C.: U.S. Department of Health, Education, and Welfare, 1973), p. 2.

[5] Roger L. Dudley, *Why Teenagers Reject Religion and What to Do About It* (Washington, D.C.: Review and Herald Pub. Assn., 1978), p. 80.

[6] *General Education in a Free Society,* p. 24.

[7] F. F. Bruce, *The Epistle to the Ephesians* (Old Tappan, N.J.: Fleming H. Revell Co., 1961), p. 85.

[8] Trueblood, *The Idea of a College,* pp. 37, 38.

[9] Gaebelein, *The Pattern of God's Truth,* p. 37.

[10] Gilbert Highet, *The Art of Teaching* (New York: Vintage Books, 1950), pp. vii, viii.

[11] Combs, *op. cit.,* pp. 196, 197.

[12] William Glasser, *Schools Without Failure* (New York: Harper and Row, 1975), p. 14.

[13] Earl V. Pullias and James D. Young, *A Teacher Is Many Things,* 2d ed. (Bloomington, Ind.: Indiana University Press, 1977), p. 128. (Italics supplied.)

[14] See George R. Knight, "Teaching: The Art of Loving God's Children," *Journal of Adventist Education,* December, 1980-January, 1981, pp. 34, 35, 43.

[15] Frank E. Gaebelein, *Christian Education in a Democracy* (New York: Oxford University Press, 1951), pp. 184, 185.

[16] This chapter does not have space to discuss the qualifications of a Christian teacher fully. The following readings, however, are helpful: Ed, pp. 275-282; 6T, pp. 152-161; CT, pp. 25-31, 64-68, 229-236.

Chapter 16

[1] Erich Fromm, *The Art of Loving* (New York: Harper and Brothers, 1956), p. 44.

[2] See R. S. Peters, *Ethics and Education* (London: George Allen and Unwin, 1970), p. 267.

[3] John Dewey, *Democracy and Education* (New York: Free Press, 1966), p. 129.

[4] Combs, *Myths in Education,* pp. 139, 140.

[5] For a fuller discussion, see George R. Knight, "Redemptive Discipline," *Journal of Adventist Education,* October-November, 1977, pp. 5, 6, 23.

[6] Figure 6 adapted from Knight, *Philosophy and Education,* p. 215.

[7] A. S. De Jong, "The Discipline of the Christian School," in Cornelius Jaarsma, ed., *Fundamentals in Christian Education* (Grand Rapids, Mich.: William B. Eerdmans Pub. Co., 1953), p. 397.

[8] Dudley, *Why Teenagers Reject Religion,* p. 89.

[9] See Reuben Hilde, *The Rod Vs. the M&M's: Plain Talk on the Principles of Discipline in Home and Classroom* (Mountain View, Calif.: Pacific Press, 1976), p. 30.

[10] Glasser, *Schools Without Failure,* p. 224.

[11] Dobson, *Dare to Discipline* (Wheaton, Ill.: Tyndale House, 1970), p. 105.

[12] Glasser, *op. cit.,* pp. 231, 232.

[13] Dobson, *op. cit.,* pp. 27-29.

[14] Glasser, *op. cit.,* pp. 25, 26.

[15] Luella Cole with Irma Nelson Hall, *Psychology of Adolescence,* 6th ed. (New York: Holt, Rinehart, and Winston, 1965), p. 541.

[16] William W. Wayson et al., *Handbook for Developing Schools With Good Discipline* (Bloomington, Ind.: Phi Delta Kappa, 1982), p. 42.

[17] Gaebelein, *The Pattern of God's Truth,* p. 91.

Chapter 17

[1] Cf. E. G. White to W. C. White, May 5, 1897, EGWRC-AU.

[2] "The Small School—How It Can Be Improved," working paper for Small School Conference, March 15-16, 1974, University of Northern Iowa, p. 1, TMC-AU. (Italics supplied.)

[3] J. Hull, "Multigrade Teaching," *The Nation's Schools*, July, 1958, pp. 33-37.

[4] E. Stanley Chace, "Multiple-Grade Grouping Compared," paper presented at the 1963 study conference of the Association for Childhood Education International at Miami Beach, Florida, p. 10, TMC-AU.

[5] Jerome Thayer, "Will My Child Suffer Scholastically if He Attends Church School?" RH, Aug. 31, 1978, pp. 11-13; Jerome Thayer, "Seventh-day Adventist Elementary School Achievement in the Atlantic Union: A Report," *Atlantic Union Gleaner*, Aug. 9, 1977, p. 3.

[6] Dennis Milburn, "A Study of Multi-Age or Family-Grouped Classrooms," *Phi Delta Kappan*, March, 1981, pp. 513, 514.

[7] Bonny E. Ford, "Multiage Grouping in the Elementary School and Children's Affective Development: A Review of Recent Research," *Elementary School Journal*, November, 1977, p. 150.

[8] Milburn, *op. cit.*, p. 513.

[9] John I. Goodlad and Robert H. Anderson, *The Nongraded Elementary School*, rev. ed. (New York: Harcourt, Brace, and World, 1963), p. 69.

[10] Alan Gartner, Mary Conway Kohler, and Frank Riessman, "Every Child a Teacher," *Childhood Education*, October, 1971, pp. 12-16. See also Alan Gartner, Mary Conway Kohler, and Frank Riessman, *Children Teach Children: Learning by Teaching* (New York: Harper and Row, 1971).

[11] Allan W. Wicker and Claudia E. Kauma, "Effects of a Merger of a Small and a Large Organization on Members' Behaviors and Experiences," *Journal of Applied Psychology*, January-February, 1974, p. 24.

[12] Goodlad and Anderson, *op. cit.*, p. 69.

[13] See the above cited studies by Hull, Chace, Milburn, Gartner, and Ford. (Chace, we should note, dissented on the point that it was clearly demonstrated that attitude toward school was improved, but he did not report it as being less favorable.)

[14] Ruth Ann Stringer, "Handbook for Teachers in One-Teacher Schools," rev. ed. (Nevada-Utah Conference of Seventh-day Adventists, 1968), p. 4, GCDEd.

[15] Chace, *loc. cit.*

[16] James B. Conant, *The American High School Today: A First Report to Interested Citizens* (New York: McGraw-Hill, 1959), pp. 77-84.

[17] John P. Miller, *Humanizing the Classroom: Models of Teaching in Affective Education* (New York: Praeger, 1976), pp. 3, 173, 174.

[18] *Ibid.* See also Roger G. Barker and Paul V. Gump, *Big School, Small School: High School Size and Student Behavior* (Stanford, Calif.: Stanford University Press, 1964), pp. 195-202.

[19] James S. Coleman et al., *Youth: Transition to Adulthood* (Chicago: University of Chicago Press, 1974), pp. 154, 155.

[20] Chace, *loc. cit.*

[21] For a provocative discussion along this line, see Stanton Legett et al., "The Case for a Small High School," *The Nation's Schools*, September, 1970, pp. 45-52.

[22] "The Small School—How Can It Be Improved," p. 4.

Chapter 18

[1] Lewis, *Mere Christianity*, p. 69.

[2] Arthur W. Spalding, "The Nature of Recreation," RH, Sept. 4, 1947, p. 13; Arthur W. Spalding, *Who Is the Greatest?* (Mountain View, Calif.: Pacific Press Pub. Assn., 1941), p. 87.

[3] Fromm, *The Art of Loving*, pp. 108, 86.

[4] Dewey, *Democracy and Education*, p. 205.

[5] *Ibid.*, p. 202.

[6] Arthur L. White, "Sports in Seventh-day [Adventist] Academies and Colleges," December, 1967, EGWRC-DC.

[7] The reader will have to decide where useful work indoors falls in this hierarchy. It might be between levels two and three.

[8] Ellen G. White, "The Avondale Health Retreat," *Australasian Union Conference Record,* July 26, 1899, p. 17. (Italics supplied.)

[9] Ron Graybill, "Ellen G. White and Competitive Sports," Jan. 24, 1974, EGWRC-DC.

[10] Fromm, *op. cit.,* p. 131.

[11] George B. Leonard, *Education and Ecstasy* (New York: Dell Pub. Co., 1968), p. 122.

[12] Ron Graybill, "Competition and the Seventh-day Adventist," *Insight,* Sept. 10, 1974, p. 7

[13] Combs, *Myths in Education,* p. 166. (Italics supplied.) For similar findings see David P. Ausubel, Joseph D. Novak, and Helen Hanesian, *Educational Psychology: A Cognitive View,* 2d ed. (New York: Holt, Rinehart, and Winston, 1978), pp. 471, 472.

[14] George F. J. Lehner and Ella Kube, *The Dynamics of Personal Adjustment,* 2d ed. (Englewood Cliffs, N.J.: Prentice-Hall, 1964), pp. 251-254.

[15] Ausubel, Novak, and Hanesian, *op. cit.,* p. 471.

[16] Schaeffer, *True Spirituality,* p. 143.

[17] C. S. Lewis, *Christian Reflections* (Grand Rapids, Mich.: William B. Eerdmans, 1967), pp. 33, 34.

[18] Graybill, "Competition and the Seventh-day Adventist," p. 8.

Chapter 19

[1] *First Annual Report of the Society for Promoting Manual Labor in Literary Institutions Including the Report of Their General Agent, Theodore D. Weld* (New York: S. W. Benedict and Co., 1833).

[2] Edward A. Krug, *The Shaping of the American High School, 1880-1920* (Madison, Wisc.: University of Wisconsin Press, 1969), pp. 1-26. See also D. C. Gilman, "A Plea for the Training of the Hand," in *Monographs of the Industrial Education Association,* January, 1888; Marvin Lazerson and W. Norton Grubb, eds., *American Education and Vocationalism: A Documentary History, 1870-1970* (New York: Teachers College Press, Columbia University, 1974); Charles H. Ham, *Manual Training and the Solution of Social and Industrial Problems* (New York: Harper and Brothers, 1886); Charles A. Bennett, *History of Manual and Industrial Education up to 1870* (Peoria, Ill.: The Manual Arts Press, 1926); ———, *History of Manual and Industrial Education, 1870 to 1917* (Peoria, Ill.: The Manual Arts Press, 1937).

[3] See Krug, *loc. cit.;* Rudolph, *Curriculum: A History of the American Undergraduate Course of Study Since 1636;* S. A. Witmer, *The Bible College Story: Education With Dimension* (Manhasset, N.Y.: Channel Press, 1962); George R. Knight, "Early Adventists and Education: Attitudes and Context," in Knight, ed., *Early Adventist Educators,* pp. 3-9.

[4] CT, pp. 203-214; E. G. White to the teachers of the Fernando school, May 17, 1903; E. G. White to those in charge of the Fernando school, May 17, 1903; remarks by E. G. White at the Los Angeles camp meeting on Sept. 17, 1902, MS 54, 1903; portion of an address given at the opening of the Fernando, California, school on Oct. 1, 1903, MS 47, 1903; cf. MS 125, 1902; EGWRC-AU. See also a critique of the problem of the Fernando school in George R. Knight, "Two Books on Adventist Education," *Spectrum,* November, 1979, pp. 53-55.

[5] In *Education,* page 217, for example, Ellen White wrote: "So far as possible, facilities for manual training should be connected with every school."

[6] E. G. White to those in charge of the Fernando school, May 17, 1903, EGWRC-AU. (Italics supplied.)

[7] Raymond S. Moore, *Adventist Education at the Crossroads* (Mountain View, Calif.: Pacific Press Pub. Assn., 1976), p. 63.

[8] Knight, "Battle Creek College: Academic Development and Curriculum Struggles"; Knight, "Ellen G. White: Prophet," in Knight, ed., *Early Adventist Educators,* pp. 27-31.

⁹ See, for example, School Committee, "The Proposed School," RH, May 7, 1872, p. 168; George I. Butler, "What Use Shall We Make of Our School?" RH, July 21, 1874, pp. 44, 45.

¹⁰ According to Paul S. Damazo, this problem has already developed. He calculates that 1,327,130 youth from Adventist homes (69.7 percent) are *"currently not attending SDA schools."* Paul S. Damazo, "Financing Adventist Education," RH, May 13, 1982, p. 4.

¹¹ E. F. Schumacher, *Small Is Beautiful: Economics as if People Mattered* (New York: Harper and Row, 1973); E. F. Schumacher, *Good Work* (New York: Harper and Row, 1979).

¹² Paul S. Damazo, "The Role of the World Church in Achieving Cost Efficiency in Education," RH, May 27, 1982, p. 7.

¹³ ———, "New Ways to Finance Christian Education," RH, May 20, 1982, p. 9. (Italics supplied.)

¹⁴ Frederick Griggs to W. C. White, Dec. 9, 1908, EGWRC-DC.

¹⁵ *The School of the Ozarks, College Bulletin: 1979-1981,* p. 28.

Index